MW01012747

SEARCHING FOR THE FOR THE STRING

SEARCHING FOR THE STRING

SELECTED WRITINGS OF
JOHN A. KEEL

EDITED BY ANDY COLVIN

METADISC PRODUCTIONS, SEATTLE

NEW SAUCERIAN BOOKS, POINT PLEASANT, WEST VIRGINIA

Books by John A. Keel

Jadoo!

Operation Trojan Horse

Strange Creatures From Time and Space

Our Haunted Planet

The Mothman Prophecies

The Eighth Tower

Strange Mutants From the 21st Century

Disneyland of the Gods

The Complete Guide to Mysterious Beings

The Best of John Keel

Flying Saucer To the Center of Your Mind

The Outer Limits of the Twilight Zone

Searching For The String

Searching For the String: Selected Writings of John A. Keel

ISBN-13: 978-1499132120

ISBN-10: 1499132123

© 2014 New Saucerian Books – Point Pleasant, West Virginia

PUBLISHED BY: Metadisc Productions and New Saucerian Books

FRONT COVER ILLUSTRATION: "Garuda Rope Trick" by E.E. Parker and Andy Colvin

BACK COVER ILLUSTRATION: Self-Portrait in Photo Booth by John Keel, New York City, 1966

CONTENTS

INTRODUCTION 7
"The Man From Twenty-Nine Palms"

EDITOR'S NOTES.. 13

CHAPTER 1... 15
The "Flap" Phenomenon in the United States – New York Fortean Society Press, 1969
Analyzing The Flaps 22
The Flaps Of The 1950s 27
The Flaps of 1966... 31
The UFOs Nobody Talks About: Deadly Fireballs in the Sky 33
The Overview... 41

CHAPTER 2... 47
Astronauts Report UFOs in Outer Space – *Flying Saucers' UFO Reports* #4, 1967

CHAPTER 3... 55
The Strange Case of the Pregnant Woman – Unpublished, October 1967
Aftermath.. 60

CHAPTER 4... 63
UFOs: 30 Years of Investigation – *Saga Magazine*, December 1976
Unidentified Former Humans: 3000 Years of Investigation 67

CHAPTER 5... 72
Are UFOs Using the Earth For a Garbage Dump? – *UFO Reports* #4 – 1967

CHAPTER 6... 80
West Virginia's Enigmatic "Bird" – *Flying Saucer Review*, July 1968

CHAPTER 7... 92
An Unusual Contact Claim From Ohio – *Flying Saucer Review*, 1968
A New Approach to UFO Witnesses 95
Is the "Electromagnetic Effect" a Myth? 98

CHAPTER 8... 103
Problems of Identity: The Aliens Among Us – *SAGA's UFO Report*, November 1977
Problems of Etymology: Ufology Terminology 106
Problems of Methodology: UFOs in 1952 108
Problems of Distortion and Distention: The Time Cycle Factor 110

CHAPTER 9... 117
The Man Who Invented Flying Saucers – *Whole Earth Review*, 1986

CHAPTER 10.. 126
A "Devil's Triangle" in Idaho? – *Saga's UFO Annual*, 1977

Chapter 11 130
    The Night the Sky Turned On – *Fate* magazine, September 1967

Chapter 12 137
    This American Town is UFO Target No. 1 – *Male* magazine, March 1970

Chapter 13 144
    The Flying Saucer Subculture – *The Journal of Popular Culture*, Spring 1975

Chapter 14 166
    Our Skies Are Filled With Junk – *Fate* Magazine – March 1969

Chapter 15 172
    22 UFO Sightings Hushed Up: Is This Flying Saucer "D-Day?" – *Male* magazine, December 1970

Chapter 16 184
    Flap Dates, Kidnappings, and Secret Bases – *New Report on Flying Saucers* #2, 1967

Chapter 17 195
    Were Flying Saucers Here Before Man? – *Argosy* magazine, 1977
    Close Encounters of the Religious Kind 201

Chapter 18 206
    The Principle of Transmogrification – *Flying Saucer Review*, 1969
    The Superior Technology 210
    The Glendale, California, Contact Claim 215

Chapter 19 221
    The Cosmic Blog – Letters To and From John A. Keel (JAK)

Chapter 20 260
    Mothman & Other Curious Conspiracies – Pt. Pleasant, WV – 2003

List of Illustrations 275

Index 276

INTRODUCTION

I had returned to my hotel room near Giant Rock, California, and had closed the door, when I heard a knock. I repressed a gasp of pleasure at seeing John Keel standing there...

Then I realized that it wasn't really he, but an almost perfect image of my friend. "You look so much like John Keel," I said, "that you could pass as John Keel's brother!"

"As a matter of fact, I *am*," he replied. As I tried to recover from the surprise, he continued:

> Nobody knows this, but John and I are identical twins. If I weren't slightly balding, you'd swear I was John himself. I guess that might be all right if I were he; I suppose he leads a pretty exciting life.

He explained why he had knocked. He had stopped at Twenty-Nine Palms not because of the 1970 flying saucer convention at Giant Rock, but for other reasons. He lived in Anaheim and was on his way north to attend an antique car show – which explained the glistening, like new, 1950s Buick that was parked near the motel office. "Then, you aren't interested in UFOs like your brother John?"

> I very definitely am. I read all of John's stuff. He sends me all of it. I also follow the subject in the papers, and occasionally buy a paperback about it. Oh, I must tell you why I happened to look you up. The desk clerk was looking at one of the magazines you gave him, and I noticed one of John's articles in it. He gave me your room number. I remembered you from talking with John about his investigations in West Virginia.

I couldn't get over the amazing resemblance of Edgar Keel to John Keel, although the manner of speech was quite different. He talked much faster than John and had an odd, "singsong" tonal quality. He said he worked for the U.S. Department of the Interior... I tried to pick his mind about John, who, although quite well known for his UFO investigations and writing, was still a rather mysterious figure, particularly in reference to his personal life. John lived in semi-isolation, either without a phone or with an unlisted number, and hinted that he was in other work besides writing.

I'd rather let John tell you about his many other activities that those of you in UFO investigation never dream of. Suffice it to say that John writes on very many other subjects, under another name that you would be very familiar with if I mentioned it. And I might also add that he holds down a very important regular job that he doesn't publicize.

He handed me some typewritten pages. "Anyhow, I must go, but you might be interested in this. I think this is a very good example of UFO sightings that may contain some validity. In fact, it's my favorite of all the reports I have read in some time." With this he departed, and avoided shaking hands (as when he first greeted me) by a quick, nervous wave of his right arm toward his hat, which seemed to be in perfect adjustment.

Then I glanced at the report, closed the door, and sat down to read it. I couldn't help being curious about the sheets themselves. They appeared to be photocopies of typewriting, but with a very odd difference. The sheets seemed to be reproduced in color, for a spelling correction showed up in blue ink. One of the sheets had reproduced a cigarette burn on the original, with a distinct brown color around the burn. The 3-M Company had developed a color photocopier around that time, although it was not on the market in 1970. The new machine, which carries a very high price tag, is sold mainly for industrial and military applications…

The report concerned an unidentified farmer of Walsh, IL, who would not give his name for fear of ridicule. On October 5, the farmer was ready to milk his cows when he noticed that the animals were agitated and extremely frightened. He looked all around for some cause of the commotion, but noted nothing abnormal. Then he saw one of them looking at the sky, and discovered a cloud-like object beaming a light toward the ground. Suddenly, another beam of light from the mysterious object shifted in his direction and enveloped him. "I felt a tingling sensation come over me, which I could not explain," the report quoted him. "While standing there in that circle of light, it just seemed as if I couldn't move. I wasn't exactly frightened in the usual sense, just sort of stunned, I suppose." Then the light went out, and the mysterious object disappeared at the same moment. Finding he could move again, and feeling normal, he turned his thoughts to the cows. It was then that he noted probably what was the most unusual facet of the incident: all five cows were on the wrong side of the barbed wire fence! Even in extreme fright, it seemed impossible for them to have jumped it…

After pondering John Keel's strange "double" (somehow I couldn't buy the "twin-brother" bit), I immediately called Keel, who made the following comments:

> I was an only child, Gray. I have no brother named Edgar, and no sister named Mary (a mysterious "Mary Keel" has figured in a number of UFO episodes). Aside from the doppelgangers described in my book *The Mothman Prophecies*, two flesh-and-blood replicas have turned up over the years. One – a dead ringer for me – used to work in Greenwich Village as a waiter. Friends who saw him reacted, "My God! Poor Keel is slinging hash!" The other appeared in a news photo published several years ago. It showed a crowd of people in a subway after an accident; a man in the front of the crowd looked exactly like me. A friend of mine cut the picture out and carried it in his wallet for a long time, believing it was a photo of me.

Before I could reply, some beeping sounds, and then a series of clicks, temporarily interrupted our conversation. "There's the Silence Group again," I joked. I was tired, but I decided to take the ufological bull by the horns and bring up a remark that Jim Moseley had made.

"Frankly, John," I began, "Jim and I had a long talk about you. He had one impression about you, which I also get. You are a better researcher than us, and a highly talented writer, and you have covered a lot of ground in the UFO field in a short time. But I somehow feel you have some theories or some information that you're holding back from all of us. Now, I presume you're writing a book, and I probably will write one, too, about the Mothman cases and all the incredible Ohio Valley incidents. I know if you have something really new and fresh, you wouldn't want to blow it in front of some other writer or editor…"

I asked him point-blank how he had learned so much in so little time.

"Simple," he explained. "I employed a particular discipline that not too many people have. I simply read practically every UFO book ever published – and you, as an editor and publisher, know that's pretty rough medicine. Some of the dullest stuff in the literary world appears between covers with brightly colored saucers on them."

"I know what you mean," I agreed. "Unfortunately I have to read them before I publish them."

"I am writing a book, which I am tentatively calling *Operation Trojan Horse*," Keel explained, "but that isn't the real reason I don't reveal everything. If that were the reason, I would tell you everything, because I know you're ethical." Then Keel became dead serious:

Believe me, Gray, something fantastic is going on – something that not even the hardcore UFO buffs are ready to believe. You've been in this crazy business for years, and you know that there are many wild and unpublicized aspects of this phenomenon – things that simply do not support the whole "extraterrestrial" idea.

When I first started digging into this, I realized that there were no real "hard facts" or genuine evidence. The whole extraterrestrial idea was built up by wishful thinkers, on speculation and circumstantial evidence. There are hundreds of bits and pieces that just don't fit that idea. Once I understood this, I tried to find a broader concept into which all the pieces could fit. So I had to literally start from scratch and work out some radical new methods for investigating these things.

I've given up all of my other work and have been spending my full time on this. I've been going into debt, and it hasn't been easy, but it's about time that somebody really attacked this mystery from every angle. I think I've got the key now, but it is going to take a lot of hard work to prove anything. In the meantime, I have to keep a lot of my findings quiet. First of all, not many people are willing to believe it. Secondly, if I reveal some of these things prematurely, a lot of crackpots and screwballs will tailor their own stories to fit my findings. I've discovered that there are many small, seemingly insignificant details in stories from all over the world that actually correlate and corroborate each other. I'm more interested in these little details than in the endless descriptions of funny flying objects.

Frankly, I've concluded that the objects really aren't very important to all of this. There are other factors that are far more important. Those are the factors I'm digging out and documenting. When the time comes, I'll be revealing these things in very small doses.

"There are a great many contradictions," I admitted, "but how can one man ever put the whole puzzle together?"

"That's the problem, Gray," he replied thoughtfully. "I suspect that the ET buffs and many of the serious UFO researchers like yourself have allowed themselves to be misled and diverted by the controversies and nonsense surrounding this subject. The buffs have worked harder at fighting the Air

Force than at investigating UFOs. Groups like NICAP have dedicated themselves to compiling anecdotes rather than facts. They've smothered themselves with what seems like a hopeless cause – trying to prove that UFOs not only exist, but that they come from outer space. You'd think that after twenty years of vain effort they would come to realize that the outer space answer is completely erroneous. It's impossible to prove, and very little observational data supports it."

"But if they aren't from outer space, where could they be from?" I pressed, intrigued.

"That's the sticky part," he continued. "They seem to be environmental, yet under intelligent control. I've done a lot of historical research and discovered that these things were as numerous in 1866 as they were in 1966. In fact, in 1866, a Massachusetts man named William Denton claimed a contactee experience very similar to Woody Derenberger's. He wrote several books about it."

"What do you mean by 'environmental,' though?"

"I mean that they seem to have always been here – that they co-exist with us somehow. Remember in the Bible, the prophet Zechariah recounts a conversation with an 'angel,' and describes seeing a 'flying roll.' The angel pointed it out to him and told him, 'That is the curse that goeth forth over the whole Earth.' That curse is still with us, Gray."

It was not a new idea, of course, but Keel seemed to be able to articulate it in remarkably convincing terms. His research was impressive and much of it was certainly unique. I could see that he was looking at the subject from a broad, overall viewpoint rather than concentrating on random lights-in-the-sky as so many other researchers were doing. He spoke knowledgeably of human history and the apparent role UFOs had played in mythology and legend in all civilizations.

"But the thing that is really beginning to bother me, Gray," he continued soberly, "is that I'm developing a gnawing suspicion that the Air Force has been right all along, and has been telling us part of the truth all along. After all, they've always claimed that there was no evidence of extraterrestrial origin, and so on. If I jumped into print with this kind of conclusion, all the buffs would scream that I've been 'silenced' or 'bought off' or some such nonsense. But I've got to admit that the Air Force's position makes more sense to me every day. Maybe the government has always realized that the 'truth' can't be proven, and that few people would believe it anyway. So they've done the only thing they could do: they've tried to play the whole thing down and dismiss it. If UFOs were around in Zechariah's time, and in 1866, they'll probably be around in 2066, too—and be just as aloof of us as they've always been. The UFO buffs keep waiting for them to land on the White House lawn, but I don't think that's ever going to happen. Instead, people like Zechariah, Denton, and Derenberger will continue to undergo wild experiences that can't be proven and which few people will want to believe. And guys like you and I will spend our lives running around trying to find all the pieces to a puzzle that doesn't seem to have any definite shape or borders."

I regretted that the intriguing conversation was ending. I yawned, looked at my watch, and only then realized how late it had gotten.

"If your ideas are valid, John," I added jokingly, "don't be surprised if there's a knocking at your door tonight, and three Men in Black attack you with a billy-club."

"I can't be bothered," he joked. "If the MIB show up, I'll just send them over to your place."

-Gray Barker (from *Saucerian Press*, 1970)

EDITOR'S NOTE

After sitting with John Keel's material for over 20 years, ruminating, I have come to a crossroads. With this third volume of Keel's "best" writings, my investigation into "Mothman" matters is beginning to feel "done." It is a good feeling, but it also means I am finally saying "goodbye" to a dear old friend. Although Keel died almost five years ago, I think it is just now beginning to sink in that he is gone. Even after his death, his "presence" was so strong that he seemingly continued to "guide" the work of myself and others in the Mothman research community. There were many physical and not-so-physical events that proved this to our collective satisfaction, some of which I briefly described in my earlier introductions.

Why should this be? My own sense is that these strong energetic impulses often come from suppression or resistance to ideas – even to the truth. When the human mind is pushed in one direction, it goes in another direction, flowing out like mysterious patterns of magnetism. In these pages, one can feel the "pushback" Keel got from the many ET believers, government "spooks," and skeptics out there. This orchestrated contention is still part of ufology today, where suit-wearing types (often former military intelligence personnel) hold endless conferences purporting to "prove" that it was the aliens, not the military, who were piloting saucers and suppressing civilian UFO investigation.

When they are not making stuff completely up, they misdirect the public with plausible-sounding conspiracies. One of these, which has come up again in May 2014, is that John F. Kennedy knew "the truth" about the flying saucers, and was killed because he was about to the announce the presence of the ETs. Of course, this is hogwash, if Keel's correspondence with Robert F. Kennedy is any indication. The real question is why *several JFK assassination conspirators were involved in ufology*, particularly in the Ohio Valley, where Keel was doing most of his investigations. By focusing on whether or not JFK believed in aliens, today's spooks effectively limit debate. If they get their way, no one will ever realize that the fields of ufology, cryptozoology, conspiracy, and "alternative" media have been – and probably will always be – infested with government agents, hitmen, willing apologists, and academic dupes.

Many of these "spooks" are writers, of course – something Keel often complained about. It irritated him that these "field spooks" were able to freely exploit a lucrative market that had been created for them by the "soap-opera spooks" on Madison Avenue: that of the potboiler, "hack" mystery novel. "Jane Austen simply put on a black suit and hat, and switched her carriage for a saucer," Keel once said. The spooks would even "send secret messages in the texts of their hack books," he claimed. And he was surely right; even more "sophisticated" personalities like E. Howard Hunt, Ian Fleming, and J.D. Salinger could not resist the temptation.

As Keel hints in the "Letters" section, Gray Barker also seemed to be involved in spooky activities. Barker's books do appear to contain those tantalizing subliminal messages adored by UFO cultists and mind-controlled assassins alike. Keel occasionally scolded Barker, but kept him close (perhaps to keep a better eye on him), drawing on their shared upbringings on farms in the Appalachian-Adirondack range. Keel saved most of his ire for Jim Moseley, who repeatedly pulled dangerous or questionable pranks and made secretive trips to South America, supposedly indirectly financed by defense-contracting profits.

My father, whose mysterious death drew me into investigating the Mothman phenomena, grew up near Keel. This, combined with my own upbringing in West Virginia during the Mothman era, has hopefully allowed me to better interpret the interactions of Keel and Barker – two very interesting and strangely similar men. When they came to my hometown to investigate why so many UFOs and Mothmen were flying around, they may have sensed that saucer-drones were being built at the plant that employed my father – which silenced anyone who "knew too much." I can't blame them for not answering every question. The terrors Keel described were very real and, at least in my case, hit home. Even as we speak, new drone factories are being built in the Ohio Valley.

Keel, of course, was a genius. His work into mysterious matters, both cultural and paraphysical, seems to shine above the rest. He was not afraid to be the lone, dissenting voice in the room. He was so driven to know the truth that he would *never* lie – a very rare characteristic. When you hear one of today's "suits" implying that Keel confabulated the facts, you are hearing the same tired propaganda that has been sapping us for over half a century. Perhaps the person who has most fought for the preservation of Keel's work is his sister, Cheryl Keaton. I would like to thank her for making certain materials available to me, for answering all of my questions about her brother (whom she dearly misses), and for allowing me to bring this wonderful material to Keel fans everywhere. It was needed.

-Andy Colvin

CHAPTER 1

"Flap" was originally an Air Force term for an ungovernable crisis. In ufology, a "flap" denotes a specific period of time during which a sudden outbreak of UFO sightings occurs. For example: if many sightings occur simultaneously nationwide on a single day, that day becomes a "flap date." A "flap" may also take place in a single area, marked by a beginning, a peak, and a decline in sightings. Such localized "flaps" can last from a few hours to several months.

Historical research by a very small group of dedicated ufologists is beginning to reveal some surprising patterns in the overall activities of the unidentified flying objects. The year 1947 did not mark the start of the "UFO era," as so many writers and students of the phenomenon have believed. "Flap" cycles have now been traced and documented back to the early years of the 19th century, and additional research may eventually demonstrate that UFO "flaps" have occurred consistently on almost a regular timetable throughout all of history.

Not only have the "flying saucers" always been with us, but they seem to have always elected to remain aloof from our organized social groups and they may have operated under many guises, following deliberate patterns of confusion and deception. As Gordon Creighton, Allen Greenfield, and other scholars have suggested, it may be that all mythology, demonology, vampire legends, leprechaun stories, etc., are actually based upon earlier "flaps" and have merely been colored and distorted by human interpretation of these events. An organized re-examination of all of man's myths and lore may yield important clues to the overall phenomenon.

I have now had an opportunity to investigate and study the numerous "flaps" of the past three years and have spent a great deal of time, effort, and money probing into the astounding events taking place in the "flap" areas. The scattered published UFO sightings represent only a fraction of the overall situation, constituting only the small, visible part of an enormous iceberg. As a journalist, I feed on facts, and I have found that there are many solid facts that have been neglected by the general field of ufology, either because those facts were too fantastic to be considered seriously within the limitations of our own environmental framework, or because so many UFO researchers have been preoccupied with the random sighting reports and have made no organized effort to compile and analyze the "big picture." We have been laboriously counting the trees in a foggy forest and have made no maps and charted no paths.

Let us concern ourselves here with that "big picture." During my visits to "flap" areas, it quickly became clear that only a small percentage of witnesses were actually reporting sightings. These "reporting observers" (ROs) do not give us a full impression of the scope of the phenomenon. After a lot of study and calculating, I have estimated that a single report may represent at least 250 unreported sightings. A single two-inch newspaper item from a remote area has often proved to be the tip-off that a major "flap" was under way there. Many newspaper editors regard UFO reports as "human interest" stories and tend to slight them or ignore them altogether. Paradoxically, the longer a "flap" lasts in an area, the less publicity it tends to receive. Both the newspapers and their readers are inclined to become bored and blasé with routine sightings during an extended "flap."

Because the UFO skeptics have been critical of the sanity and sobriety of ROs, amateur UFO investigators have devoted more time and energy to investigating the "reliability" of ROs than to investigating the actual phenomenon being reported. Actually, few people bother to report anything to the police or local newspapers unless they are quite certain that what they have seen was most unusual and unexplainable. Very few witnesses are willing to expose themselves to local ridicule and very, very few would deliberately lie to local authorities. Most witnesses prefer to remain silent about their sightings, and fewer than one percent bother to report anything directly to the U.S. Air Force, thanks to the Air Force's long-running anti-UFO campaign (and the UFO buffs' well-publicized anti-Air Force campaign).

The actual scope of the phenomenon is thus being suppressed, voluntarily, at the source, by the witnesses themselves. To worsen matters, many newspapers ignore most of the reports that come their way, concentrating on a random few turned over to them by the local police. And the local police rarely even bother to keep even a superficial record of the reports they receive during "flaps." So a tremendous amount of information is lost altogether.

By the same token, the two leading UFO organizations in the U.S., APRO and NICAP, are limited to issuing thin little newsletters every few months, and simply do not have the space to detail the many reports they receive. Most of those reports end up in forgotten files and neither organization makes an effort to compile monthly or quarterly statistical reports breaking down the sighting information they receive. They select only the most "interesting" sightings for publication, and frequently devote columns of valuable space to speculative articles, attacks against government policy, and the fostering of the personality conflicts that dominate and divide the field.

To a newsman, a radio commentator, or a scientist, statistical information is far more important than piles of anecdotes about the funny things people are reporting. The Condon Committee at Colorado University found that it literally had to start from scratch because no one had bothered to prepare statistical data in all of these twenty years. The skeptics have never been confronted with sold statistical data, and there have been too many flaws in the random speculations in the field to convince any of the hard-nosed types (who prefer to reject the entire subject out of hand).

Individual sightings are so numerous that they literally become meaningless. The data within those individual reports must be extracted, sifted, and weighed. Such data includes more than a mere description of the object. The geographical locations of the sightings are quite important, as we shall see further on. The physiological and psychological effects on the witnesses are also of prime importance, and these effects have been examined in only a handful of the 100,000 or so cases published since 1947.

If each published report represents hundreds of unreported incidents, then many millions of people have seen UFOs in the past twenty years. The tired explanations of "mass hysteria," "mass hallucinations," etc., simply cannot be applied. The USAF and the skeptics have tried to explain away the massive "flaps" as being solitary weather balloons, flights of birds, and misinterpretations of conventional objects or natural phenomena. There have undoubtedly been many mistakes, but if we had accurate statistics for these past twenty years, we would probably find that 90 percent of all sightings cannot be easily explained – or explained at all. The weight of the observational evidence is now on our side. What is needed is a concentrated effort to correlate that evidence and construct some sensible conclusions – conclusions that fit the data. Until now, most ufologists have tried to select only data that seemed to fit their conclusions.

You cannot "research" this subject by merely reading books and newsletters containing the more "interesting" sightings and written for the commercial market. You can't investigate UFOs by visiting "flap" areas a year later and staring at the sky. Such excursions are tourism, not investigation.

The obvious place to begin is with a study of the "flaps" of earlier periods, so that we can compare contemporary events with them. Newspaper clippings rarely tell the whole story. Editors and reporters are usually reluctant to describe the wilder aspects of incidents related to them by witnesses. Unfortunately, we are forced to rely upon newspaper reports for our study of the earlier "flaps," and even for our study of the more recent events of the 1940s and '50s. Naturally, some workable method is needed to organize and interpret this kind of data.

Commercial television in the United States is ruled by the Rating System. Pollsters study the viewing habits of a mere 1,200 representative families and, from such polls, they claim to understand the viewing habits of millions. Years ago, the pollsters interviewed many thousands of people to obtain their figures, but gradually they discovered they got the same results with a much smaller sampling. By 1960, the TV pollsters were concentrating on 1,900 families in all age and income groups scattered across the country. Today they are down to 1,200. In other words, if 40 percent of those 1,200 families watch a specific program on a specific night, it has been proven to the satisfaction of this multimillion-dollar industry that 40 percent of all the viewers in the country were following suit. This is a bit hard for people not familiar with polling methods to understand, but it actually works. Computers dealing with much larger samples have verified the results.

We can extend the poll method to UFO sightings, provided our sampling represents an adequate cross-section of ROs, and does not concentrate on a specific group such as policemen or airline pilots. A thousand well-investigated reports can actually represent – and represent accurately – millions of unreported sightings. A survey of 1,000 witnesses can give us the "big picture."

Our first step, therefore, is to recognize the fact that a good sampling can – and does – represent the whole. We can collect another 100,000 reports without ever learning anything or proving anything unless we can somehow extract the data within those reports. This should be our prime task as UFO researchers – extracting and analyzing rather than collecting and speculating.

There are many "unknown flaps" in the United States, and because our research methods have been pitifully inadequate, we have no way of knowing how many of these "secret flaps" have occurred, or how often. It is even quite possible that the "lull" periods were actually periods of intense activity. The late Dr. Morris K. Jessup did an entire book on the sightings of 1955 – a "lull" year. I have seen and reviewed a huge private collection of clippings and reports from 1958 – another "lull" year.

Ivan T. Sanderson lives on a farm near a small town in the western hills of New Jersey. One day in the fall of 1966, he wandered into the local newspaper office and the concerned editor showed him a bulging file of unpublished UFO reports from the local citizenry, asking for his opinion. Mr. Sanderson wrote an article on UFOs for the paper and was immediately buried in local reports from neighbors who had kept silent until then! There had been an authentic "flap" right in his own backyard – including a number of brief "touchdowns."

The sightings around the Wanaque Reservoir in New Jersey received considerable publicity early in 1966, but during my repeated trips to the area, I found witnesses who had been seeing UFOs almost continuously for two years *before* one of the objects blatantly appeared directly over the reservoir and created a "flap." That "flap" still continues sporadically, but the police and local officials are weary of the crowds and the publicity, and keep the new sightings to themselves. They haven't been "censored" or "hushed up." They are merely trying to keep interest in the phenomenon at a minimum to make things easier for themselves. This kind of voluntary "silencing" often takes place in "flap" sectors.

Unbeknownst to UFO researchers in Atlanta, Georgia, a massive "UFO flap" exploded only a few miles away in the fall of 1967. Definite, circular, metallic objects were seen daily by hundreds of people living in the vicinity of the huge Savannah River Project (it covers as much area as the city of Chicago). This plant manufactures atomic weapons and is sealed off and heavily guarded. The local newspaper editors were aware of the sensitivity of the matter, and shied away from mentioning the UFO reports they were receiving.

At approximately that same time (September through December 1967), another massive "flap" broke out in New York State. Hundreds of sightings were concentrated around Ithaca and the desolate region occupied by a semi-secret radio telescope installation. In addition, an atomic energy plant is being planned for the area, and the objects uncannily appeared directly over the proposed site. The local newspapers played the whole thing down until the "flap" subsided somewhat in the spring of 1968.

A few hundred miles south of Ithaca, another "flap" took place simul-taneously around Harrisburg, Pennsylvania. This was also a big one, but the local press barely mentioned it. There were scores of low-level sightings every night for weeks. Some were concentrated around the huge telephone installation there – a key installation for the telephone system in the whole northeast. Other sightings seemed to collect around a top-secret government project situated in the hills a few miles north of Harrisburg. Members of the Condon Committee spent a month at Harrisburg, but their public comments about the situation were vague and on the negative side.

Dr. J. Allen Hynek, the long-time Air Force UFO consultant, visited Ithaca and expressed astonishment and concern over the scope of the incidents there.

When I first visited West Virginia in December 1966, I discovered that many reliable people, police officers, community leaders, etc., had been seeing strange aerial objects for months up and down the Ohio River, but none had reported their sightings to the newspapers or the Air Force. I focused publicity on some of these cases, and hundreds of other witnesses immediately came forth. The local newspapers began to publish UFO stories, and armchair ufologists undoubtedly collected the clippings and noted, sagely, that "a big flap began in West Virginia in December 1966." Actually, as at Wanaque, the flap began months earlier, and has continued ever since. The publicity has tapered off because the editors and reporters are tired of writing the same story over and over again.

I have found many other sections of the country that have seemingly been inundated by the UFOs for months or even years, yet the local press has not carried a line about them. In other cases, such as in Wrens, Georgia, the "flaps" were of such proportions that the local newspaper editors voluntarily decided not to publish any reports, suspecting that because the objects were so real and so numerous, they had to be some "secret government device."

Since 1966, "flaps" have persisted in Michigan, Nebraska, Texas, Oklahoma, California, Mexico, Massachusetts, Connecticut, and Long Island, NY. Columbus, Ohio has had a repeated series of "flaps" for the past two years. So has Oregon and the state of Washington. We could write many enthralling pages with reports of low-level sightings, appearances of strange "giants" and "little men," landings, and weird incidents. But the sheer bulk of the reports and the general dearth of publicity, even locally, testifies to their validity, and also proves how vain it is to try to concentrate on the individual sightings.

"Flying saucers" seem to be operating consistently in the United States. Where they come from and where they go is open to debate. They do seem to move into an area and stay there for weeks or even months. Press coverage is superficial at best. UFO reports are not related to the publicity the subject receives, as some cynics have suggested. The sightings mount and subside independently of the press coverage. Often the press doesn't even begin to take the "flap" seriously until it has actually subsided.

In collecting thousands of news clips from all over the country, I have noted that sightings break out simultaneously in many sections of the country on a single day. The press coverage of the "flap" follows a day or two later. Thus, the excited farmer in Minnesota who calls his local newspaper has no idea that on the very night of his sighting, a group of fishermen in Florida and a party of housewives in North Carolina were also watching a similar object. The number of "reliable observers" mounts only when the newspapers begin reporting the "flap" at its outset, and follow it through to the peak of activity.

The general newspaper coverage has been too slight and too disinterested to give us the full data on the overall situation. It stands to reason that if one person has actually seen a strange object flying at low level over his community, others must certainly have seen it too. If a large variety of witnesses see similar objects night after night in an area, as so often happens, it seems probable that the thing is operating somehow from that area. Dr. Jacques Vallee has noted in his studies that the UFO reports seem most intense in isolated, thinly populated areas. My own investigations have confirmed this. We can take this finding one step farther and assume that in areas where there is no population at all – and therefore no reports – such as our deserts, heavy forests, the desolate regions of northern Canada, etc., the UFO activity might actually be intense beyond belief.

With the possible exception of the Colorado University project, and a very small handful of scattered ufologists, almost no practical research is being conducted into this overwhelming situation. The assorted organizations compete with each other for "scoops" and there is no collaboration or coordination between them. The very few members of the scientific establishment who have taken an interest in the subject are competing with each other for government grants, and shamefully indulge in the same kind of personal attacks and vendettas that preoccupy the amateur groups.

If the UFOs are actively hostile to us, as many ufologists now believe, we are in a sorry state in this country. The controversies and side issues have diverted us and it is questionable if any of the existing organizations, or any of the scientists currently involved in the subject, will ever be able to get down to the hard task of collecting and interpreting the data.

Our first consideration in a "flap" study should be geographical. We immediately note precise geographical correlations between early "flaps" and contemporary ones. The objects appear to return to the same isolated areas again and again, not for a few months, but for decades and perhaps centuries. Random coincidence can be discarded altogether, for the data is now too extensive and detailed.

For our pilot study, we have chosen the "flap" of 1896-97. Dedicated researchers such as Lucius Farish and Dr. Jacques Vallee have dug into old newspaper files around the country, and come up with hundreds of substantial UFO reports for those years. I am particularly indebted to Mr. Farish, who has supplied me with a great mass of material. I began by breaking this material down by dates, geographical locations, and the times of the sightings. Many of these early reports describe the same identical thing being reported today. Often several people – even hundreds – were involved in the sighting. The objects were frequently said to have "wobbled" and moved erratically. The "falling leaf" motion was often described. In a number of cases, wings and tail fins were allegedly discernible on the objects. Many of these cases have already been discussed in articles by Farish, Vallee, and in Gordon Lore's *Mysteries of the Skies*, so we won't linger over them here.

The first sighting of 1896 seems to have taken place in San Andreas, California, on Sunday, November 15, 1896. The witnesses said they observed a brilliant flying light "about the size of a saucer." All ufologists are familiar with the famous San Andreas earthquake fault, and we know that there have been hundreds of UFO sightings along that fault in recent years. Apparently it may all have begun back in 1896.

The sightings seemed to concentrate most heavily around Sacramento and Oakland. The sightings occurred almost nightly somewhere in the San Francisco area. (There was one "bastard" sighting in Tacoma, Washington, far to the north, on November 24.) The local press played up the sightings and were soon buried in apparently authentic reports. The family of San Francisco's mayor saw the object, as did many other "reputable citizens." We might note that most of the sightings took place around 7 p.m., no matter where the locale. (In "flap" areas in 1966-68, the objects have also seemed to follow a regular schedule. For example, they appeared nightly around 8 p.m. in Point Pleasant, WV during March and April 1967. Natural phenomena would not, of course, adhere to such a strict timetable.)

There were additional sightings in California during December 1896, but the "flap" seems to have built up and tapered off during that single week in November. The peak was reached on November 25, a Wednesday. The newspapers were filled with speculations about a "secret inventor" who had perfected a wonderful "airship," and they tried to keep the matter alive after the sightings subsided. But the sightings subsided nevertheless. The "secret inventor" flew off as mysteriously as he had come.

There were daylight and dusk sightings of a cigar-shaped object, and these were well publicized, leading everyone to assume that anything unusual in the sky was *that* eerie "airship." Most of the nighttime sightings were of brilliant lights, not of a cigar-shaped "airship." The sightings occurred simultaneously in scattered areas, indicating (if not proving) that more than one "airship" was involved. Powerful spotlights were frequently reported, projecting blinding beams towards the ground. There are, of course, many contemporary reports of this same thing. Colored lights were also observed, but the majority were a dazzling white.

There were also a few landing and contact reports. One man even claimed that he was taken for a fast ride to Hawaii aboard the "airship."

Now for a bit of research. If you have a copy of *Project Blue Book Report 14*, turn to Fig. 31 (p. 47), a map of the United States outlining sightings reported to the USAF between 1947-52. You will note that one of the heaviest concentrations of sightings in the entire country is centered on the San Francisco area – a total of 338, blanketing approximately the same places "invaded" back in November 1896. The sightings in these areas have been numerous and consistent through out the 1960s. We might conclude that the UFOs are especially interested in this region and have at least been keeping it under observation since 1896!

Already we have two fragmentary "facts": the objects have been repeatedly (or consistently) active in the same area for 72 years, and they were, for some reason, following a timetable – a definite plan of activity as far back as 1896. They moved swiftly into the area, and were most active in the middle of the week.

Things quieted down for several months. Then in March 1897, strange lights and aerial objects reappeared in the United States, this time in the Midwest and northern states, particularly around Michigan. Then they seemed to spread out from the Midwest. This pattern still prevails. Several recent "flaps" seem to have begun in the Midwest and fanned out.

I have laid out all the available reports from April 1897, according to dates, times, and geographical factors, and here, again, the "flap" patterns are apparent and consistent. This "flap" began with spectacular sightings over Kansas City (April 1) and Chicago (April 9), in which hundreds, perhaps even thousands, of people watched a large cigar-shaped object slowly and deliberately pass overhead. As with the California "flap" of 1896, later witnesses assumed that the strange lights they viewed were actually attached to this same "airship." It is my contention that the deliberate daytime appearances of the "airship" were a diversion to give nighttime witnesses a frame of reference for identifying the illuminated objects, many of which were not cigar shaped. The illuminated objects are the real phenomenon. The "airship" was merely a cover.

Since the April 1897 reports simultaneously cover many states and widely separated areas, we once again have evidence that many objects were being deployed. There was an outstanding number of reported landings that April, some involving police officers, judges, and congressmen. In nearly every case, these witnesses described the UFO occupants as being dark complexioned, with dark eyes, and slight stature. Dark-eyed, dark-haired females were mentioned in several of these accounts. The occupants spoke English with one notable exception. A judge in Arkansas claimed that he encountered "pilots" who looked like "Japs" and who could not make themselves understood.

A number of artifacts were dropped from these "airships," perhaps deliberately, to offer further "proof" of the mundane origin of the objects. A Canadian newspaper was tossed overboard in Michigan, as were peeled potatoes and even a shoe. Several notes, one on finely engraved stationery, were also planted in the wake of the "airship" to further substantiate the notion that a "secret inventor" was responsible for the furor.

My own personal experiences with several ingenious and carefully-planned "hoaxes" leads me to conclude that similar "hoaxes" were executed in 1897 to reduce the impact of the arrival and activities of the objects. A mystery man walked into the office of a prominent San Francisco attorney shortly before the 1896 "flap" began. He claimed to have invented a marvelous "airship" and wanted the attorney to patent it. When the "airship" sightings hit the paper, the attorney, in good faith, told the press that he had met the inventor and knew all about it. The inventor disappeared, of course, and the attorney was left holding the bag. There are extensive newspaper reports on this incident and Gordon Lore devoted a chapter to it in his book.

I suspect that the "mystery man" was an advance man for "them" and that his sudden appearance prior to the "flap" was part of the carefully conceived plan. The plan was further augmented by the mass sightings of an "airship" that resembled the dirigible-type craft than being experimented with in Europe. The ufonauts established an excellent front for their operations with this tactic. It worked admirably well and, since most people believed a "secret inventor" was behind it all, the objects were not nearly as mysterious and disturbing as they might have been.

Because such maneuvers are very common in UFO cases, I strongly recommend that every serious ufologist obtain and study a good text on psychological warfare. I was trained in psychological warfare during my tenure in the army, and I have been astonished to find that the ufonauts seem to be "following the book." It's time we recognized that something far more complex than a mere aerial survey is taking place.

The geographical factors of the 1897 "flap" are somewhat surprising. Michigan had 30 percent of all the known sightings. Texas was next with over 20 percent. In the Ohio Northern University study of 1952, they remarked that Texas seemed to be a leader in UFO incidents in that year. Most of the 1897 Texas sightings (which included several landings and contacts) took place in the northern part of the state. The very same areas still produce the bulk of the Texas sightings. Just over the border, in Oklahoma, there is an equal amount of consistent activity dating back to the last century.

The peak of the 1897 flap took place on April 17, 1897, a Saturday. You will recall that the Michigan "flap" of March 1966, took place around Ann Arbor, Michigan. There were sightings in Ann Arbor on April 17, 1897. In fact, a UFO "belt" seems to stretch between Ann Arbor in the east and Benton Harbor in the western part of the state. This is the area producing the most reports in 1897, and this same area still produces the majority of our Michigan reports.

On April 17, 1897, while Michigan was in an "airship" furor from one end of the state to the other, all hell was breaking loose in northern Texas, many hundreds of miles to the south. Several landings and contacts were reported there that night. The sightings and landings continued in Texas, Oklahoma, and Arkansas until the end of the month. They tapered off slowly in early May.

In several landing cases from the period, the grounded objects were described as being surrounded by a strange glow, and the occupants allegedly warned the witness not to get too close. Though some of the published descriptions are frustratingly vague, it is probable that these objects really did not resemble the celebrated "airship" but were discoid. If my theory of deception and diversion proves true, then the slight, dark-skinned "pilots" were probably decoys, fronting for the "Jap" types who may really be at the bottom of all this.

The full data on the events of 1897 will eventually be published. It offers a great many clues to the overall "mystery" and seems to preclude many of the popular speculations in the field. The majority of the sightings were, as I have stated, merely maneuvering lights, just as the majority of the modern reports deal with such lights. We have done ourselves an injustice by concentrating on the reports of "hard" objects (seemingly mechanical objects), which represent a minority of all reports. These "hard" objects may be no more meaningful than the "airship" that purposefully drifted over Chicago. It is erroneous to assume that "soft" objects (lights, and transparent or translucent objects that change size, shape, and color while remaining in view) are merely visible portions of "flying saucers." The "soft" objects are the real phenomenon.

Fortunately, occult manifestations have attracted a higher caliber of investigator than UFOs, and the studies of ghosts, hauntings, and polter-geists in the last century are quite thorough and responsible. Leading scientists, journalists, and clergymen have investigated and documented many of these manifestations, and they have left excellent records. I have examined much of the material and found that poltergeist "flaps" tend to either immediately precede or follow UFO "flaps," or the two kinds of phenomena occur simultaneously. I have already noted in other articles that I have found a sudden outbreak of poltergeist activity in UFO "flap" areas.

The poltergeist phenomenon seems to consist of invisible entities or fields of force that are capable of moving heavy objects, starting fires, and committing other kinds of senseless mischief. Mysterious fires often go hand-in-hand with UFO sightings. Doors in houses of witnesses in UFO areas open and close by themselves. Strange noises are heard. We must open our minds to the chilling possibility that the *real* UFOs and the *real* ufonauts may be invisible to our limited visual apparatus (the human eye can discern only a very small portion of the electromagnetic spectrum). At least one "contactee" has told us that the objects are usually invisible in daylight, but tend to glow at night and give themselves away. This may explain why the sighting ratio increases sharply at sunset and is most intense during the hours of darkness. (See Figs. 40 and 41 in *Project Blue Book Report 14* for graphs illustrating this "sunset" factor.)

It may be awesome – even insane – to contemplate the possibility that the objects can render themselves invisible. It could mean that our skies, even over our cities, could be crowded during the daylight hours and we would never be the wiser. It could also explain how the objects could "hide" from us in "flap" areas.

Our evidence thus far is fragmentary and superficial, but it shows that poltergeist phenomena parallels UFO activity.

THE FLAPS OF THE 1950S

Dr. Jacques Vallee collected and analyzed the many landing and contact reports that took place in France in 1954, and his study has given us additional "flap" data that supports the patterns already revealed in the above. Although the French "flap" began in September, it did not reach its peak until the second week in October. The high point was reached on Monday, October 11, 1954. There were many fluctuations of the sighting and landing reports during that hectic and bizarre week, with peaks being reached every other day. The sightings continued at a high level the following week, peaking again on Wednesday, October 20, and then tapering off, although there was another slight peak on Wednesday, October 27.

Dr. Vallee noted that the French landings took place in sparsely populated sectors, and that most of them occurred in the early morning hours. The landings and contacts of April 1897 also followed this pattern, the majority of them taking place around midnight or thereafter in remote ranch areas.

Since most people in rural areas are early risers, the majority of the population is in bed by 10 p.m. As we have already demonstrated, UFO reports seem to rise sharply between 10 p.m. and midnight. Perhaps it is most intense during the wee hours of the morning, when there are very few witnesses about. This would mean that the scattered reports during those hours actually represent much greater activity than we have suspected.

Perhaps the most significant "flap" of modern times was the worldwide epidemic of "flying saucers" that struck during the first week in November 1957. It marked the first large-scale demonstration of the "EM effect," and included a number of very interesting "contacts," so it is most regrettable that no ufologist or organization bothered to go through the trouble of collecting all the reports and presenting the data in meaningful form. Instead, the more interesting cases were handled individually, and no effort was made to show the correlative factors or produce a sound statistical analysis of the situation. I believe that the two most significant years in ufology were 1848 (that's right – 1848) and 1957.

NICAP's *UFO Evidence* did offer a badly organized summary of the 1957 "flap," while APRO concentrated on the sightings that occurred in Texas and New Mexico. The Levelland sightings were intriguing, but they represent only a small portion of the "Big Picture." That particular section of New Mexico has been UFO-ridden for years. (See Fig. 31, *Project Blue Book Report 14.*)

Let's review, very briefly, what happened in 1957. Sightings began to build up in October 1957. Then on Friday, November 1, there was the reported appearance of two metallic discs over Johannesburg, South Africa, and other scattered reports from Coleman, TX, Campbellsville, KY (about 200 miles from Hopkinsville, site of the famous "little man" incident of 1955); and the Sandia mountains in New Mexico. Hardly anything to get excited about.

The next night, however, was a night to remember. It was Saturday, November 2nd. Texas erupted in a series of spectacular events around Brenham, Poteet, Amarillo, and a sleepy little oil town named Levelland. Great luminous objects buzzed highways, causing automobiles to stall, radios to go dead, and television sets to jitter.

Canada joined the flap on Sunday, November 3, as did the city of Ciudad Trujillo, Venezuela, and Barahona in the Dominican Republic. A boy in Scotia, Nebraska, reported turning "numb" as a circular object, mounted with some kind of antenna, hummed low about him. At 7:30 p.m. that day, CBS-TV newsman Russell B. Day shot 40 feet of movie film of a color-changing object that was maneuvering over Deming, New Mexico. Later in the evening, a jeep filled with soldiers on guard patrol at the atomic testing site in White Sands, New Mexico, reported seeing a luminous disc low over the concrete bunkers. Five hours later, the object returned for a repeat performance in front of another jeep filled with soldiers.

The flap continued to spread. Johannesburg, South Africa, had another major sighting on Monday, November 4, with hundreds of people reportedly viewing the objects dancing around their skies. In Kodiak, Alaska, a police patrol car watched a fiery red object swoop low over a school, and while it was in view, their police radio emitted a steady "dit-da-dit" that drowned out all regular broadcasts. Earlier that same morning, in distant Brazil, an unidentified flying object buzzed an airliner outside Ararangua, and all the radio equipment on board burned out in a flash. A few hours later, a gigantic glowing form flew over the Itaipu Fort outside Sao Vicente, Brazil, and hovered so close that two sentries were severely burned. Panic reigned in the fort as all electrical power quit. And when the soldiers stumbled outside, they found their weapons became too hot to handle. Two of the men became hospital cases and were infirmed for nearly a year.

In Elmwood, Illinois, that night, three policemen watched a peculiar, red-orange object hover above the Elmwood cemetery for several minutes. They said it seemed to change shape, "fold into itself, and disappear in the sky."

The two nights that followed marked the peak of the "flap." Tuesday, November 5, they were seeing things in Dunnottar, Transvaal, South Africa, and in Canada from Ontario to Manitoba. Texas had a series of sightings in Wichita Falls, Hedley, Houston, San Antonio and Beaumont. That afternoon a TWA pilot reported seeing something he could not identify near Kearney, Nebraska. Shortly afterwards, a salesman named Reinhold Schmidt barged into the Sheriff's office in Kearney and told a wild story of having been invited aboard a strange object occupied by men and women who spoke German.

Off the Gulf of Mexico, the Coast Guard cutter *Sebago* picked up a UFO on its radar. There were other sightings in New York City, Philadelphia, Indiana, Tennessee, Missouri, Colorado, California, Georgia, Massachusetts, Ohio, Mississippi, New Mexico, and Illinois. Galesburg, Illinois, which had sightings on April 10, 1897, was revisited.

On Wednesday night, November 6, the major landings took place. A farmer in Everittstown, New Jersey, claimed that a "little man" from an object asked for his dog (note that the Russian dog, Laika, was sent into orbit on November 3, 1957). A boy in Dante, Tennessee, told reporters that a strange object had landed in a field near his farmhouse that morning, and that the occupants seemed to be talking German. (The Schmidt case of the day before had not yet received any publicity in Dante.)

Near Playa Del Rey, California, a group of cars stalled and the drivers were approached by two men with "yellowish-green" complexions. They came from an egg-shaped object on a nearby beach, and spoke English. Scores of other sightings poured in from Canada, New York State, and other regular flap areas.

Early on the morning of November 7, a truck driver near House, Mississippi, came upon a large egg-shaped object blocking the road. Two men and a woman, all about four feet tall, approached him and tried to talk to him in a rapid-fire language that he could not understand.

Friday, November 8, there were sightings in Orgueil, France, Au Sable

Forks, New York, and Lafayette, Louisiana, but the "flap" was spent. Reports became scattered, and declined through to the middle of November. NICAP recorded a total of 110 sightings between November 1 and 15. Project Blue Book later revealed that it had received 414 sightings for November, but they listed only four as "unknown."

Someone should have collected all the reports of that hectic week and written a book. Instead isolated incidents such as the Levelland sightings and the Brazilian fort case were over-publicized by the UFO press. The contacts were largely ignored by all except APRO. Reinhold Schmidt was later jailed and roundly discredited. The most important "flap" of the 20th century was thus slighted, even by the UFO buffs themselves, and the valuable information that could have been gained was lost in scattered files.

Could the skeptics have explained the sheer weight of these sightings? Many were in the form of police reports about physical things happening to the people and the vehicles involved. Here was conclusive evidence that the UFOs were real.

A reasonable "flap" study at that time would have demolished the controversy, and the ufologists could have settled down to the neglected job of finding out what these things actually were and what they were really up to.

Earlier in 1957, there had been a series of controversial contacts in South America, England, and New Jersey (the Howard Menger case). All of these "contactees" were told, in one way or another, of an impending "demonstration." That "demonstration" *did* occur. But we had been too diverted and misdirected, and too preoccupied with battling the USAF, to pay real heed. Besides, almost no one took the "contactees" seriously in those days.

And look at the remarkable coincidences: the major Levelland sightings took place on a Saturday. The whole "flap" peaked on Wednesday. The major "contacts" all occurred within hours of each other and hundreds of miles apart. The boy in Dante, Tennessee literally confirmed Schmidt's story of German-speaking ufonauts. The boy also noted that the occupants seemed interested in his dog. The New Jersey case, later that same day, confirmed that strange interest in matters canine. The latter witness described his "little man" as having a "putty-like complexion." The next morning, the truck driver in far-off Mississippi allegedly met ufonauts with "pasty" complexions.

Were all of these people insane? Had Schmidt some how got together with the Tennessee farm boy and the Mississippi truck driver beforehand and coached them? Were they all in cahoots? Not very likely.

When you review the locales of the major "flaps" of that week in November, it is surprising how many of the isolated, thinly populated sections of the country that were involved in the April 1897 sightings were also inundated in November 1957. The laws of coincidence are stretched to the breaking point.

The majority of the November 1957 sightings took place betwccn 8 and 10 p.m. In several instances, the objects returned, night after night, at approximately the same time each night.

There were "Men In Black" cases in 1957, too. And on that Wednesday night of November 6, a painter named Olden Moore allegedly saw a UFO land near Montville, Ohio. The field was found to be radioactive the next day, and odd footprints were discovered there. Had Olden Moore also made "contact?" He was whisked to Washington, D.C. a few days later by the Air Force, grilled for three days, and sworn to secrecy, according to his story.

We're forced to wonder how many other landings and contacts might have taken place that night. How much data is now lost to us forever?

THE FLAPS OF 1966

When I first plunged into this subject, full-time, early in 1966 (just before the Michigan "flap" took place), I was frankly appalled at the absence of concrete research in the field and the complete lack of "hard facts." I enlisted, at great expense, several newspaper clipping services and tediously began to collect and compile every available UFO sighting. By the end of 1966, I found, somewhat to my horror, that I have over 10,000 clippings and reports from all over the world for that singular year.

Lacking a computer, I had to develop a complicated system for cataloguing this mess and extracting the data. At that time, I had not studied the 1897 or 1957 reports, and I suppose I had been partially brainwashed by the pro-UFO books I read that year. I was "ready" to believe in the extraterrestrial thesis, even though I had uncovered all kinds of amazing things on my trips into "flap" areas, and was beginning to realize that the ET concept simply did not fit much of the data.

Painstakingly, I sorted out apparent hoaxes (they were remarkably few in number), and the vague reports of lights seen high in the sky. Using the "poll method," I settled upon about 730 excellent sightings as being representative of the whole, and I studied them very carefully. I catalogued the known sightings from every day of the year in 1966, broke them down by states and times, traced them on maps, and tried to build up the "Big Picture."

As my study progressed, I noticed that when a "flap" occurred in a specific state, it seemed to go from border to border, but did not overlap into the adjoining states. It was almost as if the UFOs were using our maps and operating in one state at a time. This finding automatically ruled out natural explanations, such as meteors.

There were many "flap" dates in 1966, but let's just consider one. While Michigan was winning all the publicity in March of that year, Wednesday, March 30 produced major sightings in South Carolina (there was a "flap" there), Ohio, Iowa, California, New Jersey (the Wanaque reservoir again), and Long Island (an "electromagnetic effect" case).

"Flaps" took place each month that year. And they seemed to move systematically from state to state. My trips taught me that clippings were a very inadequate barometer, so I made friends with policemen, sheriffs, and newspaper editors wherever I went. They fed me new reports continuously, and most of these reports went unpublished. I was buried in data. Sightings would break out simultaneously, in a dozen states, on a single date. I reached a point where I could frequently predict the geographical location of the next "flap" in advance.

Then, when I started analyzing the historical "flaps" and digging into hitherto undiscovered sources of information, I returned to my 1966 study and found that the "flaps" were consistent, and had occurred repeatedly in the same areas, not only in the 1940s and 1950s, but in the 19th century as well. My misgivings about the extraterrestrial thesis grew into a certainty that it was erroneous. The phenomenon had to be terrestrially based. How, why, and by whom remained unanswered, but we have to take this thing a step at a time, which is what I've been trying to do.

Later I applied what I had learned to some of the major flaps of 1967 and 1968, and the patterns were clearly repeated. The UFO buffs have been looking for evidence of another kind. They want "hardware" and landings on the White House lawn. All the while, they have been overlooking a mountain of real evidence. The same kind of evidence used to prove the quantum theory. The same kind of evidence used to send killers to the electric chair. Correlative facts. Facts that can be tested and verified in new cases, and which are confirmed globally.

THE UFOS NOBODY TALKS ABOUT: DEADLY FIREBALLS IN THE SKY

On the night of Monday, April 25, 1966, a very slow moving "meteor," greenish and trailing a long tail, gracefully arced over Canada and floated southwards over the Atlantic seaboard from New York to the Carolinas. It was so brilliant that it actually lit up the ground over which it passed, and moved so slowly that many excellent photographs of it were taken by amateur and professional photographers along its path. It looked like a "meteor," but it certainly didn't act like one. If you were out-of-doors anywhere along the eastern seaboard between the hours of 8 and 9 p.m. that night, you may have seen this thing yourself. It was visible throughout most of New York State, including New York City.

Thousands of miles away, in the far-off Soviet state of Tashkent – at the same latitude as New York (exactly on the opposite side of the earth from the northeastern United States) – a Soviet scientist named Galina Lazarenko was awakened at 5:23 a.m. on Tuesday, April 26, 1966, by a brilliant flash of light.

"The courtyard and my room were brightly lighted up," she said later. "It was so bright that I could clearly see all the objects in my room."

Simultaneously, an engineer named Alexei Melnichuk was walking down a Tashkent street when he heard a loud rumble followed by a brilliant flash of light.

"I seemed to be bathed in a white light that extended as far as I could see," he recalled. "I was forced to shield my face with my hands. After a few seconds, I took my hands away from my face and the light was gone."

A few seconds later, the great Tashkent earth fault shuddered and buckled, and a tremendous earthquake struck, killing 10 and leaving 200,000 people homeless. As the dazed and terrified residents staggered into the rubble-strewn streets, they saw strange "glowing spheres, floating through the air like lighted balloons."

There is a nine-hour time difference between our Atlantic seaboard and Tashkent. We were watching that "meteor" cruising majestically overhead at exactly the same time that a brilliant and inexplicable flash of light was announcing the impending disaster in Tashkent. These correlations are precise. There is no room for error. Our "meteor" and the Tashkent earthquake occurred simultaneously, at exact opposite sides of the earth!

What kind of a coincidence is this? A "meteor" appears on one side of the earth, and a disastrous earthquake strikes exactly opposite. Science does not have the answer. In fact, most scientists making a study of earthquakes admit that they don't even know all the questions.

An hour before the Tashkent earthquake, a schoolteacher living near the fault said that her dog began to howl, and that when the earthquake began, the dog ran anxiously to the door before each shock struck. Scientists have long been puzzled by the apparent ability of animals – particularly dogs and horses – to sense impending disasters.

Another "meteor," followed by earth tremors, zipped in over the Gulf of Mexico early on the morning of Wednesday, March 27, 1968. It was first sighted by the crew of the tanker *Alfa Mex II*, who described "two or three objects in the center of a bright ball of fire." The crew of the Mexican warship *Guanajuato* also reported seeing a flaming object, and the men on both ships said that the waters of the Gulf were churned into fountains of spray after the object passed. This could indicate that whatever it was, it was exerting a direct gravitational pull.

At 2:10 a.m. that morning, residents in Veracruz, Mexico, about 25 miles from the ships' positions, were awakened by a deafening rumbling noise. "Before I had a chance to realize what was happening," Senora Angelita de Villalobos Arana, 40, told investigators, "it was as bright as day, and the terrible noise kept on. I felt cool, then cold. The light got brighter."

Within minutes, the streets of Veracruz were filled with hysterical people. They thought the end of the world had arrived, as the sky filled with unearthly light, and the ground trembled. The strange "meteor" loomed over the scene, seemed to dip towards the ground, then rose again and shot off.

Mr. Ernesto Dominguez, head of the Mexican Department of Meteorology at Veracruz, conducted a careful investigation and collected all the reports. "This probably was not a meteorite," Dominguez stated in his official report.

> We cannot say for sure just what it was. We do know that it
> did not fall to earth or collide with the earth. Its trajectory
> was curved. Imagine a jet or a spaceship suddenly going out
> of control and plunging down directly toward earth. Then
> – as if control was regained suddenly – the object or objects
> suddenly veered away from the earth, only moments before
> collision point, and went out over the Gulf of Mexico. But I
> think it did not fall into the sea. It could have gone upward.
> A meteorite would hardly do such a thing.

These peculiar "meteors" and green fireballs have been turning up in increasing numbers for the past fifteen years. They usually look like the astronomer's concept of "meteors," with a long tail dangling behind, but their maneuvers alone rule out the simple natural explanation. They are far more numerous than the intriguing "flaying saucer" type reports of metallic circular objects. In fact, the reports of mysterious lights and unlikely meteors outnumber the "saucer" reports by almost ten to one. Furthermore, they pop up year after year in the same isolated, thinly populated areas. Natural meteors could hardly be so selective. And meteors don't change direction or angle of descent.

Some of our funny "meteors" also cause electrical blackouts.

Towards sunset on the evening of Friday, April 18, 1962, a giant reddish object appeared over the northern part of New York State, apparently moving down from Canada in a southwesterly direction. Air Force radar locked on to the object and carefully followed it, across a dozen states, as it sped westward. Then, at 7:30 p.m., a brilliant flash, followed by deep rumbles and earth tremors, occurred in southwestern Nevada. Shortly afterwards, an unidentified circular machine landed near a power station outside Eureka, Nevada, and the lights went out for thirty minutes.

Lieutenant-Colonel Herbert Rolph of the North American Air Defense Command Center at Colorado Springs, Colorado, faced a throng of excited newsmen that night. He admitted that NORAD's radar had tracked the object all the way across the U.S. and added: "A meteor can't be tracked on radar – but this thing was!"

What are these "things," and why don't we know more about them? The real problem lies in the "scientific attitude" many have. Because the objects resemble meteors in appearance, astronomers have automatically dismissed them as such, and have never made a concerted effort to study these piles of reports, filled with obvious contradictions. If the thing passes over at a high altitude, glows, and hauls a tail, then it must be a meteor, according to the reasoning of astronomers.

But the non-conforming "meteors" are nothing new. They appeared repeatedly throughout places like Nebraska, Michigan, Canada, and New Mexico during the 19th century. One professor, C.A. Chant of the University of Toronto, made a study of the strange "train" of meteors that flashed across Canada on the night of Thursday, February 9, 1913. Unlike natural meteors, the fiery red objects traveled slowly across the sky in a straight, horizontal line. They glided majestically out of the northwest and sailed away to the southeast.

"Other bodies were seen coming from the northwest," the Professor wrote, "emerging from precisely the same place as the first one. Onward they moved, at the same deliberate pace. In twos or threes or fours, with tails streaming behind them, they came. They traversed the same path, and were headed for the same point in the southeastern sky."

Very odd meteors, indeed!

More recently, on Sunday, September 15, 1968, a brilliant luminous object buzzed the New England states, moving slowly enough so that thousands of people were able to get a good look at it. As usual, the astronomers quickly dismissed it as "a meteor." However, that same week, a new "flap" of UFO sightings erupted in several states, from Nebraska to Virginia. It is a curious coincidence that our "meteors" manage to turn up during the same periods when thousands of witnesses are also getting close-up views of other strange lights, cigar-shaped objects, and those troublesome "flying saucers."

Not only do our "meteors" refuse to obey the laws set down for them by our learned astronomers, but they also have an unnerving habit of traveling in formations with military-like precision.

The late Morris K. Jessup, a professional astrophysicist, was especially interested in the fireball-comet-meteor reports, and did study them extensively. In his book, *The UFO Annual* (1956), he described many of the "meteor" reports of 1955 and had this to say (p. 96-97):

> We are having an influx of fireballs, and these have had an unusual amount of attention because of their numbers, brilliance, and the kelly-green color of some of them. There does, indeed, seem to be something queer about them. For the record, it might be stated that the green fireball flurry did not originate in the U.S., but apparently in Sweden (1946). This was a few years ago, before the great intensity of interest in UFOs or saucers. They were then thought to be Russian rockets or missiles; and to this day, we cannot prove that they were not Russian. In the U.S., the green fireballs made their debut in New Mexico, and were thought to be associated with atomic energy experiments. Now, however, they have spread over much of North America and, frankly, we don't know what they are nor why, nor from where.

As we have noted, the majority of all UFO sightings are of spherical or shapeless blobs of very intense light (so intense that many witnesses complain of "eyeburn" afterwards – the searing of the cornea, similar to the sunburned eyes you can suffer at a beach). The soft diffused light of "swamp gas" is quite different from these objects, as is normal starlight. In addition, the objects have a talent for going through all the colors of the spectrum in front of the startled witness. Most often they are described as turning green, then fiery red just before descending or ascending. When traveling in a straight line overhead, they are usually a brilliant orange or a glaring white. Since the advent of manmade satellites, many people actually mistake UFOs for satellites instead of the other way around, as the skeptics would have us believe. At present there are only two manmade satellites that are visible to the naked eye, and both are so small and so dim that you must know where and when they're going to appear in order to be able to see them. Those big, brilliant white "stars" moving across the sky during the summer months are *not* satellites.

The author has collected and studied hundreds of those neglected reports, and some startling patterns have come to light. In the majority of all these cases going back to the 19th century, the objects (if they are "objects") have consistently appeared from the north and followed apparently *controlled* courses southwards.

A surprising number seem to enter the U.S. from the section of Canada lying north of Michigan.

Our UFOs and "meteors" do follow precise patterns that can now be predicted to some degree. The state of Nebraska has a long history of UFO sightings. During the heavy but little-publicized "flap" of July-August 1966, some definite patterns emerged. On Tuesday, July 5, 1966, at 10 p.m., a group of four witnesses viewed "a large octagon-shaped object with colored lights. The light dimmed and brightened, and the object swooped twice over a field and then went back into the air." This took place three miles northwest of Norfolk, Nebraska.

On July 9 and 10, there were sightings in North and South Dakota, the states north of Nebraska. On July 11, there were several sightings in Iowa, the state bordering Nebraska on the east. The South Dakota sightings took place in the southwest corner of the state, close to the Nebraskan border. If we had been able to collect this data fast enough, we could have successfully predicted that a "flap" was due in Nebraska and that, statistically, the odds were that it would take place on a Wednesday night at 10 p.m. (the majority of all UFO sightings occur around 10 p.m.).

Shortly after 10 p.m. on Wednesday, July 13, 1966 (10:05 according to a newsman witness and another person), a blazing object hurtled across the skies, heading southward over York, Nebraska. Perhaps their watches were wrong, or perhaps they got a preliminary glimpse of the thing that would be seen by many thousands five minutes later at 10:10 p.m. At that time, scores of people in Muny Park, Cozad, Nebraska, saw "a very bright object with multicolored smaller bright 'stars' trailing it." They all agreed that it appeared in the northwest and headed southeast.

If it had remained on this course, it would have angled straight across Kansas and all the Kansan reports would have described a northwest to southeast course. However, a flood of reports from Kansas, including sightings by policemen, attorneys and many others, said that the "meteor" traveled northwest to northeast. This meant that it had *changed course* and had skirted the Nebraska-Kansas border.

There was a particularly heavy concentration of reports from central Nebraska, from small communities such as Scotia, Ord, Burwell, Comstock, Arcadia and North Loup. All these were consistent, describing the object as passing from southwest to southeast. Another cluster of sightings was reported from the Omaha areas on the eastern tip of the state. These all stated that the object was traveling from southwest to southeast.

A larger picture can be drawn from this. The "meteor" came from the northwest, from Wyoming perhaps, executed a slight turn south of Cozad, and moved along the Nebraska-Kansas border towards Missouri-Iowa. Then it turned again and headed northwards towards Illinois.

The sheriff of Warren County, Illinois, was sitting in front of the police station in Monmouth, Illinois that night when he observed a fiery orange ball arcing across the sky towards the northeast. A few minutes later, he received an excited phone call from a Galesburg, Illinois woman who said she and her three children had been driving along the U.S. 34 bypass when they saw a green light seemingly skirting the treetops. A white-colored fire seemed to burst from it, she said, and it appeared to dive towards the ground in the northeast. Thinking that a small plane might have crashed, she stopped at the nearest farmhouse and called the sheriff. He rushed to Monmouth Park, the area of the sighting, but found nothing. Eight other persons called radio stations and newspapers in the area to report similar sightings. All agreed that the object was green with a red ring around it, and trailed a short red tail. One other person, besides the sheriff, reported seeing an orange object. Everyone reported that it first appeared in the southwest and traveled northeast.

What lies to the northeast of Illinois? Michigan, of course.

A few minutes after 11 p.m. Michigan time (10 p.m. Nebraska time), Jack Westbrook and Charles Frye of Willis, Michigan, were walking across Rawsonville Road when Mr. Frye exclaimed: "Look at that!" Both men saw what appeared to be a silver disc with one red and one white light on it. They estimated that it was no more than 1,000 feet high. The object moved forward swiftly, stopped, seemed to reverse itself, circled around, moved up and down, and finally shot out of sight. They said they watched it for about seven minutes and heard no sound.

Were the Monmouth, Illinois and Willis, Michigan, sightings of completely different objects totally independent of the Nebraska "meteor"? This is a possibility, of course. But it is equally possible, and probably very likely, that a UFO – or a group of UFOs – passed from Wyoming, crossed Nebraska, and then turned northwards into Illinois and Michigan.

Mr. Charles Tougas of the Meteorite Recovery Project at Lincoln, Nebraska, was the man the press turned to for an answer. He said that special cameras had recorded the event. He estimated that the "meteor" had appeared somewhere near McCook, Nebraska, and had plummeted to Earth somewhere outside of Phillipsburg, Kansas. A search for it was launched at Phillipsburg, but the object was never found. If the object had enjoyed such a very brief life span, and had traveled such a very short distance in the western part of the state, it is very unlikely that it would have been so clearly seen in the Omaha sector, hundreds of miles eastward, and that all the witnesses would have described it as moving to the southeast. And it certainly would not have turned up in Illinois – still further to the northeast.

The "meteor" explanation simply does not work in this case. There are too many "ifs," and too many unnatural coincidences.

All the descriptions were uniform. A newsman in Brewster, Nebraska, described it as being "the size of a basketball; the white fore-end changed colors, going from blue to green, trailing a long tail." A young witness on a ranch near Scotia, Nebraska, described it as being "a bright, whitish-yellow light." Brilliant white lights were mentioned in a scattering of reports, but the overall consensus was that it was green or "blue-green with a red band around it." Kansas viewers thought it was green.

Only two groups of witnesses reported hearing any sound. Both were located in the central Nebraskan cluster. People driving near Arcadia said they saw "a flashing red light" and heard "more than one explosion." Mr. George Bremer of Ord reported the same thing. (Viewers of that 1913 "meteor chain" in Canada said that the objects were low enough in the atmosphere to displace air as they passed.)

One week prior to the Nebraska "flap," a "green object with a long white tail" appeared over Muskegon, Michigan, traveling a horizontal path from east to west. It was seen by police officers and other reliable witnesses. The date was Wednesday, July 6, 1966. The time was 11 p.m. (making it 10 p.m. Central Daylight Time in Nebraska). At 10 p.m., Monday, July 11, a round blue object was observed over Lake Erie by witnesses in Ashtabula, Ohio, facing in the direction of Michigan. Some noted that it seemed to have a long tail. One person described it as "a round ball of bright blue light with an outer rim of pale gold." It appeared to descend westward.

When we drew a great circle on a map of the U.S. looping through Nebraska and curving up through Monmouth-Galesburg, Illinois to Michigan, we found that the other end of the curve cut across the northeastern part of Wyoming. A quick review of our clippings and general report data revealed that that very section of Wyoming had a UFO "flap" a few days before the Nebraskan "meteor" arrived. Extensive UFO activity was also reported further to the northwest that month, around Glacier National Park in Montana. Brilliant, fast-moving lights appeared there nightly on precise schedules, passing from the northwest to the southeast. This course would have carried them to the Wyoming "flap" area and, if extended along a perfect curve, would have continued into Nebraska to the McCook-Cozad sector.

So the plot thickens! Our Nebraska "flap" of July 13 was merely part of an overall "flap" involving several states. All of the sightings fitted neatly into a perfect circle beginning in northwestern Montana, looping through the central states, and curving upwards through Illinois and Michigan, and back into Canada. If we continue the same circle into Canada, we find that the uppermost part of it would rest in the densely forested and thinly populated regions of Manitoba and Saskatchewan. Both of these provinces have had long UFO "flaps" in 1967-68. The majority of the seemingly random sightings can be fitted into this "Great Circle Route." London, Ontario, in the east, would be a part of it. The continuous flap areas of Ohio, Indiana, and Pennsylvania would lie just southeast of the circle.

But it doesn't all stop with this one circle. Other circles are evident, some interlocking, other apparently independent of the main "routes." If you refer to your maps or a globe, you will see that the latitudes of 80 to 60 extend from northern Canada southwards, encompassing all of New England and the continuous flap areas of New York State, Pennsylvania, etc., into that section of the Atlantic known as "the Bermuda Triangle." As the same latitudes continue into South America, they cover the flap areas of Venezuela, Peru, Chile, and – most important – the Salta-to-Bahia Blanca sector of Argentina.

At least some of the "flying saucers" and "meteors" are coming down to us from Northern Canada's isolated, unpopulated, and nearly inaccessible areas. They move along geometric courses, going from point to point along a great circle, and by collecting all available sightings we can sometimes even predict where they are going to turn up next.

Aime Michel's "straight-line theory" works for short distances (usually about 200 miles) along these routes, but it is necessary to extend the route on a curve for long distances.

It is probable that the objects originate – that is, they begin their flights – somewhere between Victoria Island and Baffin Island in the Far North. We might mention that the Eskimo tribes of the Far North have ancient legends that claim they were originally flown to these inhospitable regions from some point far to the south. Contrary to the theories of the evolutionists, the Eskimos have dark skins and Oriental features. Strange that they have failed to turn pale or chalky white in a land where the sun is absent altogether for six months out of the year, and where the bitter cold forces them to overdress and thus remain sheltered from the sun's rays during the sunlit months.

THE OVERVIEW

Aside from the charts and graphs compiled by Captain Ruppelt's Air Force teams in the early 1950s and Dr. Vallee's basic work, we have no practical indices to overall UFO activity. No research of any real worth has been done to data in the United States. The compilation of the endless sightings has no value unless all this material is adequately indexed and catalogued. We have even failed to make logical studies of big "flaps" such as the November 1957 sequence. Individual sightings are meaningless and often misleading. When a report comes in from an obscure town in Utah, say, I want to know if any other reports had come from that same in 1952, '57, or even 1897. I want to see if that town fits into the overview.

We must recognize that the phenomenon is continuous, not sporadic, and that the objects return to the same areas year after year, century after century. Who has studied the history of Socorro, New Mexico? No one. Chances are excellent that other incidents have occurred in the Socorro sector (within 200 miles), not only in 1964, but also in 1952, 1947, and possibly even in 1897.

This kind of systematic research is tedious, unglamorous, and often frustrating, but it must be done. It cannot be done by one man or 100. Everyone interested in ufology must contribute. Every ufologist should become an expert on the history of his own particular locale. Every ufologist must dip into the yellowing pages of the old newspapers in his area, and into the Indian legends and ghost tales. Every ufologist must carefully compile every sighting ever recorded in his area, no matter how irrelevant or unsubstantial it might seem. As I have now demonstrated, an apparent "meteor" sighting – the kind of thing usually ignored by most UFO buffs – can provide a vital link in a chain of events that can reveal important patterns.

This data must then be distributed freely to other ufologists in other areas, so that it can be studied and compared. Gradually these key patterns will become clearer, and we will build up a substantial body of statistical evidence that will enable us to clearly define the source and nature of the phenomenon.

It is scandalous that so little actual research has been done in the past twenty years. If you review the publications of 1948 and 1952, as I have done, you will immediately see that we have been standing still. We have been devoted to the "cause," not to the subject. Even worse, the very valid - and very advanced – work of men like Morris Jessup and Meade Layne has literally become lost and forgotten, because we have buried ourselves in controversies and nonsensical issues.

Last year, a foreign TV producer came to me after he had traveled across the U.S. interviewing UFO witnesses and UFO buffs. He was quite disheartened. "You know," he groaned. "This has been going on for twenty years, and I haven't been able to find a single expert – real expert – on UFOs in this country." Nobody knows what is going on because nobody has made a logical, objective, systematic effort to find out.

On March 3-4, 1968, a major UFO "flap" exploded in 25 states. Automobiles were pursued by luminous objects in several areas. In West Virginia, the objects remained in view for several hours. The sightings began about 8 p.m. and continued until 4 a.m. the next morning. Many of the "flap" areas under scrutiny in my studies were affected.

The reports trickled in for weeks afterwards. The Air Force, however, explained this one away as being the disintegration of a Soviet rocket, and many UFO buffs accepted this without question. When a rocket breaks up and re-enters the atmosphere, the small fragments burn out within seconds and are rarely visible over a large area – if they are visible at all.

Obviously, what is needed is a central organization capable of collecting and correlating such "flap" data quickly and accurately. These incidents are "news" for only a few days, sometimes for only a few hours, so speed is essential if the "truth" is going to be released to the public. Weeks after the March 4 "flap," *The New York Times'* anti-UFO science editor, Walter

Sullivan, wrote a piece "explaining" it. He backed up his story by quoting NICAP's erroneous statement that UFO reports were on the decline in 1968.

If a comprehensive study of that "flap" had been prepared, it might have swayed even Mr. Sullivan. Unfortunately the "flaps" are so frequent and numerous that I have not been able to devote my limited time and resources to this kind of study exclusively. As a reporter, I know that any news feature on a "flap" must be issued as soon as possible. It is a waste of time to try to get editors to publish such things weeks or months later.

Although there have been numerous attempts at "flap" studies over the years, it was not until John Fuller's close and thorough study of the Exeter, New Hampshire cases, in 1965, that the ice was broken. The validity of a "flap" study was proven by Mr. Fuller's book, which did more to demolish skepticism in the phenomenon than anything written previously. Dr. Vallee's examination of earlier "flaps" has also been extremely important and has given us much valuable information.

The more we review the events of the 19th century and early part of the 20th century, the more correlative data we will have to lead us closer to that elusive "truth." It stands to reason that the random reports published in those earlier years represented many thousands of sightings. There was no UFO "subject" in those days, and the occasional published reports were treated as "human interest" items, not as part of an idiotic controversy. In poring over the back issues of *The New York Times* and other newspapers across the country, I have found that there were substantial "flaps" in the 1920s and 1930s – particularly in the years 1922, 1930, 1934, and 1937.

Patient research is required to collect and correlate all of this "lost" data. Hundreds of researchers should be engaged in this type of historical study, but very few are making the attempt. This is not a problem for scientists per se. It rightly belongs in the hands of scholars and historians who are trained to evaluate the validity of such documentation, and who can apply the standard methods of scholarship to its correlation and presentation. Thousands of bits and pieces must be unearthed and assembled in a methodical manner, in the same way that archaeologists spend months or years collecting bits of pottery from the sand, and reassembling them.

Unidentified flying objects have been active for centuries, clearly concentrated in the same areas, year after year. (I have found that old American Indian legends describe essentially the same things that are happening today in former Indian territories such as Oklahoma.) The "flaps" are not random. The objects follow a rigid timetable that could be interpreted and understood, with proper research. Ancient records substantiate the notion that the objects have always been a part of our earthly environment.

Ufologists must begin with a thorough study of human history, not with a study of the endless descriptions of objects that are rarely identical to each other in appearance.

Captain Ruppelt's Blue Book team computerized the 434 "unknowns" of the 1947-52 era, and tried to develop a "model saucer." They found that the descriptions were so varied that they had to settle upon 12 basic types. However, they did evolve some general categories, which happen to verify the independent studies of Ohio Northern University and of Otto Binder.

In 1966, an American tabloid, *The National Enquirer*, subscribed to clipping services and attempted to break the sightings down superficially by shape and locale. Despite its sensational reputation of earlier years, *The National Enquirer* has actually been doing an accurate and responsible job of reporting on the UFO phenomenon in the U.S.

Since the objects are plainly so numerous, and so varied in size and shape, I do not feel that we will ever learn anything concrete by merely studying the descriptions. In a sense, it is like trying to classify all the fish in the ocean by counting and describing the sea life turned up in a single net. As I have already noted, the "soft" objects actually far out-number the "hard" ones, and we may have made a serious mistake in concentrating our efforts on the "hard" sightings.

We must also take into account the apparent deceptions, diversions, and "hoaxes" that seem to be carefully engineered by some unknown group, to lead us astray and keep us in confusion. Ufologists must study psychological warfare and police investigative methods so that they will be prepared to cope with such deceptions and recognize them for what they are.

There is a tremendous amount of evidence that proves that "they" don't want us to know too much about their nature or origin. Perhaps they have always been communicating with us indirectly, in ways that are hard for us to understand, and impossible for our science to comprehend. There appears to be a direct linkage between "occult" phenomena and the techniques being employed by the ufonauts to communicate with contactees.

In many recent cases, the ufonauts have demonstrated that they know the full details of the lives of specific individuals. They have demonstrated that they are at least aware of our political boundaries, and that they can operate on timetables that correspond to our own time cycle. In innumerable instances all over the world, witnesses have claimed that many of the elusive "pilots" look very much like us, and can breathe our air and speak our languages. Over the years, hundreds of scraps of metal and other substances have been dropped from UFOs, and nearly all of it consists of earthly materials, notably aluminum, magnesium and silicon.

In an unpublished portion of the enigmatically annotated "Varo Edition" of Dr. Jessup's *Case For The UFO*, one of the anonymous marginalia writers commented on Jessup's repetition of a rumor that a "flying saucer" had crashed in the Soviet Union, and was being examined by Russian scientists. The notation-writer laughed at the notion, stating that if it were really true, then Russia would have cornered the world's diamond market.

What does *this* mean? We can go back to a letter published in *The Sacramento Bee* on November 24, 1896. A writer, who signed himself "W.A.," expressed some contactee-like opinions on the "airship" and stated:

> The airships are constructed of the lightest and strongest fabrics, and the machinery is of the most perfect electrical work. Aluminum and glass (silicon), hardened by the same chemical process that forms our diamonds, contribute the chief material of their most perfect airships. When in use, these vessels, at a distance, have the appearance of a ball of fire, being operated wholly by the electricity generated on such vessels.

We have not yet been able to simplify all the complex and contradictory factors inherent in the "flap" data. We can only point the way to additional research. There are many bewildering psychological aspects that must be examined by qualified psychologists and psychiatrists. Again and again, I have encountered amnesia victims and people who have experienced dramatic changes in IQ and personality after a UFO experience. The number of people now claiming telepathic "contact" is unbelievably large, and many of these cases correlate favorably with each other.

Contactees in widely separated areas have detailed identical conversations with the ufonauts. The same questions are asked of these people. None of these questions have been published, so the chances of deliberate hoaxing on the part of the alleged witnesses are slight. Also, people who claim to have been taken aboard the objects have described certain (unpublished) things seen inside the craft. (Mrs. Betty Hill described being "examined" by a machine which probed her with wires in the same manner that Carroll Watts, in Texas, claimed to have been probed by a multi-wired machine in 1967.)

Whatever is happening now has apparently been going on for many years unnoticed. And we are still not sufficiently organized to truly investigate and understand this phenomenon. We have just been counting the fish that have fallen into our net. The subject has been exposed to so much ridicule that it has attracted largely teenagers and individuals who are not equipped to cope with such a diversified and complicated situation. The "extraterrestrial" concept has gripped our imaginations and led us to rule out many of the salient facts. We cannot apply human logic to this situation.

Consider what Zechariah, in the Bible, said about his conversation with an "angel." When the angel provided Zechariah with a vision of a "flying roll," and he expressed wonderment, the angel reminded him that the flying object was "the curse that goeth forth over the face of the whole earth." (*Book of Zechariah*, 5: 1-3)

The Oruro Festival, which takes place in the Gran Chaco region of South America each year, features the Oruro birdman (pictured) and the Virgin Mary; the two join forces to fight dark spirits emanating from inside the earth. Most of the sightings of Mothman in Seattle have occurred in a specific park where rare parrots from the Gran Chaco region have migrated. During the coincident Mothman/UFO sightings in Point Pleasant, West Virginia, thousands of bags of quebracho bark from the Gran Chaco region were stored a couple of miles away from the TNT Area, at the Defense Logistics Agency (DLA) site (see page 54). The DLA is still active today, and is said to house a collection of minerals so valuable that their combined sale would "alter the world minerals market." Was "Mothman" the angel who spoke to Zechariah?

CHAPTER 2

You never read about it in your local newspaper, but during the last
successful manned space shot – the flight of Gemini 12 in November of
1966 – astronauts James Lovell and Edwin "Buzz" Aldrin reported seeing
four unidentifiable flying objects near their orbit.

"We saw four objects lined up in a row," Captain Lovell told a press
conference on November 23rd, "and they weren't stars I know." Several
orbits earlier, he explained, they had thrown *three* small plastic bags of
garbage out of the spacecraft. He hinted that these *four* starlike objects
standing in a neat row were, somehow, that previous trio of non-luminous
garbage bags.

The black gulf of space around Earth is now filled with all kinds of
garbage. Over 1,000 pieces of debris, dead satellites, and assorted
manmade junk are loping around up there. There is even an astronaut's
glove and a very expensive camera, both accidentally lost during manned
flights, barreling along in unplanned orbits. All of these things are
carefully tracked and indexed by an expensive and elaborate radar and
communications network that has bases all over this planet. They even
keep a careful watch on three *unidentified* satellites that were discovered
last fall. These satellites come as close as 204 miles to the earth, and then
wobble outwards to a maximum distance of 6,930 miles. Both the United
States and the Soviet Union deny ownership of them, and their actual size
is a classified secret.

Back in 1960, the Pentagon announced Project Saint, a plan to send
specially equipped satellites into space to pursue and identify such mysterious objects. Perhaps a Project Saint spy is bumbling around up there,
trying to focus its TV cameras on the three intruders, but no further data
has been released.

One thing is certain: there are a great many unexplained objects maneuvering around the outer limits of our atmosphere and, for some odd
reason, no one in authority cares to say very much about them. All of our
astronauts, and most of the Russian cosmonauts, have closely observed
and photographed many of these things. Whatever they are, they are
frequent visitors to our rocket-launching sites. If they are manufactured
vehicles operated by some "alien" intelligence, there are many indica-

tions that they have been closely observing our space program with great interest.

"We have two bright objects up here in our orbital path," astronaut John W. Young radioed shortly after going into orbit in Gemini 10 on July 18, 1966. "I don't think they're stars – they look like we are going right along with them."

When the Manned Spacecraft Center in Houston requested a bearing on the objects, Young replied: "They just disappeared. I guess they were satellites of some kind."

Disappearing satellites seem to be a constant hazard to the men we hurl into space. Astronauts Frank Bormann and Jim Lovell got a good look at another unidentified interloper during the second orbit of their GT-7 capsule on December 4, 1965. "We have a bogey at 10 o'clock high," Bormann announced calmly. The officials in the ground control station asked him to take a closer look, to see if it were a booster rocket.

"We know where the booster is," Bormann responded. "This is an actual sighting."

An actual sighting of what? Aside from this brief bit of dialogue recorded on Tape #43 of the Gemini 7 flight, there has been no further comment from NASA or the astronauts.

Another member of the world's most exclusive club – men who have had a chance to watch UFOs in outer space – is Gordon Cooper. While flashing over Australia on his 15th orbit, during his flight of May 16, 1963, Cooper informed ground control that a glowing green object with a red tail was approaching his spacecraft. Whatever it was, it was also visible from the ground. Personnel in Muchea, Australia, estimated that it was at an altitude of 100 miles. Millions of people heard Cooper's report on radio and television, but once he was back on terra firma, he refused to comment on it.

In June 1965, astronauts James McDivitt and Edward White reported seeing "a mysterious object in space" over China. Again, millions heard their original report on radio and television. According to an Associated Press dispatch on June 11, 1965, they also observed unidentified objects over Hawaii and Eastern Asia. Recently, James McDivitt stated: "I don't know what it (the UFO) was and, so far, no one else does, either."

One of the first Americans to sail into the upper atmosphere aboard the X-15 high-altitude rocket plane, the late Joe Walker, not only saw a formation of six cylindrical objects at an altitude of 246,700 feet in the spring of 1962, but his automatic cameras photographed them. These movies were later shown at a single press conference, but copies of the pictures never were released. Walker told the press that one of his appointed tasks on the flight was to look for unidentified flying objects. (The author was shown a blow-up of one of these pictures at NASA headquarters in Washington, D.C. recently. Unfortunately, it was so grainy that it cannot be reproduced clearly.) In later interviews, Walker shrugged off the pictures, saying that he didn't "feel like speculating about them."

Major Robert White established an altitude record on July 17, 1962, when he flew the X-15 to 314,750 feet. He howled into the microphone, "There are things out there!" as a large, gray-white object appeared and paced alongside his plane (he was traveling at 3,832 miles per hour). The object moved ahead of him and finally glided over his canopy. His report was carried by the wire services and was even mentioned in *Time* magazine.

Colonel John Glenn, the first American to make an orbital space flight, created a sensation when he told of seeing swarms of "fireflies" in space. All of the other astronauts, as well as the Russian cosmonauts, have mentioned this phenomenon. NASA scientists say that the tiny, luminous particles are as small as 25 microns in diameter. Scott Carpenter claimed that he produced these particles from his spacecraft when he rapped on the hatch. Gordon Cooper reported that the "fireflies" emerged from his jet nozzles. NASA contends that the things may be bits of ice formed by the steam ejected from the spacecraft's life-support systems. Such theories, however, fail to explain the clouds of these particles that Bormann and Lovell reported as having appeared *several miles in front of* the GT-7 spacecraft, and *moving at right angles* to their path.

(Tiny UFOs have been repeatedly reported over the years. One large cluster of flying discs, silver colored and measuring only 3 *inches* in diameter, were described by the crews and pilots of several bombers of the 384th Group during a raid on Schweinfurt, Germany in October 1943. These baffled men later told intelligence officers that their planes flew through the cluster without suffering ill effects. The full story of this astounding incident is detailed in Martin Caidin's book *Black Thursday*, an account of the Schweinfurt raid based on official Air Force records.)

In addition to their puzzling encounters with unidentified objects in space, our astronauts have reported many other oddities that have gone unnoticed by the general press. They have made a careful study of a phenomenon called "nightglow" – bands of luminosity surrounding Earth that apparently are not visible from the ground. Astronaut Wally Schirra described seeing a large, luminous patch hovering in space above the Indian Ocean. Cooper saw a similar glowing blob of enormous size high above the atmosphere over South America. Since both men said that they could see stars below these "patches," it is clear that these glowing masses were in space and were not part of the normal "nightglow" phenomenon. Astronauts have also reported these "patches" over Tamanrasset, Algeria and Maui, Hawaii. What are they? NASA scientists are still pondering.

All of the astronauts have also experienced a peculiar smudging on the outside of their spacecraft windows. In a number of flights, these smudges became so severe that the pilots had to close the visors on their windows and fly blind. What could smudge a window in the vacuum of outer space? They're still working on that one, too.

Strangest of all are the many "bugs" that plague the communications systems of our spacecraft. As everyone knows, all of the systems used in spacecraft are in duplicate, so that there is always a backup circuit if the main circuit fails. Even so, we have suffered all kinds of difficult-to-explain failures.

During his fourth pass over Hawaii on May 15, 1963, Gordon Cooper's transmission to ground control was interrupted by an "unintelligible, foreign language." This sudden interference on the broadcasting channel reserved exclusively for space flights has never been explained. Nor has the "foreign language" ever been identified or translated.

Unexplained radio interference on June 1, 1966 caused delays in launching an ATDA target vehicle. Soon after the satellite was finally blasted into orbit, all of the radio and television networks interrupted their broadcasts with this statement: "The Defense Department has announced that three unidentified flying objects are in orbit with the target vehicle." Astronauts Thomas Stafford and Eugene Cernan were slated to follow it immediately in their space capsule, but they were kept on the ground for two days while Air Force experts solemnly explained that the UFOs were probably part of the plastic shroud that covers the rendezvous device (despite the fact that the *plastic* shroud would *not* give a radar return). However, when the astronauts finally went into orbit and reached the ATDA vehicle, they found the plastic shroud completely in place. It had, in fact, failed to open and disperse as planned. There were no further comments from the Air Force or the Defense Department.

Unidentified flying objects were observed in the upper atmosphere long before our space program really got underway. And sightings were numerous around the White Sands Proving Grounds when a handful of men were toying with captured German rockets after World War II. As far back as 1945, when government specialists were scouting areas for a future rocket-launching site, peculiar flying lights and circular aircraft were being reported around Cape Canaveral (later renamed "Cape Kennedy").

After Dr. Lincoln La Paz of the University of New Mexico sighted an unknown object orbiting the earth in 1953, the U.S. Army assigned Dr. Clyde W. Tombaugh to conduct a search for it. Dr. Tombaugh is the astronomer who discovered the planet Pluto in 1930. Although the results of his study of "mystery satellites" have been buried in Pentagon red tape, it is known that he discovered three of the things up there, but little was heard about them.

Then, in December 1957, Dr. Luis Corrales of the Communications Ministry in Venezuela photographed one, somewhat to his own aston-ishment. Sputnik 1, the first manmade satellite, had been launched two months earlier, and Dr. Corrales was taking pictures of Sputnik II as it passed over Caracas. His photograph showed a trace of a second, unknown object closely following the Soviets' dog-carrying satellite.

Two huge objects pursuing a polar orbit appeared in space on January 4, 1960, causing quite a stir in scientific circles. Neither the Soviet Union nor the U.S. had succeeded in launching anything in a pole-to-pole orbit at that time. These objects were photographed by the satellite tracking station of the Grumman Aircraft Corporation, and were studied by observatories throughout the world. They were estimated to weigh at least 15 tons. The biggest Soviet satellite launched up until that time weighed 2,925 pounds (less than one and a half tons), and the largest U.S. satellite was a puny 450-pounder.

"It's not a meteor," Frank Judson of the Adler Planetarium declared, "because it's much too slow. And it's not an artificial, manmade satellite; of that we are certain. The object travels from east to west; every artificial satellite ever put up has traveled from west to east. That's the only way in which we can take advantage of the earth's rotation."

Other mystery satellites of gigantic size appeared briefly at altitudes up to 20,000 miles. *Newsweek*, *Life*, and other news media labeled the things "the Black Knights." There is no record of where these things went. They may still be up there, "classified" by bewildered scientists.

While astronomers were trying to figure out what was buzzing around in space, our rocket technicians were trying to cope with unidentified objects operating closer to home. On January 10, 1961, a large unknown object followed a Polaris rocket aloft. The tracking station at Cape Kennedy was thrown into confusion when their radar locked onto the mysterious stranger for fourteen minutes.

Four unidentified objects closed in on an unmanned Gemini capsule on April 8, 1964, and followed it for one complete orbit around the earth, according to Major Donald E. Keyhoe, head of NICAP. On January 5, 1965, several witnesses, including Dempsey Bruton, Chief of Satellite Tracking at the Wallops Island, Virginia NASA rocket station, reported that a bright, circular, yellowish-orange object appeared in the area shortly after an Arcas rocket had been launched. Bruton estimated that it was traveling at speeds up to 8,000 miles per hour. He dutifully passed on full details of the sighting to the U.S. Air Force, who later announced that the incident offered "no evidence of any superior technological development."

Soviet scientists have experienced similar problems with these strange intruders. Although solid information about the Russian space program is hard to come by, some details have trickled through the cracks in the Iron Curtain. We know that many Soviet satellites have either *disappeared* altogether or have been de-orbited mysteriously. And there are continuing rumors that several cosmonauts have lost their lives in manned space flights.

During the Seattle World's Fair in 1962, Colonel John Glenn and cosmonaut Gherman Titov held a press conference together. When a reporter asked Titov if he or his colleagues had ever seen any flying saucers in space, the Russian launched into a lengthy monologue. He allegedly described several incidents in detail, but his translators asked that his comments be kept "off the record."

Moscow correspondents claim that widespread rumors tell how a three-man spaceship orbited in October 1963, was surrounded by a formation of fast-flying discs that jarred the cosmonauts with powerful magnetic fields, and almost brought the flight to a disastrous climax.

Soon after cosmonauts Pavel I. Belyayev and Alexei A. Leonov went into orbit in March of 1965, Moscow radio proudly announced that they would be making a "prolonged flight." But after only 18 orbits, the spaceship crashed back into the atmosphere, plunging into a snow bank 873 miles northwest of their planned target area. The craft came down in a ball of fire, which burned off the antenna and prevented the two men from radioing their location. They almost froze to death, trapped in their capsule, before rescuers located them.

A few days later, the luckless duo faced a press conference in Moscow, and revealed that they had seen an unidentified "satellite" shortly before disaster struck their spacecraft. As usual, the *Tass* report on this press conference was ignored by the American press, even though newspapers in all other parts of the world carried it.

From these and countless other incidents like them, it appears that both the U.S. and Soviet space programs are under close and continuous surveillance.

This surveillance is so thorough that it seems to have included the minor rocket experiments of teenagers. In the summer of 1966, a group of young amateur rocket builders fired a primitive, homemade "spacecraft" from a field in Virginia. It soared 3,000 feet into the air and then drifted back to Earth, dangling from a makeshift parachute. Less than 24 hours later, five adult witnesses reported seeing a circular craft surrounded by an eerie glow as it landed *in that very same field!* Was it a coincidence, or did a flying saucer actually visit that spot to find out if there was some kind of secret rocket launching base there? We will never know the answer.

Somewhere in NASA, there may be a heavily locked file containing part of the answer to these continuing mysteries. Our astronauts and rocket technicians have now had many years in which to observe and study the enigma of the unidentified flying objects. Persistent rumors of mysterious attempts at sabotage circulate around our rocket launching sites. Some of these rumors, leaked to the author by insiders, hint that UFO activity is frequently blamed for peculiar mishaps. The celebrated "EM effect" – the electromagnetic interference that is said to exist when UFOs are present – has frequently been blamed for disruptions in communications.

But would the "EM effect" alone explain the mystery of 1962-64, when four different U.S. satellites all mysteriously stopped transmitting radio signals back to Earth? Months later, they mysteriously resumed transmissions. Technicians were baffled as to why the radio backup systems failed. They never did find an adequate answer.

The year 1967 got off to a grim start for NASA when three astronauts died in a sudden fire aboard a Gemini capsule during a dry-run on the launchpad. A few weeks later, a Russian cosmonaut was killed when something went awry with his orbiting spacecraft. Ufologists around the world are now speculating about the meaning of all of these events. They ask: "Are our efforts to leap off of this planet being deliberately thwarted?"

We can only hope that none of this is as ominous as it seems. Perhaps our technology is not yet advanced enough for that giant leap into outer space. And maybe those luminous patches, starlike objects, and other things reported by our astronauts are merely still-unknown natural phenomena after all.

While NASA technicians and officials strive to reorganize and redesign our space plans, those mysterious unidentified satellites continue to wheel silently across our skies. Every few minutes, one of them passes over you.

Early satellites and aerial drones were tracked from a secret naval command base in Sugar Grove, West Virginia. A few miles from Sugar Grove, privately owned satellite dishes (top) download digital data from millions of phones and computers, which are relayed down from satellites (and reportedly intercepted by the naval base). The owners of these dishes also controlled the TNT Area in Point Pleasant, suggesting that satellites and drones were manufactured there. Down the road from the TNT Area, at the DLA facility, five large warehouses sat for decades, filled to the brim with thousands of bags of quebracho bark from the Gran Chaco region of South America. In 2012, removal of the bags began. The bark was transferred to new white bags (above, far right) and shipped to China. Mysteriously, the bags appeared to be radioactive when tested with a Geiger counter.

CHAPTER 3

The following case is one of the most astonishing "contact" stories ever to come to my attention. I must explain at the outset that it is based entirely on the testimony of a woman I have never met. But there were many details in her story that have appeared in cases I have investigated in other states. In the past three weeks, I have spoken to this woman for hours on the telephone, and have carefully cross-examined her. I believe that she is telling the truth as she knows it, and that this whole situation deserves thoughtful attention. For reasons that will be obvious, I cannot reveal her real name or address. However, this information is in my files.

On Sunday, September 24, 1967, a woman named Pat was attending a Lutheran church in a small town on Long Island, about an hour's drive from New York City, when she was approached by a young lady who appeared to be East Indian. She was wearing a sari-like gray garment, had a dark olive complexion, and dark Oriental eyes. She purportedly told Pat a few very personal things – things that Pat says were not even known to her own husband. Pat was annoyed and disturbed by this brief conversation, and moved to another pew. The Indian woman followed her and tried to resume the conversation, but Pat ignored and evaded her. Later, Pat described the incident to a friend of mine on Long Island.

The next day, September 25th, an unidentified woman phoned the entertainment editor of *Newsday*, a large Long Island daily, and related the details of the encounter. Pat, however, denies emphatically that she made the call. She has not seen or heard from the Indian woman since.

On Tuesday, September 26th, at 5 p.m., I received a call from a woman whom I shall call "Helen." Helen lives in another section of Long Island, some distance from Pat. Since *Newsday* did not publish Pat's story (or any stories like it), it is improbable that Helen could have known anything about it. Helen told me that she had heard me on a Long Island radio station a few weeks earlier. She remembered my name, and had gotten my number by calling the telephone company. She began her story in the classic way: "You'll probably think I'm crazy, but…" She sounded sincere, and apparently was a young housewife in her twenties. She had an uneducated, regional accent, but was articulate and straightforward.

At about 3 p.m. that afternoon, she said, she had heard a strange humming sound outside her house, and had looked out a window. (Her home is surrounded by trees in an isolated section on the outskirts of a small town. There are no other houses nearby.) Hovering about 100 feet in the air above the trees, close to her house, she saw what she described as a "gleaming, disc-shaped object." It was quite large, but there were no discernible features – no windows, fins, or identifying insignia. She claims that she was never at all interested in flying saucer stories, and so she was rather astonished by this object.

While she was staring at this thing, her doorbell rang. She opened the door, and was confronted by an Indian-like lady about 5'9" tall, wearing a gray sari. She had a "snake bracelet" on one arm, and there were beads around her neck. Her face was dark and Oriental-like, but was quite pleasant, and she spoke in a very quiet voice.

"Hello, *Pat*," the Indian woman addressed her.

"I'm sorry, but my name *isn't* Pat," Helen answered. "You must have the wrong house."

"No, this is the right house," the woman said. She then proceeded to tell Helen something very personal and surprising about herself. And then she asked if she could have a glass of water (so that she could "take a pill"). Helen admitted her, and gave her the water. The woman also asked for something very unusual, and Helen gave it to her. (Note: this "something unusual" has cropped up in a number of other cases I have investigated. It has never been published, and I am withholding a description of it here.)

There was very little conversation between the two women at this time. The Indian woman thanked Helen and left, walking into some nearby bushes. A moment later, the hovering disc shot away. Helen did not see the woman enter or leave the object. She pondered the whole incident for several minutes, and then decided to try and locate me.

I was, understandably, quite suspicious of this first phone call. During our conversation, there was a considerable amount of static and interference on the line. But I was impressed by Helen's ability to come up with certain specific details that are unknown to the general public. There was one detail in particular that was especially significant to me.

On Saturday, September 30th, Helen called me again around 6 p.m. She said that the Indian lady had visited her again, about an hour before. Now the mystery deepened. The two women talked together for several minutes, and the Indian woman mentioned, by name, some "silent contactees" known to me, but totally unknown to Helen. She declared that she was *not* "Princess Owl Moon" (a hoaxer who has been running around Long Island claiming to be from the asteroid Ceres), but would not identify herself or state where she was from.

During this conversation, I pumped Helen for details about her life and background. She told me some interesting things that coincided with patterns I have uncovered in other "contact" cases. She also revealed that she was living alone, being separated from her husband only recently. She had a ten-month-old baby, and was *also* six months pregnant.

I re-questioned her about the first incident, cross-examining her and trying to trick her in different ways. She passed these tests with flying colors, and I became more convinced of her honesty.

Heavy static developed during our discussion. She revealed that she had felt slightly nauseous for a day or so after the first encounter, and that the following night, she was awakened by the sound of a baby crying somewhere in the house. She got up and was baffled to find *her* baby sleeping peacefully. She could not locate the source of the sound.

At 9:30 p.m. that evening, Helen called me again. She sounded very frightened. A large black car was parked outside of her house at that very moment, she said, and two strange men were taking pictures of her house with some kind of odd camera. She was able to watch them through the window as she talked to me. She gave me a thorough description of them. Both were just under six feet tall, and they were dressed in black trousers, black turtlenecked sweaters, and broad-brimmed black hats. Their complexions were dark. They were using some kind of large camera with a flashgun, which flashed red when they took pictures. At first, she said, she thought they were clergymen, because of their black garb. But for some reason, they frightened her very much. Then she told me that shortly before they had arrived, she had received a phone call from the Indian woman, who now identified herself as "Chloe." Chloe warned Helen to lock all of her doors and windows, and to stay inside.

These Men in Black (MIB) have been reported all over Long Island, and Helen's description of them was already very familiar to me. At that time, however, none of the details of these MIB cases had been publicized. So it is unlikely that Helen could have heard about any of them. Unbeknownst to her, a great many things were happening to other people all over Long Island at that time, and I was gravely concerned over a rash of serious incidents involving "silent contactees" who were communicating with me. I was quietly making plans for another extended trip to some of the "trouble" spots.

On Sunday, October 1st, Helen called at 5:45 p.m. to give me the details of another visit from Chloe. She told Helen that she had visited "ten different homes in the last 24 hours." She again made a number of remarks about silent contactees who were known to me, but unknown to Helen. (Because of certain dangers involved, I have set up a complicated system of codes to be used by all of the contactees I uncover. For example, these contactees are given codenames and codephrases to identify themselves. It is all very James Bondish, but quite necessary, unfortunately.) Chloe referred to some of these contactees by the codenames *I* had given them. Helen, of course, did not know what she was talking about.

Meanwhile, the MIB were very active on Long Island and, to add to the confusion, there were random reports that *West Virginia's celebrated Mothman was now being seen on the tip of the island* – Montauk Point. Also, ships in the Atlantic were reporting huge luminous "cigars" discharging small globes of light, which sailed toward New York and Long Island. (Many of these same orbs have also been appearing in the Ohio Valley.) On Long Island and in neighboring Connecticut, the globes were cutting nightly capers.

(During my frequent treks out to Long Island, I have seen several of the objects myself, and have collected some mind-boggling eyewitness testimony. One family swears they saw a circular object land and deposit two normal looking, human-sized beings, who were picked up by a big black car and driven away. Similar incidents have been reported in South America, France, and England, but this is the first one I have come across in the U.S.)

More and more people were now calling *Newsday* to report the activities of the elusive "Princess Moon Owl." Long John Nebel, WNBC's famous radio personality, heard of the "princess" somehow and called me, wanting to know how to locate her for his show. The whole situation was getting more complicated and confused daily. A woman on Long Island had an encounter with an olive-skinned gentleman in a greenish suit in May of this year, who called himself "Aphloes." I finally figured out that it was from the word *aphlogistic*, derived from Greek, meaning "a lamp giving light *without* flame."

I decided to drive out to Long Island on Tuesday, October 3rd, but at 8:30 a.m. that morning, I received a phone call from a woman – a total stranger – who read a short statement to me advising me not to make the trip that day. This baffled me, because I had kept my plans a secret from my friends in New York, and no one on Long Island knew exactly when I intended to arrive. As it happened, I had to cancel my plans anyway. Things were developing elsewhere. That day, a large black car containing three men in black suits attempted to *run down* Mrs. Mary Hyre, a newspaper reporter in West Virginia and a close friend of mine. An identical attempt was made on the life of a "silent contactee" on Long Island *that same afternoon.*

The next day, October 4th, as I was preparing to leave the city, I received another phone call from Helen. She said Chloe had instructed her to locate a certain Long Island motel, at 9 p.m. the previous night, and ask for me. It was the motel where I often stayed on these trips. Helen had actually gone looking for the motel, which is several miles from her home, but had been unable to find it.

I drove out to Long Island that afternoon and did check into that motel. The desk clerk greeted me by announcing, "We had a reservation for you last night; and a lot of people have been calling you." But I had made *no* reservation, and I certainly did not expect anyone to be calling there for me. Shades of Kenneth Arnold in Tacoma!

I busied myself with investigations of the new MIB cases. No one attempted to call me at the motel while I was actually there. As I was driving out that evening, I noticed a slow moving, flashing light in the sky, traveling along a route parallel with my car. Four UFOs appeared over nearby Huntington, NY that night, hovering and bobbing low in the sky. They were seen by hundreds of people, including several police officers.

Unlike my previous trips (where I had personal encounters with big black Cadillacs and their black-suited drivers), nothing too unusual happened. I returned to New York City late Thursday night, October 5th. As soon as I entered my apartment, my phone rang. It was Helen. She said she had received a visit from Chloe and a dark-skinned man in a gray suit. *They told her that the baby she was expecting belonged to them!* Then they made an incredible proposition. They produced a sheet of paper – a legal contract of some kind – and asked her to sign it. If she signed, they said that she and her small child would be "taken to another planet," where they would all be well cared for and quite happy.

Helen was stunned with disbelief. She told me that she was receiving only small sums from her husband, and that life was very difficult for her. She was leading a sad and lonely life, and she was obviously seriously thinking about accepting this proposition. I cautiously advised her to think it over, very carefully, before taking such a step. It was evident that these two people had given her a convincing sales talk. She was very impressed with their sincerity. She now believed that they were very real, and that they were actually from another planet.

We talked for over two hours, and then suddenly the line was cut off. I did not hear from her again until Monday afternoon, October 9th. Then she told me the most astounding story of all. She said they had visited her again, late Thursday night, after our conversation. She had told them that she had decided not to sign. She went to bed at 1 p.m. that night. *The next thing she knew, it was Monday morning, October 9th.*

She could remember *nothing* that had happened over the weekend, except for one strange detail. An image was firmly planted in her mind. She clearly remembered seeing a gigantic glass structure, red and transparent, but she could not recall anything else. When she awoke, she had a slight headache, her feet were sore, and her legs ached as if she had done a lot of walking. Everything in her house was in place, just as it had been when she had gone to bed four nights before. Even her hair was put up the way she had it when she had retired. Her small baby was alert and well taken care of.

At 11 a.m. that morning, she said Chloe had paid her a short visit and had told her that it would not be necessary for her to sign the paper after all. "They" had "examined" her over the weekend, Chloe said, and "everything was all right."

Helen is, of course, disturbed and confused by all of these events. She complains that she is having trouble with her memory in other areas. I suspect that she will soon forget all about this strange interlude – that it will all seem like a vague dream to her. Like so many others, her life has been briefly touched by the "aliens."

We cannot, however, predict how all of this will affect her unborn child. Nor can we estimate how many other isolated, unfortunate mothers-to-be may have undergone similar experiences. Perhaps we should all re-read the great British science-fiction novel, *The Midwich Cuckoos*, and Trench's comprehensive book, *The Sky People*. The answers may lie in our genes and not in the skies.

AFTERMATH

Helen's baby was born at 10:30 p.m. on Saturday, October 28, 1967 – the same evening she was visited in her home by the Men in Black. She had called me while they were there, and through her, I was able to ask them questions. (A transcript of this bizarre conversation is in my files.)

At about 9 p.m. that evening, after the conversation had ended, a large black car arrived at Helen's home and transported her to an isolated house. She does not remember the trip at all, either going or returning.

Incredibly, several other women, all known to me as "silent contactees," were *also* at the house. According to Helen, all were pregnant, *and all had their children that evening.*

Before the children were born, telephone contact was established with me by another woman present. For three long, unbelievable hours, I *supervised* the birth proceedings by "remote control." I spoke to each woman and could clearly hear the sounds of the babies as they were being born. I referred to my various medical books and gave instructions over the phone. I have tape recordings of the entire sequence of events.

Two "aliens," a man and a woman, assisted with the births onsite. The female alien remained in a trancelike state and served as the "control." The man handled the actual deliveries, following my instructions.

Four children were born, including Helen's. They apparently all looked alike, were dark-skinned, and had Oriental features. Two of these children died later. There were several crises during this birthing operation. One of the women began to hemorrhage uncontrollably. The alien man produced (from his *car*) a small, boxlike instrument that stopped the bleeding instantly.

Another woman went into hysterics. The babies were born within minutes of each other. All of the mothers returned to normal *instantly* after giving birth. They were able to walk about and talk normally immediately afterwards. All were in fine, healthy shape when I spoke to them the next day.

Helen named her baby after me. Several such babies have now been named after me, or have been given names suggested by me.

Shortly after the children were born, a group of hostile alien women entered the house and tried to gather up the children. On my instructions, these women were ejected forcibly.

There have been many similar births in recent months, usually involving Catholic girls in their late teens or early twenties. Many of them were unmarried. The average gestation period is *six weeks.* Some girls have been "used" repeatedly and have given birth to more than one child.

As of this writing (February 8, 1968), I have lost track of a number of these women. They have moved or disappeared soon after their involvement. I am still in touch with Helen, however. She has moved three times since October. Some of the children have been hidden in orphanages or moved to other sections of the country.

I know of many other "controlled" births in other states, and am keeping close tabs on several of these children.

The material in the transcripts indicates that these were "staged" incidents meant to convey a couple of ufological "truths" to me. Nearly all such direct confrontations with the ufonauts and MIB are "staged," and therefore meaningless. Most contactee experiences fall into this category. Elaborate charades are often played out for the contactee's benefit. In some cases, these charades are meant to *replace* the memory of actual events. What actually happened is often quite different from what the witness remembers.

The "events" that occurred earlier in the evening, prior to the trip to the birthing house, were unusual and important. Barring an elaborate conspiracy involving many people, there is absolutely no possibility that Helen could have known of the actions of the other silent contactees in my orbit, and then put them into a narrative "told to her" by the MIB.

She could not have known of the stories of, say, another contactee's stolen ring, how a contactee had ripped a phone out of an MIB car, or that a Man in Black had been "captured." (I have been involved, directly or indirectly, with other MIB "captures.") Nor could she have known about my own encounter with a black Cadillac earlier that day.

Outsiders with no experience in these matters will find all of this difficult to believe or understand. The individual entities do not, by our standards, seem too bright. Many of their conversations are conducted on a childish level. They try to speak in our vernacular, using slang terms like "stupid broad," etc. They are evasive, and they are prone to telling us what they think we want to hear; or what they think we will accept.

The witnesses are the victims in all of this, since they cannot remember everything that happened. But the events they do remember seem totally real to them. Therefore, there are no grounds for believing that Helen was making all of this up or putting me on.

Sometimes, things can get *very* complicated.

CHAPTER 4

June 1977 will mark the 30th anniversary of Kenneth Arnold's famous sighting of flying discs over Mount Rainier in the state of Washington. Although there were innumerable sightings earlier that year, "June 24, 1947" has become the accepted date for the beginning of modern ufology. Private pilot Arnold is also credited with introducing the term "flying saucer." Several years later, Captain Edward Ruppelt of the U.S. Air Force's Project Blue Book coined "unidentified flying object" (UFO).

For the past 30 years, thousands of people have spent part of their lives, and a lot of their money, acting as amateur investigators of the UFO phenomenon. An entire generation has grown up surrounded by comic books, movies, and television dramas concerned with the questions raised by the flying saucer mystery. Today's young people accept the presence of strange objects in our skies as easily as they accept jet airplanes and manned flights to the moon. Flying saucers have become as real as ballpoint pens to millions of people all over the planet. Nearly every nation on Earth hosts at least one civilian organization devoted to the study of "the problem." Several noted scientists and top government officials, particularly in Europe, have publicly expressed their concern over the UFO situation.

But what have we actually learned from the phenomenon in these 30 years? What real effect have these mysterious intruders had upon our society and our sciences?

There are many impressive parallels between the flying saucer mystery and the fairy faith of days gone by. Thousands of humans once saw the "little people," and millions believed steadfastly in their existence. However, the fairy myth had little real impact upon our civilization, and probably made no tangible contribution to our progress. UFOs, on the other hand, have had a resounding, though subtle, effect on the last generation. Their mere presence has caused us to contemplate cosmic questions that were once the exclusive property of science-fiction writers. It is even probable that if UFOs did not exist, we would not have broken our backs – and our wallets – sending men to the moon, and sophisticated probes to Jupiter and beyond. If nothing else, the arrival of the flying saucers over Mount Rainier made us aware of our pitiful smallness in a vast universe.

After 30 years of study and observation, we still do not know where UFOs come from, why they are here, and who is behind the phenomenon. But we have learned a great deal about ourselves in the process of trying to study them. This sudden self-knowledge may be their greatest gift to us.

Unfortunately, on another level, the existence of UFOs has spawned an industry that may not be so beneficial. One question that is rarely asked about the flying saucer mystery is: "Who profits?" The major result of the UFO enigma has been the interest created in "extraterrestrial" life. In 1950, no reputable astronomer or scientist was even willing to speculate on the existence of life on other planets. Most sneered at the whole idea as a "fantasy." Ten years later, however, nearly all of the leading astronomers and cosmologists were writing reams of articles and lecturing enthusiastically about the possibility of life on other worlds. Suddenly, exobiology (the study of "alien" life) has become a "respected" science.

What brought about this dramatic change? Did the scientific community suddenly accept flying saucers as proof of extraterrestrial life? Hardly. The answer is both ancient and disappointing: *Money*. It suddenly became very profitable to study extraterrestrial life. The government, NASA, and the leading foundations began handing out generous grants to scientific institutions and individual scientists to search for "proof" of life somewhere "out there." There was "gold in them thar spaceships" hovering in the night skies!

NASA was created for three reasons. First, the Russians were ahead of us in space technology, and we wanted to catch up, primarily for military reasons. The "space race" of the early 1960s was outwardly a matter of prestige – a public relations performance. We finally beat the Soviet Union to the moon, but only because they gave up the effort after losing several cosmonauts in accidents. Secondly, President John F. Kennedy had the notion that space exploration could become a substitute for war. By channeling vast sums of money into the space program, he thought he could switch our economy from making the machines of war to making the machines of space. (The nation had, and still is, largely dependent on a military economy since the early days of World War II.) Thirdly, NASA was assigned the task of "searching for extraterrestrial life." This, too, was largely a public relations gambit designed to appeal to the public's imagination and justify the enormous expenditures.

The space program gobbled up four billion tax dollars per year during its peak years, but most of this money was fed back into the economy through the burgeoning aerospace industry. Hundreds of thousands of workers, engineers, and technicians were employed by the program.

And thousands of scientists and astronomers, accustomed to struggling along on the pittances they received from their universities and colleges, suddenly found themselves eligible for sizeable grants, commissions, and profitable part-time consultancies. The gravy train had arrived at last, and no one was really bothered by the fact that its engine was a flying saucer.

In contrast, the ominous Central Intelligence Agency and the shadowy National Security Agency were trying to make ends meet on a paltry $11 billion tax dollars per year during that same period. Millions were spent on assassins hired to rub out Fidel Castro and other foreign leaders – hardly a notable contribution to our economy or our world prestige.

In 1966, I trudged around Washington, D.C. trying to find someone who knew exactly how much was being spent for the non-hardware research in exobiology. Many astronomers were being paid large sums to calculate the number of probable planets in our galaxies. Biologists, zoologists, and anthropologists were experimentating with plants and animals to find out how they would fare in an alien environment. Statisticians and mathematicians by the hundreds were hard at work on the problem with their computers and Ouija boards. But no official in Washington seemed to know what the exobiology budget really was. The best estimate I could come up with was that we were spending about $150 million annually on these matters.

That same year, the U.S. Air Force reluctantly handed $300,000 to Colorado University to begin a UFO study. The figure was later upped to $500,000.

Paradoxically, the effusive search for extraterrestrial life was worth at least $150 million, but the search for a flying saucer – which could conceivably prove, conclusively, the existence of such life – was only worth a miserable half-million!

The rest, as they say, is history. The Colorado Project was a monumental disaster, and the grandiose search for extraterrestrial life slowly fizzled out. We were left with great piles of reports, all negative, and mind-boggling probability tables that only proved that if extraterrestrial life existed somewhere in our galaxy, the odds against our locating them – or their locating us – were staggering. Radio telescopes, built at enormous expense, did discover clouds of *known* chemicals in outer space – chemicals that the exobiologists optimistically call "the building blocks of life." But since it is safe to assume that everything in our galaxy is composed of essentially the same kind of matter, this find was not particularly revealing.

In the early 1970s, NASA's budget was cut back sharply and the great search for alien life quietly folded. The scientists who had been living in luxury apartments in Houston and Cape Kennedy glumly packed their bags and moved back to their old apartments in little college towns. Engineers and technicians who had expected aerospace to be their life's work found themselves standing in unemployment lines.

In the 1950s, the pioneer ufologists were convinced that flying saucers came from Venus and Mars. The space program proved otherwise. Venus is too hot and gaseous to support life as we know it, and Mars is apparently as dead as our moon. The famed contactees of yesteryear were all proved wrong. George Adamski, who died broke in 1965, had claimed he had seen trees and rivers on the moon when a flying saucer had transported him there. Our astronauts found only dust and rocks. Others who had allegedly visited Mars described great cities and friendly people. Our space probes found only dried riverbeds and huge craters.

The "scientific" frenzy of the early 1960s now seems like a sad job. We mobilized our best brains in the 1940s and built an atom bomb in a mere five years. We mobilized science again in 1960, and reached the moon in less than a decade. But we are still alone. In fact, we are more alone *now* than then. In 1960, we hoped that our solar system was shared by some other intelligent life. In 1977, we know that we are an island – a cosmic oasis – in a great sea of black emptiness. It cost us dearly to find this out. And we may never be the same.

The world of 1947 seems very distant and naïve now. In those early days, the pioneer ufologists cried out for an organized exploration of space. When that exploration became a reality in the 1960s, the ufologists somehow hardly noticed. The flying saucer syndrome had generated complex and foolish causes, and for many people, those causes became more important than the study of UFOs themselves. A very small handful of indefatigable researchers, widely scattered throughout the world, have made the only real contributions to our understanding of the UFO phenomenon. The rest have spent 30 years engaging in polemics and feuds, and indulging in evangelism, trying to convince a still dubious world that wonder "brothers" from outer space are coming to save us from ourselves. A few manage to earn a living by lecturing on the subject to anyone willing to pay to listen. But most will die as broke as Adamski. Overall, we don't know much more about the phenomenon today than Kenneth Arnold knew when he first gaped at those shining discs wobbling around the mountaintop.

We know only what they are *not*, and where they *cannot* be from. We know that the expenditure of money alone will not provide any answers. We could buy our way to the moon, but we have proved we cannot buy proof of extraterrestrial life.

That proof must lie in some other direction, beyond the tables of probability, beyond the charts of radiowave frequencies collected from outer space, beyond experiments with turtles in oxygen-less tanks – somewhere out there in the night, where people are still staring at strange lights bobbing in the darkness. Those same lights led us forth into mankind's greatest collective adventure. But now that that adventure has ended, will those lights and objects also fade into myth, or will they still be there in 2007, 2037, and 2067? Will we know more about them then than we know now?

UNIDENTIFIED FORMER HUMANS: 3000 YEARS OF INVESTIGATION

We probably will *not* understand the UFOs any better 300 hundred years from now. All we will know that is that they keep showing up in the same "window areas" year after year, century after century. These areas of highly strange activity are often located on old sacred spots such as mounds and tumuli. The presence of these physical relics makes us hopeful that answers will someday be found, but science shows little interest in their meaning. Unfortunately, we know as little about our past as we do about our future. How can we hope to conquer outer space when we do not even know our own history?

Here's a surefire bet. Ask you friends to name the first child of European parentage to be born in North America. If they say "Virginia Dare," they lose. Miss Dare, daughter of Ananias and Elinor Dare, was born on Roanoke Island, off the coast of Virginia, on August 18, 1587, and every schoolbook names her as the first American. But actually, she was a latecomer. The title really belongs to Snorre Karlsefni, son of Torfinn Karlsefni, who was born in Newfoundland in the year 1020.

Snorre's father was a Viking. The ruins of the house he built in the New World were rediscovered by archaeologists a few years back. In fact, Viking longhouses have been found far inland in Canada, and Viking artifacts have been dug up all over the U.S. Many hardy Scandinavia explorers visited North America centuries before Columbus set sail. Their expeditions are outlined in the ancient Viking histories, which also describe the Indians (whom the Vikings called "Skraelings"), their food, and their weapons. Physical evidence of their visits (including written records in the form of carved runestones) is ample and impressive. But even the Vikings weren't the first. They, too, were late arrivals. North America was populated thousands of years ago by a race of people whose origin is completely unknown. They brought with them a technology equaling, or even surpassing, the European cultures. Some Indian tribes feared them; others worshipped them and imitated them.

The ancient Egyptians, Chinese, and other civilizations knew of the existence of North America, and even included our continent on their maps. A cartographer in Lisbon, Bartholomew Colombo, collected many of these ancient charts in the 15th Century, and made the mistake of showing them to his opportunistic brother, Cristoforo. Cristoforo, a man with a reputation for being a liar, couldn't read maps very well, but he thought he saw a route to the rich, isolated lands of the Far East. He talked the Spanish crown into financing an expedition. The rest is history. Cristoforo Colombo ("Christopher Columbus") didn't know where he was going, misidentified the place when he got there, and when he got back to Spain, he still didn't know where he had been. The people who drew the charts he used knew far more about the world's geography than he did.

At least one group of Indians had made the same trip, in the opposite direction, 1,500 years earlier. Two historians, Pliny and Pomponius Mela, claim that a boatload of red-complexioned people arrived on the German coast in 62 B.C. It sounds as if some adventurous American Indians discovered Europe long *before* the Europeans risked "falling off the edge of the world" and "discovered" America! And if a small band of Indians could make the long journey in 62 B.C., there is no reason why the Phoenicians, Egyptians, and other early peoples could not have visited North America long before that.

When the first Europeans landed in New England, they were surprised to find ancient stone towers, great manmade mounds of earth, and other strange structures dotting the landscape. Many of these important monuments were torn down and plowed under in the early years of colonization. But new discoveries continue to be made. In the 1930s, hundreds of miles of fine roads, some 40 feet in width, were found in the Southwest. The Indians didn't have horses or the wheel, and thus had no real need for roads.

Dolmen (standing stones) and massive Stonehenge-type structures are also scattered across the U.S., and like their many counterparts in Great Britain, Denmark, France, and Portugal, were built with mathematical precision. Modern scientists believe they were used as astronomical observatories. The American Indians were mostly nomadic hunters, and lacked the advanced knowledge necessary to build such structures.

The ancient American builders also left a massive system of irrigation canals, so intricate and so carefully surveyed and laid out that their construction seems far beyond the abilities of the Indians.

Throughout the Mississippi and Ohio Valleys, there are all kinds of ancient structures and traces of a civilization that may have been comparable to the early civilizations of the Indus Valley, in India, and the Nile Valley in Egypt. Stone cities up to 8,000 years old are now being unearthed in the Mississippi Valley. Excavations into the lower layers of some of the so-called "Indian" mounds have turned up metal artifacts of iron, copper, and various alloys. The American Indians had no knowledge of metallurgy then, and were limited to hammering ax heads out of flint and meteoric iron – a substance so rare that the axes were used only for religious and ceremonial purposes. Yet suits of copper armor, carefully and expertly worked from copper tubing, have been discovered in some mounds. Skeletons with copper noses were apparently part of the burial preparations, which were as delicate and complicated as the Egyptian mummification process.

In the Great Lakes region, a huge network of ancient copper mines can be seen. Some of these mines were in use 2,000 years ago, and would have required thousands of workers to extract and process the ore. Indian culture centered around stone arrowheads and animal skins, not mining and metallurgy.

Oil was a virtually useless liquid to the Indians; they used it only in medicines, and in small quantities. The first important modern oil well was discovered at Titusville, Pennsylvania in 1860 but, later, very ancient shafts were discovered there, indicating that someone had been drilling for oil hundreds – maybe thousands – of years before. Tools, ladders, and construction methods similar to those found in the old copper mines around Lake Superior were also unearthed at Titusville. Another ancient oil well was discovered at Enniskillen, Canada. And a "worked" lead mine was found on a farm outside of Lexington, Kentucky. Apparently, North America was a beehive of industrial enterprise thousands of years ago.

Indian myths and legends tell us that large parts of this continent were once inhabited by strange white men. The tribes around what are now the states of Kentucky and West Virginia claimed that a bizarre group of "moon-eyed people" once lived there. They had pale skins and large round eyes so sensitive to light that they rarely ventured outside during the day. They lived in villages of stone houses, which they guarded fiercely. The Indians learned to avoid them and, in fact, the rich, fertile hills of West

Virginia were never settled by the Indians, because it was the "land of the moon-eyed people."

Modern armchair anthropologists have speculated that the moon-eyed people may have been remnants of the famous "Lost Colony" of Roanoke. Soon after Virginia Dare was born, she, her parents, and the entire Roanoke Island colony disappeared. When supply ships arrived from Europe, they found the island deserted. The nearest Indian tribes were not hostile, and were also baffled by the mass disappearance. The only clue left behind was a meaningless word carved into a tree: CROATOAN.

For 500 years, the Vikings maintained a large settlement on Greenland and then, like the Virginia colony, the entire population suddenly and mysteriously vanished. Had they simply migrated *en masse* to North America?

Indian legends about tall, blond, pale-skinned gods abound. Some of these gods sound like armor-clad Vikings. But others were supposedly dressed in long, flowing robes. In the West, the Paiutes speak of sacred plateaus where these gods reside. They were said to be equipped with magical rods that caused the skin to prickle and *induced paralysis*. In some legends, these gods are described as having the power of flight. They rode the night skies in great metal "birds."

The Eskimos, who bear an interesting resemblance to the ancient Olmecs of Central America, maintain that they were originally flown to the far north in "metal birds." The Navajo have a legend that their ancestors, the Anasazi, flew to South America on a great bird.

Could it be that the Americas were once the location of an advanced, Atlantis-like civilization? Like the Virginia colony and the Greenland settlement, the Olmecs and Anasazi vanished suddenly and mysteriously.

Aside from the moon-eyed people and the blond gods, the Indians also had to contend with *giants*. The Delaware Indians believe that their tribe once lived in the West, but migrated eastward. In those days, the land east of the Mississippi was inhabited by a race of giants who built many cities and fortifications. They were called the Alligewi. Both the Allegheny River and mountain range were supposedly named after them. The migrating Indians asked permission to pass through the Alligewi country, but were refused. So, the Indians went to war against the giants, and eventually drove them out. The Alligewi are said to have fled westward, down the Ohio River and up the Mississippi, into Minnesota. Bones of people seven to ten feet tall were found in the Minnesota mounds in the last century.

In South America, the natives of Ecuador retell an old story of how a tribe of giants landed on their shores in reed rafts and tried to take over. From the knee down "they were the size of an ordinary man," and their eyes were "the size of small plates." These giants slaughtered the Indians and attacked their women, but were finally killed by some cosmic disaster – a meteor struck their settlement and destroyed them. Were these the Alligewi from North America, looking for a new home?

The hard physical evidence found all across our continent indicates that an advanced culture thrived here long before the Indians made their mythical migration across the Bering Straits from Asia. Because the mounds, henges, and towers are strikingly similar to constructions found in Europe, Asia, and even remote Pacific islands, we can speculate that this culture was once worldwide. It probably reached its zenith before the Ice Age 10,000 years ago, and then degenerated in the wake of the geological calamities. That early culture mapped the whole planet, and fragments of those maps were handed down through the centuries, until they reached Columbus. The giants, who had once built the puzzling monoliths and pyramids that still stand on every continent, gradually reverted to a fierce, uncivilized state, driven by the urgent need to survive.

Eventually the giants were driven from their ancient homeland by the Native Americans. Some may have managed to flee to the interior of South America. To this day, there are rumors and stories about tribes of fair-haired, Amazonian giants living in isolated jungle cities of stone. We think of them now as "gods" from a far-off time, and there is now a lot of speculation that they may have come from a distant planet. But it is more likely that these "ancient astronauts" were merely survivors of a long-forgotten golden age, prior to the cataclysms. For a time, they influenced early man, and were even worshipped by him.

Atlantis may not have sunk into the ocean. You may be living on it.

CHAPTER 5

ARE UFOS USING THE EARTH FOR A GARBAGE DUMP? – *UFO REPORTS* #4 – 1967

Spring had come to the quiet back hills of West Virginia. On the evening of Thursday, April 20, 1967, three adults and two small children were sitting in front of their small bungalow on Plantation Creek Road, a narrow strip of ruts and mud-holes a few miles outside of the little town of Pliny, enjoying the unseasonably warm weather. Suddenly, around 8:15 p.m., something came sailing out of the clear, starlit sky and crashed to Earth directly in front of them, barely missing a little three-year-old girl playing in the winter-brown grass.

"We could see for miles," one of the witnesses told me four days later. "There weren't any planes around. There just wasn't any place for that thing to come from. And if it had fallen a foot off, in any direction, it would have hit one of us. And from the way it hit the ground, I'd say it would have really hurt."

"The thing" was a large, tightly packed ball of finely cut metal foil, which splatted against the ground with a loud thud, and spread out over an area about two feet square. It must have been slightly larger than a softball before impact. The startled children gleefully pounced on the glistening mess, which resemble short strips of very thin Christmas tree tinsel. But the alarmed mother hauled them away from it. Within minutes, both the mother and the two children were covered with a red rash, which they said lasted for several hours and itched fiercely. The men, disturbed by this reaction, feared that the substance might be radioactive, so they covered it with a rubber doormat and called the state police.

The next day, Corporal R.W. Porterfield of the Winfield station of the West Virginia State Police drove into the hills, sought out the family, carefully collected most of the foil from the ground, and sent it off to the Criminal Investigation Laboratory in Charleston, WV for analysis. West Virginia was in the midst of an amazing orgy of flying saucer sightings at the time, and everyone was very interested in anything that appeared in the sky or fell from it. While roaming up and down the Ohio Valley collecting material on these incidents, I had also come upon several "falls" of this metal foil. I already had several samples of it in my briefcase.

A large quantity of the stuff had been found spread over several acres of farmland on Sandhill Road in Point Pleasant, West Virginia in November

1966. Dozens of UFO sightings and several brief landings had been reported in that immediate area. Additional samples had turned up in Pennsylvania, Michigan, Indiana, New Hampshire, and several other spots where UFO sightings were especially intense. All of the samples were identical: very short, (about two inches long) strips of shiny, silvery tinsel slightly wider than ordinary steel wool. In West Virginia, they called this "outer space grass," and in some places, disgruntled farmers had to shovel it up before they could proceed with their spring plowing. It has a tendency to mat into clumps and fall in concentrated masses. Usually, it was found after one of those mysterious, bobbing white and red lights had slowly and silently passed over. Such lights were as common as fireflies in the fall of 1966 and Spring of 1967. The most recent appearance of the strange material took place in Amagansett, Long Island in early July of 1967. Several small piles of the foil were found there by Mrs. Bernice Lester, and samples were forwarded to me. They proved to be precisely similar to those collected in West Virginia.

Accompanied by Mrs. Mary Hyre, a jovial woman with 25 years of experience as the West Virginia correspondent for the Athens, Ohio *Messenger*, I interviewed the people on Plantation Creek Road and learned that they, like so many others in the state, had been watching strange aerial objects nearly every night.

"We see these things all the time," one farmer told us. "They look like big orange balls of fire. I guess they must be some of those satellites we're putting up."

That rang a bell. I remembered that two piles of this metal foil had been found at Lapeer, Michigan on December 9, 1965, shortly after numerous witnesses had reported observing a bright orange sphere that seemed to dump something out as it went by. (Incidentally, manmade space satellites appear as tiny pinpoints of light moving rapidly across the sky. They are most difficult to see with the naked eye, unless you know the exact time and place and watch for them.) Mounds of this foil material have also been repeatedly found in the Pocono Mountains of Pennsylvania. And a few years ago, layers of this stuff were found strewn over the greens and trees of a golf course near Camden, New Jersey.

Checking with other farmers living along that West Virginia ridge, Mrs. Hyre and I discovered that Mr. and Mrs. Charles Hudson had come upon a small quantity of "space grass" in their orchard only a week before that mysterious ball had plopped down on their neighbor's lawn. It was, Mrs. Hudson pointed out to us, lying directly over a telephone line that was buried in that orchard. (Many telephone companies are now burying their lincs instead of stringing them on poles.)

"We didn't give it much thought," Mrs. Hudson remarked. "We didn't even bother to pick any of it up, until after that ball of it came down and very nearly hit the little girl."

In the state police station at Winfield, Corporal Porterfield said that there had been two small strips of paper mixed in with the samples he had collected. He described this paper as being extremely thin, unevenly cut to about four inches in length, with a glossy brown finish. Unfortunately, these pieces got lost somewhere along the way. But Lieutenant R.J. Barker of the Criminal Investigation Bureau in Charleston ran a spectrographic analysis on the foil sample and, on April 28, revealed that the "particles submitted are composed of aluminum and traces of magnesium." The material was not radioactive or magnetic.

The results of his tests came as no surprise. On September 7, 1956, a large circular machine flew low over Chosi City, Chiba, Japan, and hundreds of people stood agape in the streets. They reported that it ejected enormous quantities of metal foil, which drifted down over the buildings and parks. One of the witnesses, a dentist named Masatoshi Takita, collected a large sample of the material and sent it to the Industry Promotion Association in Tokyo for analysis. UFO buffs around the world held their breaths, hoping that the long awaited "physical evidence" for the existence of extraterrestrial flying saucers had finally been found. They were disappointed when the laboratory revealed that the foil was composed of aluminum, lead, silicon, iron, and copper – all rather mundane, earthly materials. The pieces were four to five centimeters in length, one millimeter in width, and ten microns thick – identical to the West Virginia samples. However, since hundreds of people had seen the stuff fall out of a saucer-shaped craft, there seemed to be little question that it had come from a flying saucer.

Aluminum is not mined, but must be manufactured by extracting it from bauxite. A check with the Kaiser Aluminum Company in Hillside, NJ, and the Aluminum Association in New York revealed that the common aluminum foil sold by the roll in supermarkets consists of 99% pure aluminum with minute amounts of magnesium, zinc, copper, silicon, iron, and other random impurities making up the remaining 1%.

Nothing very startling there. Unless, of course, the UFOs were buying aluminum foil in supermarkets, shredding it, and dumping it out all over the American landscape.

Since it has been repeatedly proven that this space grass is plain old

Yankee aluminum, there is one other possible source for it. In his investigation into the mystery, Corporal Porterfield had called up the Air National Guard base in Charleston and had been told that the foil was just "chaff," and that Air Force planes "use it to foul up radar on training flights." The explanation made sense, and Corporal Porterfield was willing to forget the whole business. But *I* wasn't.

On my way back from West Virginia, I stopped at the Pentagon in Washington, D.C. and confronted Lt. Col. George P. Freeman, spokesman for the Air Force's Project Blue Book, with the space grass mystery. Colonel Freeman, a placid, balding man with years of experience in Air Force Public Relations, has been struggling to restore the Air Force's good image after the "swamp gas" fiasco of a year ago. He was most cooperative.

"We get a lot of this 'chaff' in the mail," he admitted. "And we send it on to Wright-Patterson Air Force Base (headquarters for Project Blue Book), but it's just the stuff used against radar on training flights."

If that's all it is, I asked, why did he bother to forward the mailed samples to Wright-Patterson at all? Colonel Freeman stared at me wearily. Then I asked if I could see a sample of foil used by the Air Force for radar purposes. "We don't have any of it here in the Pentagon," he said. "You'd have to go to an Air Force base to get some."

"Fine," I responded willingly. "I'll do just that."

He patiently explained that I would be wasting my time. Soon after the development of radar during World War II, our planes began using strips of tinfoil as a countermeasure. This material was cut into long, wide pieces and packed in boxes. As our bombers flew over Germany, the gunners would periodically dump the boxes out of open ports. As the tinfoil fluttered down, the enemy's radar beams bounced off it and it produced false images on their radarscopes. It was a reasonably effective countermeasure for a time, but as radar became more sophisticated, this technique became obsolete. Besides, the rapid advance in the design of military aircraft made it impractical. The planes flew too high and too fast, and there were no longer openings or "windows" from which the chaff could be dumped.

By the time the Korean War rolled around, we had developed electronic gadgets that did the same job, and did it better. All modern military planes are equipped with these "black boxes," which, according to an Air Force release, are "transmitters designed to radiate interfering signals that either block the receiver or obscure the targets on a radarscope, distort or deny the sound on radio, provide erroneous guidance signals to missiles, place false targets on radarscopes, or alter the course on navigation devices."

Tossing boxes of tinfoil out of a lumbering B-17 is one thing, but throwing "chaff" out of a modern jet-bomber hurtling across the skies at 800 miles an hour is something else again. Here's what the Air Force says about that:

> The "chaff" strips are called "tuned" or "resonant" devices. At the lower radar frequencies, these strips become excessively long. Because of this, they are not easily packaged or dispensed from modern, high-speed aircraft. In order to overcome this difficulty, a second form of reflector called "rope" is employed. Rope, unlike chaff, is a roll of thin aluminum foil or tape, several hundred feet long, which gives strong reflections at low radar frequencies when it unravels in the air. These are called "untuned" or "non-resonant" devices. Modern packages of these expendable reflectors contain both rope and chaff. Since rope is no longer packaged separately, the term "chaff" now describes the complete bundle or unit of reflective material.

In all of the cases in which these very fine and very short pieces of metal foil have been found, not a single piece of this "rope" has been discovered, nor even seen. Since it is now supposedly packaged together with the short chaff, one might ask why these strips "several hundred feet long" have failed to come down with the short chaff. What's more, the "chaff" samples picked up throughout the world stick together in clumps and would not disperse easily, no matter how they were released in the air. The pieces are always found matted together, and such clumps, regardless of length, would certainly fail to reflect to radar in the manner presumably intended.

Colonel Freeman, at my insistence, arranged for me to visit a secret radar installation in New Jersey where I could discuss the matter with experts. He asked the officers there to present me with some samples of the actual "chaff" and "rope" used on Air Force missions. So my next stop was at a setting straight out of a *James Bond: 007* movie: a huge, windowless, concrete building surrounded by a high metal fence, and heavily guarded.

An officer met me at the gate and escorted me through a labyrinth of empty gray corridors, past a gigantic chamber that looked like the War Room in *Dr. Strangelove*, and into a cluttered office where I was faced by a group of taut-lipped officers and enlisted men. A young sergeant spread out a newspaper on a desk and produced a small, beat up paper sack.

"You'll never know what we went through to get this for you," he smiled as he dumped the sack onto the paper.

"What's so difficult about obtaining a sack of aluminum foil?" I asked. The stuff he had poured out was identical to my West Virginia samples, except that it seemed coarser and stiffer, as if it were very old.

"We have to find this on the ground," one of the officers explained.

"Find it? I thought you fellows were dumping it out of your planes all the time!"

"We just keep it around to show it to trainees, so they'll know what it looks like," the sergeant said.

I had the uneasy feeling that this was some kind of put-on.

"Well, how is this stuff packaged?" I asked. The spokesman for the group, a captain, looked at me blankly. "Does it come in boxes, tubes, cartridges, or what?"

"We can't give you that information," he answered warily.

"Then can you tell me how it's dispersed?"

"I think they drop it out of a chute," the captain said slowly.

"Fine. You have a lot of planes here. Could you show me one of those chutes?"

They looked at each other helplessly. I picked up a strand of the "chaff." The whole clump stuck to it. "Since it sticks together like this," I went on, "it looks like it wouldn't disperse well, if at all. I'd like to know how you get it spread out."

"It's released out of a chute," the captain repeated.

"Is it packed in balls or what?" An air of silent tension settled over the group. "Is it wrapped in paper tape?"

"No, they don't wrap it in tape," the captain said unhappily. "It's just dumped out of a chute."

I started to gather up some of it. "I'd like to take a sample of it," I told them, "to compare with other samples."

"We can't let you have any of it," the captain replied quickly. "It's classified."

"You mean you 'classify' aluminum foil?"

"The length of it can tell someone the length of the frequencies our radar is using," he muttered.

I held up a piece of it. It was about an inch and a half long.

"That's a mighty short wavelength," I noted. Nobody smiled. "Why don't we take a pair of scissors and cut one of these up. Then I won't be able to sell it to the Russians."

"I'm sorry. We can't do that."

"But the Pentagon promised that you would supply me with a sample."

"I'm sorry," the captain said. "This is classified material, and I can't release any of it to you."

When I left that concrete wonderland, empty-handed, I was reasonably convinced that this "chaff" was as mysterious to the U.S. Air Force as it was to me. Since it was being found in such large quantities, it should have been a very easy thing for a major radar installation on an important Air Force base to produce fresh samples of both "rope" and chaff," *if* the stuff were actually being used by the Air Force.

The next day I called Major Hector Quintanilla, Jr., head of Project Blue Book at Wright-Patterson in Dayton, Ohio, and asked him about "chaff."

"We get a lot of it here for analysis," he told me.

"Could you send me a sample, along with a copy of the results of your tests?" I asked.

"Oh, it's nothing but tinfoil," he declared flatly.

"Tinfoil! Thanks a lot, Major." I hung up. Project Blue Book was obviously on the job. I made a note to send them a junior chemistry set for Christmas.

There are no regular Air Force bases in West Virginia, and only a couple of National Guard units. More specifically, there are no known radar installations in the state. Therefore, there would be little purpose in dumping out "chaff" and "rope," even on training missions. Reporters in West Virginia have failed to find any of this aluminum foil, in any condition, at the National Guard units.

However, there is a huge Kaiser Aluminum factory on the banks of the Ohio River south of Ravenswood, WV, which employs almost 5,000 people. Ravenswood is a hotbed of UFO reports. As a matter of fact, almost everyone there has seen at least one flying saucer in recent months. Many have complained of the now familiar aftereffect – burnt eyes, similar to the results of staring into a bright welder's torch without wearing protective glasses. One resident, Lester Holly, has kept a careful log of local sightings. According to his records, unidentified flying objects buzzed Ravenswood on March 1, 7, 9, 10, and 17, and on April 15 and 17 of this year.

More important, scores of employees at the Kaiser Aluminum factory have reported a long string of fascinating incidents. I spent two days snooping around the immediate area and interviewed many of the workmen. Since Kaiser is involved in making classified parts for military airplanes, and since the Air Force allegedly informed the plant's management that the objects reported were nothing more than stars and good old reliable "swamp gas," these witnesses were all afraid to allow their names to be published.

One Kaiser employee claims that one night in mid-March, he was driving a truck out to the garbage dump behind the factory when his engine suddenly quit, his radio went dead, and the ground around him lit up with an eerie glow. He climbed out of the cab and looked up, and was astounded to see a large, brightly illuminated disk hovering directly above him. He ran all the way back to the factory in near hysteria, and refused to return to his truck that night. Numerous other workmen have repeatedly reported seeing low-altitude UFOs around that garbage dump, as well as above the factory's water tower and over the factory itself. They tell the story of another man who quit his job, on the spot, after watching three small, reddish circular objects join a large, luminous cigar-shaped thing directly over the plant.

I visited that garbage dump to see if Kaiser Aluminum was throwing away any waste products or shavings that might resemble "outer space grass." But all I found was garbage.

So we are still left with the mystery of the aluminum strips. While the Air Force is trying to take the blame, they can't produce any proof that they are actually using these tiny strips, nor can they present a convincing case for the possible need of such material in the modern Air Force. On the other hand, if the UFOs and flying saucers are dumping "chaff" all over the landscape, why? Are these tailings the curious byproduct of some unknown manufacturing process going on in our skies? If so, why don't the mysterious UFO pilots – if they really *are* the culprits – dump their garbage in the remote forests of Canada, or the vast desert wastelands of the Middle East? The farmers of West Virginia are tired of cleaning up after them.

CHAPTER 6

Approximately 100 miles west of Flatwoods, West Virginia, site of the celebrated appearance of the "Flatwoods Monster" in 1952, a new kind of creature materialized in 1966, and has apparently been lingering around Point Pleasant, West Virginia ever since. Unlike its predecessor, the Point Pleasant critter is equipped with a pair of wings, and is reported to be able to fly as fast as a speeding automobile without flapping them! Local citizens refer to it as "The Bird," but newspapermen from coast to coast have labeled it the "Mothman."

Whatever it is, the "Bird" has managed to frighten a great many people and confound a wide variety of scientists, biologists, and ornithologists. Since December 1966, I have visited Point Pleasant five times, and have interviewed many of the witnesses at great length. Some of their lives have been drastically changed after their fleeting experiences with "Mothman." I have kept in constant touch with many of these people, and have carefully compared developments in West Virginia with the UFO developments in other sections of the country. There is now no doubt in my mind that Mr. Mothman is related to unidentified flying objects in some very special and terrifying way.

Although winged creatures are no strangers to ufologists and have appeared repeatedly since 1878, they – if we can call them "they" – have never before returned consistently to one area, as they now seem to be doing in West Virginia. In almost half of the sightings between November 1966 and November 1967, the creatures either pursued automobiles or made direct approaches to the occupants of parked cars. This is not only a familiar UFO pattern, but is an apparent behavioral trait of the tall, odious, hairy, and manlike "Bigfoot" creatures, which turn up every year in California, Michigan, and many other places around the United States.

Perhaps we should start entertaining the possibility that *all* of these assorted and very elusive creatures are not only related, but that they are also cunning *disguises*, and that the masqueraders are, in fact, more than just curious about the products of Detroit. "They" may have a special interest in the occupants of the automobiles being approached, and they conceal that interest – their true purpose for existing at all – by manifesting themselves in weird guises. There is now mounting evidence to support this somewhat outlandish notion.

The people in Mothman country are *not* hillbillies. Many of the witnesses are intelligent, well-educated people enjoying fine reputations in their community. The Point Pleasant area of West Virginia is quite industrialized. There are many large chemical factories lining the Ohio and Kanawha rivers, employing highly skilled labor. Another factor in their favor is that they are part of the "Bible Belt," and are highly religious. Point Pleasant, a town of about 5,000, has 22 churches and *no* bars serving alcohol.

A "winged man" was first reported in Scott, Mississippi on September 1, 1966. Scott is on the Mississippi River, several hundred miles south of the point where the Mississippi joins the Ohio. Mothman's apparent new home in West Virginia is the area where the Kanawha River joins the Ohio. More than a third of the sighting reports have come from the immediate vicinity of the TNT Area, a World War II ammunition plant located just north of Point Pleasant. The TNT Area consists of several hundred wooded acres adjoined by the Clinton F. McClintic Wildlife Station, a 2,500-acre animal preserve that is heavily forested, very hilly, and laced with artificial ponds and lakes.

The TNT Area contains over a hundred large, concrete domes all sealed with heavy steel doors. Some of them still contain stores of high explosives and are fenced off. There are no guards and no activity in the area today. Former explosives factories now lie in ruins there, as do two large abandoned power plants. A vast network of tunnels is spread out underneath the site. Most of these tunnels are sealed off now, or are filled with muddy water.

The "fourth" Mothman sighting occurred at midnight, November 15, 1966, directly outside one of the abandoned power plants. Mr. and Mrs. Roger Scarberry and Mr. and Mrs. Steve Mallette were driving along the rugged dirt road that passes by the plant, when they suddenly saw a gray figure as tall as a man, which had large, eerily glowing red eyes and wings. It turned and shuffled awkwardly towards the door of the old plant, they said. Badly frightened, they accelerated and fled the area. As they hurtled towards Point Pleasant at over 100 mph, all four claimed that the creature appeared overhead and flew along with them without flapping its wings! They reported the incident to the police. Deputy Millard Halstead drove out to the area with them. The creature was gone, but Halstead's police radio began to emit a strange sound – like a speeded-up phonograph album, he said later.

This was the beginning of a long and bizarre chain of events. The Scarberrys, who were living in a trailer home at the time, began to suffer a series of poltergeist manifestations. Although Mr. Scarberry is now in the U.S. Army and his wife, Linda, lives with her parents in Point Pleasant, the poltergeist seems to have moved with her. Her parents, Mr. and Mrs. Park McDaniel, have been having unusual problems with their telephone, and they suspect it may be tapped by some unknown party. Strange lights have appeared in the McDaniel home in recent months, and objects have moved of their own volition, or seemingly so.

On January 11, 1967, Mrs. McDaniel saw the "Bird" herself, in broad daylight. She was outside her home when she observed what appeared to be a small plane flying down the road, almost at treetop level. As it drew closer, she realized it was man-shaped object with wings. It swooped low over her head and circled a nearby restaurant before going out of sight, she told me later. I might add that Mrs. McDaniel enjoys a fine reputation in Point Pleasant and works in the local unemployment office. I have often been a guest in the McDaniel home, and they show no signs of being overly imaginative.

Both Linda and her parents state that they have received visits from people whose descriptions tally with those of the legendary and contro-versial "Men in Black" or "MIB." Their reports of these incidents were among those that led me to take the MIB seriously. Their last visit from the MIB was on December 23, 1967.

(A Man in Black of slight stature systematically visited several of the people I had interviewed. All witnesses described this man as resem-bling an Oriental, such as a Thai or Burmese. His speech was slow and parrotlike. He apparently could only hear the witnesses when they looked directly into his dark, glassy eyes. He identified himself as "Jack Brown." All witnesses said that he was primarily interested in what I had been doing in the area, whom I had been talking to, and where I had gone. He drove a white station wagon that made a lot of noise, as if the muffler was broken.)

The McDaniel home lies just off Route 62, which leads past the TNT Area.

In the majority of the Mothman cases, the witnesses managed only a brief glimpse of the creature. Its most outstanding feature seems to be its glowing red eyes. Few witnesses have been able to describe the Bird's face, but most have noted the eyes and have admitted being terrified by them. While some people have claimed that Mothman was brown, most have described it as being grayish in color. All witnesses seem to agree that the wings do not flap in flight, making its incredible speed all the more unaccountable. Those who have seen it walk say that it shuffles or waddles. Those who have seen it take off claim that it rises straight up, like a helicopter.

Tom Ury, 25, of Clarksburg, West Virginia, was driving along Route 62 at 7:15 a.m. on the morning of November 25, 1966, just above the TNT Area, when he saw a large gray figure floating above a field next to the road. "It came up like a helicopter and veered over my car," he said. He stepped on the gas and accelerated to about 75 miles per hour, but the Bird not only stayed with him, but also *circled* casually above his speeding car. He described it as being about six feet long, with a wingspan of eight to ten feet. Like most of the others, he didn't get a look at its face. He was too frightened. He was driving a convertible, and he was afraid it was going to come down on him.

Another witness swears she saw Mothman's face, but has been unable to find words to describe it. "It was horrible, like something out of a science-fiction movie," Connie Joe Carpenter told me the first time I interviewed her.

According to Connie, a quiet, sensitive 18-year-old, she was driving home from church at 10:30 a.m. on Sunday, November 27, 1966, when she saw a tall gray figure standing on the deserted greens of the Mason County Golf Course outside New Haven, West Virginia. The figure suddenly spread a pair of ten-foot wings, took off straight up, and flew directly at her car. It had large, round, fiercely glowing red eyes, she said, which gripped her. She couldn't turn away. "It's a wonder I didn't have an accident," she commented.

The apparition swooped over her car and she sped up, in near hysterics. The next day, her eyes were reddened and almost swollen shut. When I interviewed her two weeks later, they were still red and watery. (UFO witnesses often suffer from this eye malady for several days afterward. This is the only case in which a "Mothman" witness has had this problem, however.) As with many of the other cases, this first incident was only the beginning of the nightmare for Connie.

Early in February 1967, Connie married Mr. Keith Gordon, and they moved across the river to a two-family house in Middleport, Ohio. They did not have a telephone. At 8:15 a.m. on February 22nd, Connie left the house to go to school. As she started to walk down the street, a large black car pulled alongside. Since all young people today are very automobile conscious, she said she could positively identify it as a 1949 Buick. The occupant of the car opened the door and called to her. Thinking that he was seeking directions, she approached him. He was a young, clean-cut man of about 25, she told me later. He was wearing a colorful "mod" shirt, no jacket, and had neatly combed, thick black hair. He appeared to be suntanned, and spoke with no noticeable accent.

When she reached the car, the driver suddenly *lunged and grabbed her arm*, and ordered her to get in with him. He did not get out of the car. She fought back, and there was a brief struggle before she broke away. She ran back to the house (the other apartment was deserted, the occupants having gone to work) and locked herself in, completely terrified. Later in the day, she thought she heard someone on the porch, but she did not look.

After her husband came home from work, she told him the story. He said that *he* had also seen the Buick cruising around the neighborhood. Neither of them had ever seen the driver before.

Connie remained indoors the following day, February 23rd. At 3 p.m., she heard someone on the porch again, and there was a loud knock at the door. She cautiously went to the door. There was no one on the porch, but a note had been slipped under the door. It was written in pencil, in block letters, on a piece of ordinary notebook paper. "Be careful, girl," it read, "I can get you yet."

That night, Connie and Keith went to the local police. They turned the note over to officer Raymond Manly.

One curious and significant thing that Connie noticed about the car involved was that despite its obvious vintage, it appeared to be brand new, inside and out. It was not just well kept, she assured me, but "brand new." (Many MIB witnesses and "silent contactees" have told me of their experiences with old cars that looked new inside and out, and even had a "new car smell.")

The Middleport police force is small (the town has a population of 3,400) and somewhat lethargic. In March 1967, I visited their office and asked to see their file on the case. The police chief produced a printed form containing Connie's name and address, and one scribbled line: "Dark Buick, young man." He told me no such car existed in Middleport, and that it was obviously a case of some maniac trying to abduct a young girl. Officer Manly assured me that he was keeping the house under constant surveillance. I had to break the news to them that the Gordons had moved back to the West Virginia side of the river shortly after the incident, and no longer even lived in Middleport. Despite my sheaf of credentials from leading magazines and the North American Newspaper Alliance, both men were overly suspicious of me, and asked me repeatedly if I really wasn't from "the government."

Officer Manly conveniently lost the note somewhere along the way.

Connie and Keith moved in with Connie's mother, Mrs. Faye Carpenter, in New Haven temporarily. On the night of March 22, Connie was awakened in the middle of the night by a long beeping sound, which she said appeared to be coming from directly outside her window.

On December 22, 1967, a "Man in Black" type visited Connie and Keith, and talked to them for about two hours. Mrs. Carpenter was present at the meeting but, strangely enough, she can remember only the man's entrance into the house, and his departure. She does not remember *any* of the conversation that took place. For the past year, there have been repeated poltergeist manifestations in her home – strange noises, objects that have been in one place for years suddenly falling off shelves, and so on. She has also been receiving many odd telephone calls. The phone rings and there is nobody there, or there is heavy static and strange mechanical sounds during conversations – familiar patterns of phone harassment. Mrs. Carpenter leads a quiet life and has received no publicity of any kind. Like everyone else in New Haven, she has seen a number of UFOs in recent months.

A witness to Mothman's "fifth" appearance, Mrs. Marcella Bennett of Point Pleasant, has also suffered a series of traumatic experiences following her encounter.

At 9 p.m. Wednesday, November 16, 1966, Mrs. Bennett drove out to the TNT Area, together with Mr. and Mrs. Raymond Wamsley, to visit Mrs. Ralph Thomas, whose family is one of the few living in the area amongst the "igloos." Mr. and Mrs. Thomas were not at home, but three of their children, Rickie, Connie, and Vickie, were. Not knowing this, and having heard of the "monster" sighting the night before, the Wamsleys decided to pull a prank and rap on the windows. They got out of their car quietly and started towards the house. Mrs. Bennett was carrying her two-year-old girl, Tina. As she got out of the car with her sleepy burden, she suddenly gasped. A giant gray figure with blazing red eyes seemed to rise up from the ground behind her car, staring directly at her.

Horror swept the trio, and they all started to run for the house. But Mrs. Bennett stumbled, dropped her child to the gravel, and stood transfixed.

"It was as if she went into some kind of trance," Raymond Wamsley observed later.

After a prolonged and agonizing moment, Mrs. Bennett managed to scoop up the now screaming Tina, and staggered to the house. Hysteria overcame the entire group as the creature moved onto the porch. They frantically called the police. The "thing" was gone when police arrived.

Mrs. Bennett came close to suffering a nervous breakdown after the incident. She could not discuss the experience at all for several weeks afterwards. She refused to see me for months, but finally, mutual friends talked her into meeting with me. During that first interview, she was laconic and quite reluctant. She hinted that the "monster" had returned, and that she had seen it in the immediate vicinity of her house. But it was not until November 1967 that she really granted a fruitful interview.

She had been cautious during our earlier talk, she said, because "something kept telling me to be careful – that you were from the government." (This anti-government paranoia is one of my biggest obstacles in my research. We can thank the organized UFO groups for this unfortunate public attitude, which undoubtedly cuts the Air Force and government off from much important information.)

Mrs. Bennett recalled that she and the Wamsleys had been watching a strange, large, red light dancing around the sky as they drove through the TNT Area to the Thomas' place. At that time, no one in Point Pleasant was UFO conscious, so they didn't know what to make of it.

In the months following the incident, the Bennett home was tense. Mrs. Bennett suffered from bad dreams and heard strange noises, ranging from footsteps on the roof to the sound of things being dropped in empty rooms. On one occasion, she heard what sounded like a woman's piercing scream directly outside the house. (I have heard both the footsteps on the roof and the pan-dropping phenomenon during my travels. The latter sounds as if a big metal pan has been dropped somewhere in the house. The sound of a "woman screaming" has also been frequently described to me. In some cases, the witnesses have said it "sounded like a dog being torn apart.")

Early in December 1966, Mrs. Bennett was driving along a deserted backroad with Tina, when she became aware of a red Ford Galaxy following her. It was driven by a large man who appeared to be wearing a very bushy "fright" wig. She slowed, hoping the vehicle would pass. Instead, it tried to *force her off the road*. She stepped on the gas, and the other car accelerated and shot down the road ahead of her, disappearing around a bend. When she circled the bend, she was alarmed to find that the Ford was now parked crossways on the dirt road, blocking it. Badly frightened, she warned her daughter to hold on, and she jammed the gas pedal to the floor. The other driver, seeing that she didn't mean to stop, pulled over hastily and let her pass. She has never seen him before – or since.

On my first visit to Point Pleasant, in December 1966, I was baffled to find that the newspapers and the police had not received a *single* "flying saucer" report. But in a matter of hours, I discovered that many people had been seeing mysterious objects throughout the summer and fall of 1966. Accompanied by Mrs. Mary Hyre, the local AP stringer and reporter for the Athens, Ohio *Messenger*, a daily with a large circulation in the area, I tracked down and interviewed several UFO witnesses, and she wrote newspaper pieces about their stories. As soon as the stories appeared, the dam burst. Scores of people, ranging from hill farmers to prominent local officials, came forward with UFO stories of their own.

I prowled up and down both sides of the Ohio River, visiting other towns and uncovering many other good UFO sightings. It was apparent that a major "flap" was taking place there and that it was unnoticed by the press, largely because most of the witnesses were reluctant to come forward. But once the door was opened, UFO mania soon gripped the whole region. Since then, Mrs. Hyre has received as many as 20 new sighting reports a day.

I saw so many strange lights and objects myself that I actually lost count. Sightings ran the full gamut, from "flying bird cages" (one of those passed low over Point Pleasant early in March 1967, and was seen by hundreds) to giant reddish cigars and great spheres that displayed a penchant for hovering over nearby dams and factories. There were dozens of auto pursuits and innumerable brief landings reported, including several around schoolyards.

It would be impossible to recount the situation here. People living on high ground told me of being awakened in the middle of the night by loud thumps against their houses. There was a widespread outbreak of poltergeists cases. Television sets went haywire; new sets "burned out" immediately after they were installed.

Much of the UFO activity seemed to be concentrated in the TNT Area itself. Police officer Harold Harmon told me of seeing a large, dark, metallic object hovering over a pond in the wildlife preserve one night in early March. He said that they watched it for several minutes as it rocked "like a boat on the waves" and glided silently past, just above the treetops.

Harmon was with me on the night of March 31, 1967, when all hell broke loose. Police radios all up and down the Ohio Valley were useless that night, jammed by inexplicable static. The Mason County Sheriff's radio transmitter was destroyed by fire at 7:30 p.m., and the auxiliary transmitters wouldn't work. In front of Harmon and several other witnesses, I flashed a powerful light at some strange looking "stars" overhead, and astonished everyone when the "stars" suddenly skittered about the sky, changed colors, and flew on up the Ohio.

People in the vicinity of the TNT Area began to have the usual trouble with their telephones. By the middle of March, the objects were following a regular schedule, appearing in the TNT Area every night at 8:30 p.m. – *at treetop level*. They were seen by thousands, and were photographed by newspaper photographers and television crews. And yet none of this was mentioned in the national press, except for a seven-part newspaper series I wrote for the North American Newspaper Alliance in June 1967.

As usual, a rash of mysterious fires broke out. An abandoned building in the TNT Area burned to the ground one night in March *in a pouring rain*. Firemen could not figure out how it got started.

Another mystery took place in a large cemetery on the outskirts of Point Pleasant. Huge tombstones were found knocked down in neat rows. Together with the police, I examined the damage. Many of the stones had been securely bolted and cemented in place. Some of them were cleanly broken off. A number of the larger stones must have weighed many hundreds of pounds. At first, the police suspected teenaged vandals, but it would have taken tractors and heavy equipment, plus a lot of very hard work, to inflict such damage. Similar "pranks" have occurred in other cemeteries throughout the country, always in heavy "flap" areas. (In accordance with routine police procedure, reporters were asked to refrain from mentioning the cemetery damage while an investigation was being done. Police kept the cemetery under close nightly surveillance for several weeks. Strange lights were frequently seen there, rising straight up.)

The enormity of this situation – and there are now hundreds of Point Pleasants in America – has been ignored by the newspapers and neglected by the UFO buffs, who devote themselves to collecting random descriptions of flying objects. It is time for us to stop misleading ourselves and buckle down to the job of investigating the "flap" areas and the strange things that happen to the people caught in them. There is a definite correlation between poltergeist activity and other seemingly "occult" manifestations, and the UFO phenomenon itself. There is also the disturbing possibility that terrestrials or terrestrial-type beings are directly involved with the phenomenon itself.

By using the standard journalistic procedure of in-depth interviewing and steady follow-up of important cases, I assured myself of the reliability of the witnesses and the reliability of their reports. None of these people had ever heard of the "Men in Black," and few had any knowledge of poltergeists. Most them tried to fit their experiences into a religious framework.

During my visits to "Mothman" country, a number of prominent local businessmen, teachers, and others came to me to tell me – in strictest confidence – of their own experiences with the "Bird" and UFOs. All of them described essentially the same thing. But there were a couple of notable exceptions, where the witnesses may have actually seen some kind of huge and unclassified "normal" bird. It may sound preposterous, but there is reason to believe that large, unusual birds may have been *imported* into the area, to spread confusion and to reduce the effect of Mothman's presence. In late December 1966, a rare arctic snow owl was shot by a farmer in Gallipolis Ferry, West Virginia. This creature was two feet tall and had a five-foot wingspan. "Mothman" witnesses converged on the farmer for a look at the owl, and all of them declared that it in no way resembled what they had seen.

In July 1967, another rare bird turned up. This one was a turkey vulture, and it stood over a foot tall. It was found by a group of boys near New Haven, West Virginia. Again, the Mothman witnesses looked and shook their heads. But the big question is: How did the rare arctic snow owl and turkey vulture make their way to Point Pleasant in time to coincide with the Mothman sightings?

(We might also ask how deflated weather balloons manage to turn up conspicuously in UFO flap areas, often landing on the front lawns of prominent citizens. This kind of coincidence is becoming too common. Either the UFO skeptics are right – or somehow involved in these charades – or we are all being made the victims of a gigantic plot to deceive and confuse us.)

There are no bears in Mason County, but in November 1966, Mr. Cecil Lucas saw three bearlike creatures sniffing around an oil pump in his field. His farm is located a few hundred yards from the McDaniel home, and is on the banks of the Ohio. When he came out of his house to investigate the situation, the dark, hairy forms ran off – erect – towards the river, disappearing into a thicket. No "bears" have been seen before or since by anyone else. In talking with Mr. Lucas, I was impressed with his forthright honesty. Besides, why should anyone make up a story about little bears?

All of this is a rather inadequate summary of the situation in Point Pleasant and in West Virginia. The story is not over yet. Mrs. Hyre and the police continue to receive at least one new UFO report daily. Mothman's appearances have been less frequent, but the MIB activity seems to be continuing throughout the Ohio and Kanawha valleys.

In March 1967, I called both the Pentagon and Wright-Patterson Air Force Base and made a direct appeal to them, asking that they at least perform a token investigation in West Virginia. Nothing was done.

Dog disappearances and the mutilation of cows and horses are now common in West Virginia and Ohio. Newell Partridge of Doddridge County said his television started "acting like a generator" on the night of November 15, 1966, and his German shepherd dog, Bandit, "started carrying on something terrible." Partridge shined a flashlight into the field and saw something "like two red reflectors." The dog's hair stood straight up, and it ran into the field. It was never seen again. The police are baffled.

In the past three years, over 20 *people*, all teenaged boys, have vanished suddenly without a trace in Braxton County, home of the "Flatwoods Monster."

One final "Bird" sighting is of special interest. At 10:30 p.m. on the night of Friday, May 19, 1967, two women were driving along Route 62, heading north from Point Pleasant. As they passed the C.C. Lewis farm near the TNT Area, they say they observed a dark form with two brilliant red lights on it. Apparently it was circling a tree. From the general shape, they believed that it was a winged object slightly larger than a man. Suddenly, a larger red light appeared and floated toward the dark figure. The two seemed to merge, and then the large, combined red light flew off to the north.

The two women returned immediately to Point Pleasant and excitedly reported what they had seen. Both were convinced that they had watched Mothman rendezvous with a UFO! At 3 a.m. that morning, several residents reported seeing a brightly glowing UFO land in a field near the junior high school in Point Pleasant. Some of the witnesses reported watching it for twenty minutes before it rose slowly into the night sky and disappeared.

If this report is accurate, then it would appear that the UFOs and "Mothman" could indeed be related.

In November 1967, I visited Point Pleasant again. Even though sightings had subsided somewhat, I saw another UFO hovering over the TNT Area, as did several other people. In talking with the residents, I learned of a peculiar new epidemic. Mrs. Ralph Thomas, Mrs. Mary Hyre, and a number of others claimed they had been having disturbing dreams. Mrs. Hyre said she had dreamed of people crying for help in the icy waters of the Ohio River. Mrs. Thomas said her dreams were also of a terrible disaster on the river. A mood of ominous foreboding seemed to have gripped Point Pleasant.

On December 15, 1967, the suspension bridge that joined Point Pleasant with the Ohio side of the river suddenly collapsed, taking with it 17 trucks and 40 passenger vehicles. Among the scores of people who died were several UFO witnesses, including Marvin Wamsley, teenaged nephew of Mr. and Mrs. Raymond Wamsley.

Within an hour of the bridge collapse, twelve UFOs appeared in the TNT Area, according to the testimony of the James Lilly family, who were experienced UFO-watchers. No UFOs were seen in the vicinity of the bridge, however.

Point Pleasant, West Virginia is a microcosm. All of the complex ground-level factors inherent in the UFO phenomenon can be found there. We might even consider the possibility that some UFOs are actually *based* somewhere in the almost inaccessible back hills of West Virginia. Aside from National Guard units, there are no known military installations in West Virginia, and no radar nets to locate the interlopers. Police forces in the Ohio Valley are small and overworked. There are only two FBI agents assigned to cover the entire sector.

After 9 p.m. at night, the major portion of the population is sound asleep. Point Pleasant's Main Street is completely deserted after 7:00 p.m. In short, West Virginia is most vulnerable to any kind of invasion.

Perhaps an invasion has already begun.

Several childhood Mothman witnesses from West Virginia had premonitions of the 9/11 attacks, and several local adults had close encounters with Mothman just before or after the attacks. Just after the Twin Towers fell on September 11th, 2001, this photograph of "Mothman" was taken by a photographer whose identity still remains unknown. Analysis of the photograph indicates that it was not "photoshopped," and may indeed be genuine. Other witnesses in New York City reported seeing Mothman on that day, and reports of Mothman sightings in New York go back more than a century.

CHAPTER 7

I myself investigated this strange case, which was reported in the Youngstown, Ohio *Vindicator* of July 20, 1967. The contact claimant is the Reverend Anthony De Polo of Indianola Road, Boardman, Ohio. He is the assistant pastor of the Bethel Assembly of God Church in Boardman.

At about 1:30 a.m. on the morning of July 18, 1967, Reverend De Polo was awakened by a very loud noise: the "type you hear on television science-fiction programs." This oscillating sound began at a low pitch and then rose to a high whine, until it was no longer audible. However, he said that he continued to experience pressure in his eardrums. He assumed that the sound has risen to above 20,000 cycles per second – the high range of human hearing. This strange noise followed this pattern, rising and falling, three or four times. At a certain point in this curve of sound, he distinctly felt that a mental message was somehow being conveyed to him. This message was more a feeling than actual words, but he interpreted it to mean: "Go downstairs."

He headed for the stairs, curious but unafraid. When he reached the foot of the stairs, he looked out of a window facing west and there, standing in the driveway between his house and his neighbor's, he saw what he later described as a five-foot-tall figure wearing a luminous "space suit." The surrounding glow made the figure very distinct.

Something compelled him to step out onto his porch and take a closer look at this strange being. The eerie whine began again, and he received a second message: "You have nothing to fear. I will not harm you; and I know you will not harm me." He started to step towards the figure when the whining sound began again, and he received a third message: "Danger. I must go."

At this point, the good Reverend looked up at the night sky. There was no "spaceship" in sight, but he noticed that the sky was strangely illuminated "like the light from a mercury vapor lamp, such as they use on the turnpike." A fourth message was passed on to him, but he is not willing to divulge its contents.

When he returned his eyes to the driveway, the "spaceman" was gone. In the exact spot where he had been standing, there was a formless blob of light – not figure-shaped – which faded out and vanished in a short while.

Reverend De Polo claims that he was completely unafraid throughout this experience, and that he went directly back to bed without saying anything to his wife about it. "I fell asleep immediately," he noted. He decided the next day to say nothing about this incident, unless other witnesses came forward and reported the same thing.

De Polo describes the figure as wearing a silver suit that was "more refined and less bulky than those our own astronauts wear." Apparently, it was snugly fitted to the being's form. There was a trace of a belt around its middle. The being wore five-fingered gloves and a transparent helmet. He could see that the "spaceman" had human features, but he did not get a close enough look to describe them. Nor could he tell whether the being's skin was light or dark. He did not see any tubes, tanks, or other attachments to the suit.

Reverend De Polo is in his late thirties, possesses three degrees in psychology and philosophy, and has been a college teacher. He seems to be of above-average intelligence, is very articulate, and tells his story in a straightforward manner. I interviewed him at length by telephone. He does not tend to embellish, nor does he invent details to answer unexpected questions about his experience. I personally believe that this is an exceptionally good witness, whose story should be taken very seriously.

After other witnesses reported seeing UFOs that night, De Polo told his wife about his experience, and mentioned it to a reporter. The Youngstown, Ohio *Vindicator* mentioned him in their UFO story of July 20, but did not describe his contact.

Two weeks later, a group of men arrived at his home and identified themselves as "scientists with B.F. Goodrich in Akron, Ohio." They said they were making a serious study of the UFO phenomenon and asked for the full details of his story. He told them everything, including the contents of the fourth message. When he was finished, the spokesman for the group told him that other contacts of this kind had been made, and that they fit a common pattern. "Other people have received similar messages," they said, "and we want to compare notes." They then asked him to keep the contents of the fourth message to himself, otherwise someone else might use the information to lead them astray. When their study was completed, the spokesman continued, they would turn over all the relevant information to him.

They then requested him to give a speech at a private meeting of Goodrich scientists the following week, on August 15th. Employees of B.F.

Goodrich were quietly researching the whole subject. Reverend De Polo obliged them and did visit their plant, where he addressed a large and responsive group. Afterwards, they asked many probing and intelligent questions. They said that they were going to file his full report with the Condon Committee in Colorado.

In my telephone conversation with Reverend De Polo on August 17, I asked a great many background questions and, as is usual in this type of case, found a repeat of many of the patterns now so familiar to me.

He told me that his television had occasionally emitted unusual "bleeping" signals over the past few months. (I have heard this many times in various places around the country, and classify it as "phase one.") Probing deeper, I learned that a few months ago, he had called in a TV repairman because his set was picking up *voices counting off numbers*, and he thought he was "intercepting a ham radio operator from somewhere nearby." (This number-counting on radios and televisions is "phase 2" in the contactee pattern, and is often followed by "phase three": direct *phone calls* in which strange, distant-sounding voices continue to recite numbers in patterns.)

Reverend De Polo has received "hundreds" of phone calls since that night, but all were from people who had also seen a UFO. He has not received a single crank call of any kind, nor has he received a number-counting call. (Looks like they skipped "phase 3.") He has not been subjected to any hoaxes or ridicule.

When asked if he has heard any strange noises inside his house since his "contact," he paused and told me that only last night, he had heard what sounded like a baby crying at around 2 a.m. He had wandered through several rooms, but could find nothing that could be making such a noise. (This baby-crying phenomenon has been reported to me in cases in West Virginia and Long Island.) Earlier in the evening, he and his wife had heard a loud crash in another part of the house, but could not find the source.

I asked Reverend De Polo a few questions about his family background. "I've traced my family all the way back to biblical times on my mother's side," he said. But there is no Indian or Egyptian strain in his family that he knows of (both of these lineages tend to experience a higher incidence of paranormal events). He was born on May 5th, ruling out the odd "March birthday pattern" of contactees.

The Reverend has had a longtime interest in ESP, and he has had numerous experiences that convinced him that he may be telepathic.

He would not reveal the fourth message, but he did imply that it concerned a possible return visit from the being. It may have been a statement about others being contacted in the same area. It was *not* a message about the end of the world, or problems with our atomic experiments.

Around 9:15 p.m. on July 4, 1967, a mysterious cloud of luminous gas moved down Market Street in nearby Youngstown, Ohio, at ground level. This gas caused eyes to water and produced dizziness and choking. Respiration equipment had to be rushed to the area to aid victims of the gas. (Similar clouds of gas have turned up in Naples, Italy, Charleston, West Virginia, and southern Long Island in recent months.) Youngstown is only a few miles from Boardman.

There have been many UFO sightings around Boardman in recent months. On the night of Rev. De Polo's alleged experience, July 18, 1967, witnesses in southern Youngstown reported hearing eerie sounds "resembling a dive-bombing plane, a screaming noise," at 1:20 a.m. One witness said that it was cigar-shaped, and was flying just above the treetops. He described it as being "a metallic silver blue," and estimated its length to be about seven feet. A powerful odor, resembling the smell of hot tar, clung to the air. While he watched, the thing turned green, then orange-red, and flew off southwards in the direction of Boardman.

A NEW APPROACH TO UFO WITNESSES

The celebrated "scientific method" has proven to be totally unworkable in the case of UFO interpretation. After twenty years of application, we have produced nothing more than a rather meaningless census of unidentified objects. Were we to go through the expense of feeding this mass of fragmentary data into a computer, we would – based upon past experience – probably come up with an equally meaningless mass of statistical data.

We know, for example, that in thousands of reports, the objects have shown an ability to change color. Therefore it is totally irrelevant that 400 green objects, 600 yellow objects, 280 red objects, etc., were sighted in any particular month or year. The green objects could have been red in *other* phases. Nor is the altitude of the objects important. Since we are dealing with *flying* objects, they could have been at 500 feet (and colored green) at one observation point, and could have been at 6,000 feet (and colored orange) at another point five miles away. Their speed is just as variable and just as meaningless to the overall picture. In essence, all sighting data is worthless once it has been reasonably established that an object did exist and was seen.

To continue to collect such data at random is obviously a futile, expensive, and unproductive task, as the U.S. Air Force discovered in the 1950s. "Explaining" individual sightings is not worth the cost and effort involved. And the long delay in explaining individual sightings tends to eliminate any intelligence value. One substantial sighting proves that the UFOs exist; 10,000 substantial sightings don't prove it any further. After arriving at the basic conclusion (that the UFOs are real), the next logical step is to determine precisely what they are doing here.

It is improbable that anyone at this late date will ever come up with tangible physical proof of anything. But if the objects are busying themselves all over the world, they *must* be doing something. The UFO researchers have failed to try to determine what that something is. They have been sidetracked by speculations on the "technology" involved, the "galactic" source of the objects, and the motives behind "government suppression." We will never really learn about the mechanics of a "flying saucer" until we actually catch one. If the source is extraterrestrial, then we don't have much of a chance of pinpointing it. Furthermore, there's nothing we could do about it once we did locate the source.

There is only one thing left that can be rationally investigated: the purposes behind their activities. What are they really doing that requires frequent touchdowns in remote areas? What requires the widespread and furtive nocturnal activity? Therein lies the secret to the UFO mystery...

While the objects are fascinating, they are merely vehicles. And vehicles, as we all know, are used to *transport personnel and material* from one point to another. The incredible scope of the activity of these vehicles rules out simple explanations such as an "aerial survey of Earth." These things are operating in great numbers, far greater than those indicated in the haphazard reports.

Wherever I traveled, police officers and high school officials invariably took me aside, one by one, and asked the same three astounding questions, urging me never to mention that they asked. I heard these questions again and again. The governor of a state asked me these questions, and two days later, a dirt farmer on a remote backroad came up with the same identical queries:

1. Can the UFO occupants walk through walls?

2. Can they make themselves invisible?

3. Are there any documented cases of them having kidnapped people?

These are, you must admit, very far-out questions. The mere fact that people everywhere are asking them indicates that something very frightening is going on. These aspects are only whispered about by the ufologists themselves. They received little or no publicity until the publication of Ivan Sanderson's book, *Uninvited Visitors*, in the fall of 1967.

If that gives you pause, consider the fact that "poltergeist" phenomena breaks out in flap areas and continue long after the flap subsides. We must reconsider our whole approach to the UFO phenomenon. "Science" has proven to be inadequate. It appears that we have misinterpreted many "occult" happenings for centuries. There may be a basic force at work that unites the UFOs with the occult – a deep interrelationship. The UFO buffs scoff at the "occultists," and vice versa. There has been no attempt at coordinating the various fields of belief. The time has come for us to find the links, if they exist.

Today, ESP is widely accepted. It has long been a part of occultism, and now it is a tangible part of the UFO mystery. Now we must carefully consider the possibility that trance mediums are not communicating with "the dead" but are, in fact, serving as mediaries for the same playful entities that throw heavy pieces of furniture around. Parapsychologists claim poltergeists always operate in the presence of children, usually a boy or girl at the age of puberty. So contemplate this: in the majority of the cases I have investigated in which low-level objects have closely pursued automobiles, there was either a child in the car, or the driver or one of the occupants was a schoolteacher. Then look at the growing number of close sightings around schools all over the world, including many touchdowns in schoolyards.

There is no simple "extraterrestrial" conclusion. The truth is undoubtedly infinitely more complex. It may lie completely outside of the recognized and much-touted sciences. The only way to find out what is happening is to perform in-depth studies of *everything* happening in the flap areas. This requires standard police and journalistic procedure, not haphazard "scientific" collating of lights-in-the-sky reports. People throughout the U.S. are now caught up in a science-fiction nightmare. We must come to realize that we are dealing with a phenomenon that has all of the implications of "science fiction." We can no longer dismiss the weird and the seemingly irrelevant.

Somebody – or something – is walking through a lot of walls these days. And the ufologists are so busy peering through telescopes that they have removed themselves from the true situation, whatever it may be.

Let's stop trying to "prove" the existence, origin, or mechanics of the objects. We've played around for decades and gotten nowhere. Put aside your personal beliefs and prejudices. Throw away those useless sighting forms and find out what the witness had for breakfast, what kind of phone calls he's been getting, and prod his memory about his childhood. You may be astonished at what he comes up with. And after you've talked to enough people and visited enough flap areas, your astonishment will turn to abject horror.

You'll throw all your books on astronomy and exobiology into the garbage can, and you'll find yourself reconsidering the entire UFO "problem."

IS THE "ELECTROMAGNETIC EFFECT" A MYTH?

Between the years 1817 and 1821, a strange and sinister influence settled over the farm of John Bell in Robertson County, Tennessee. Flying lights "like a candle or lamp" were frequently seen flitting about the yards and fields near the old farmhouse, and a voice from an apparently invisible source heckled the family and carried on extensive dialogues with visitors and curiosity seekers. The full story of the celebrated "Bell Witch" has been carefully documented and is too long and complicated to even outline here. But it deserves careful study since it, and the many other cases like it, may provide important clues to the overall UFO phenomenon.

According to Dr. Nandor Fodor, General Andrew Jackson was one of those attracted to the Bell homestead during the period of the "haunting." As General Jackson's horse-drawn wagon approached the area, the wheels suddenly seemed to freeze, and the straining horses were unable to budge it. Jackson dismounted and examined the wheels and axles, and was unable to find any reason for this sudden problem. The wheels simply would not go around. As he stood there, scratching his head in bewilderment, a "sharp metallic voice" suddenly rang out from behind some nearby bushes.

"All right, General," the voice announced. "Let the wagon move." To everyone's amazement, the wheels began to turn again.

The incident was recorded as just another manifestation of the "Bell Witch," and was shrugged off by investigators who were more concerned with proving that the phenomenon was caused by an "evil spirit" or a "dead soul" than with assembling all of the variegated activities and observations taking place in the area. Actually, if this particular story is true, it may be the first concrete example of what has now become known as the "EM effect" (electromagnetic effect), even though no electrical apparatus was involved. General Andrew Jackson went on, of course, to become the seventh president of the United States (1829-37). The "Bell Witch" eventually was alleged to have caused the death of John Bell before it disappeared into the limbo from which it had come. But during one of its many "conversations," it was said to have declared, "I am a spirit from everywhere – Heaven, Hell, the Earth; am in the air, in houses, any place at any time, have been created millions of years; that is all I will tell you."

Tales of the occult stick in the craws of most ufologists, particularly those who have spent years vainly seeking "hardware" that would conclusively prove that UFOs are extraterrestrial vehicles. Now a growing band of serious researchers are beginning to examine the hitherto ignored occult records for hidden factors that might relate supernatural events to the UFO phenomenon. Some are beginning to suspect that a large part of the phenomenon is actually a terrestrial condition, and that many of the objects have either always been based upon this planet, or have in some totally incomprehensible way coexisted with us throughout our history. In this current phase, most of the scientifically oriented ufologists have attempted to oversimplify the phenomenon and place it within the framework of our contemporary understanding of the physical universe.

Many thousands of people have heard "sharp metallic voices" since General Jackson's wagon came to a dead halt in the hills of Tennessee. These voices have reportedly emanated from the flying saucers, from caves and abandoned buildings, and even from telephones. At the same time, there have been hundreds upon hundreds of reports of automobile and airplane engines suddenly stalling in the presence of UFOs, and countless power failures have been blamed upon the objects.

Ufologists have accepted the speculation that these events are caused by a powerful magnetic field that allegedly surrounds the craft, the theory being that these powerful fields cause the generators of motors to shut down temporarily. In 1967, then Ford Motor Company, working on a grant from Colorado University, conducted experiments regarding the effect of magnetism on automobile engines. It was concluded that a magnetic field strong enough to stall an average car would also be strong enough to bend and twist the automobile itself. Magnetism alone does not seem to be the answer to this phenomenon.

Certainly a magnetic field would not have had much effect upon the largely wooden wheels of General Jackson's wagon.

In the fall of 1967, a New York television producer, Mr. Dan Drasin, observed an unidentified flying object near Point Pleasant, West Virginia.

He attempted to "signal" the object with a powerful flashlight charged with brand new batteries. The flashlight went out instantly, according to Mr. Drasin, and would not operate again until the object had passed out of sight. In later experiments, I tried to cause a similar flashlight to malfunction by placing it in a powerful magnetic field. The results were negative.

On one occasion, in the spring of 1967, I had observed a UFO in West Virginia, together with other witnesses, and had attempted to photograph it with a battery-operated movie camera. The camera would not work. The object remained in view long enough for me to change the battery pack. The camera still would not work. Again, as soon as the object was gone, the camera functioned perfectly.

In another interesting incident, Mr. Willard Henderson of Belpre, Ohio reportedly observed a large, luminous, cigar-shaped object hovering above a dam on the Ohio River in the summer of 1967. He directed the spotlight mounted onto his car at the thing, and his light immediately went out. Later, when we inspected the spotlight, we discovered that the wiring was inexplicably burnt out, suggesting a focused or directed power surge *that did not affect any other part of the automobile.*

Although magnetism undoubtedly plays some role in the mechanics of the flying saucers, it does seem as if there are various other factors involved in the "EM" cases.

There is a hillside near Melville, Long Island where UFOs have frequently been observed in the past two years. Teenaged UFO buffs in the area told me that battery-powered cameras and tape recorders refused to function there. I visited the spot several times, and discovered that my own equipment failed there, too, although compasses and magnetic detectors did *not* reveal any unusual magnetic aberrations.

Throughout 1967, there were over 1,000 unexplained telephone failures in the U.S., often involving whole counties. In my interviews with telephone company personnel around the country, I learned that they were baffled because "the wires just don't seem to conduct current." Similarly, when a massive, four-state power failure struck the Northeast on June 5, 1967, the personnel at the Kittatinny Power Plant in northern New Jersey claimed that their equipment did not shut down, but simply stopped "as if it had frozen." The Kittatinny plant was in no way connected with the other power plants that failed, at that same time, in other states. There had been frequent, almost daily UFO sightings in the Kittatinny Mountains throughout that period.

Obviously, the electromagnetic explanation is not applicable to this kind of incident. In some of these cases, we seem to be dealing with a basic paralysis of electrons. It may even go deeper and involve a temporary alteration in the basic properties of matter.

An intense field of radioactivity could cause electrical drains, but such a field would almost certainly affect the human beings present, and traces of radiation would be left behind in the flashlights, automobiles, etc. There are, of course, many excellent cases in which intense radiation was found at landing sites, but there relatively few cases in which vehicles or people suffered detectably from such radiation.

To paralyze the flow of electrons in a wire, battery, or flashlight, the conductive properties would have to be altered in some manner. A strong field of magnetic induction would produce a power surge that would overload the circuit and burn out the equipment. But very few "burnouts" are being reported. Was it coincidental that Mr. Henderson's spotlight burnt out the instant he tried to focus it on a UFO? If the UFO somehow extinguished the light, why wasn't the rest of the wiring in his auto similarly affected? Why wasn't the delicate mechanism of my camera burnt out in a like manner?

Possibly the UFO occupants can direct this *molecular paralysis effect* (MPE) in somewhat the same way that they seem to have been able to paralyze human beings. Perhaps the same device or technique is used on both animate and inanimate objects. General Jackson's wagon wheels may have been "frozen"" by the same identical force that brought the massive generators at Kittatinny to a sudden halt. In other words, a basic alteration of physical properties took place in both cases. Magnetism could not have been employed on Jackson's wagon, and it may be erroneous for us to assume that magnetism was used at Kittatinny.

If earthly matter is composed of energies from the low end of the electromagnetic spectrum, then perhaps entities composed of energies from the other end of that spectrum might actually have the power to tamper with and alter the physical properties of terrestrial substances. If the matter of our world can be manipulated freely by such entities, then we would have an explanation for many of the manifestations that have always been classified as "supernatural." Such entities might conceivably be able to walk through walls. Anyone seeing them doing so would automatically regard them as "ghosts."

The numerous cases in which compasses and magnetic instruments have reacted to the presence of the unidentified flying objects have led us to believe in the electromagnetic effect theory. But it all may be just an *effect*, not a cause. We have noted in the U.S. that an unusually high proportion of landings and low-level sightings have occurred in areas of magnetic deviation. We must now ask ourselves if the objects and their occupants may not merely be taking advantage of such deviations in some manner – exploiting "window" areas.

Owatonna, Minnesota is such a window area. There were poltergeist manifestations in Owatonna in 1880, "airship" sightings in 1897, and UFO and MIB "flaps" from 1966 to the present. A study of the Indian lore in window areas like Owatonna has revealed that these peculiar manifestations probably can be traced all the way back, long before the white settlers arrived. The "EM effect" should be studied in these window areas. If these areas are gateways to the ufonauts' mysterious universe, we may be able to somehow find a key.

But we will never solve the riddle through speculation. If the objects are composed of matter radically different from our own, then we cannot hope to unravel the problem based upon the physical properties of Newtonian science. We know that many of the objects are able to move at fantastically high speeds without displacing the air and producing sonic booms. This, in itself, is a strong clue that the objects could be composed in such a way that they can pass *between* the molecules of air, just as the entities seem to pass through solid walls.

The objects may also take advantage of the magnetic currents and deviations of this planet, riding these currents as a glider rides the updrafts of air surrounding hills. Such a propulsion system seems far beyond our present scientific framework.

As the objects traverse these magnetic currents, they may cause a displacement, as a ship displaces water, and it may be this displacement that our compasses and instruments have been detecting.

The more sophisticated manifestations such as car stallings, power failures, and so on may have nothing to do with electromagnetism, and may not be as accidental as we have led ourselves to believe.

Suppose there was a UFO beyond the hill where General Jackson's wagon halted? And suppose that the entities felt he had to be stopped until the area could be cleared?

CHAPTER 8

PROBLEMS OF IDENTITY: THE ALIENS AMONG US – *SAGA'S UFO REPORT*, NOVEMBER 1977

From the mountains of northern Sweden to the hills of Tennessee, one of ufology's most persistent rumors has been enjoying a rebirth in this "lull" year of 1977. The rumor first began circulating in 1950, only three years after flying saucers had suddenly burst onto the scene as a topic for discussion and investigation. In the 1960s, the rumor swept the world and became an accepted truth to many respected ufologists. But its basic premise was so obscure and preposterous that many rejected it and forgot all about it until the upsurge of landings and contacts in 1973. The rumor is that the ufonauts are conducting *biological* experiments on human beings, and may even be creating an army of pseudo-humans by using the sperm and ova from unsuspecting earthlings.

Certainly the evidence is mounting rapidly now, as more and more investigators take an interest in the once shunned "contact" cases. In the mid-1960s, I visited several college communities in the northeastern U.S., and collected a series of incredible reports from sincere young men and women who claimed they had been abducted by UFOs and subjected to sexual experimentation. The males said that their sex organs had been examined, and special instruments had extracted semen from them. The females claimed they had either been forcibly raped aboard UFOs, or that instruments, usually long needles, had been inserted in their lower abdomens to remove substances from their ovaries.

Only two cases of this type received any publicity: the Villas-Boas incident in Brazil in 1957, and the Betty and Barney Hill abduction in 1962. However, *neither* case had been published when I came across the first witnesses to inform me of these bizarre occurrences. Today, only a few such cases have appeared in UFO literature, and are still unknown to the general public.

Early ufologists, however, knew of such experiments, and based their "hybrid theory" on them. Essentially, the theory asserts that there are people living among us today who are crossbreeds – half earthling, half extraterrestrial. These people are allegedly loyal to, and controlled by, the ufonauts. They are hybrids. The time will come, the theory states, when a large part of Earth's population will be hybrid.

There's more… Many women involved in close encounters with UFOs become pregnant soon afterwards, although they have no memory of anything beyond a simple UFO sighting. Some are more than a little astonished by their unexpected pregnancies. I have kept in close contact with several of these women and followed the developments with great interest. The children they produced seem exceptionally bright, and are frequently surrounded by poltergeist manifestations in their early years. Otherwise, these offspring appear to be normal. In more than one case, the woman's husband was disturbed by the fact that their child did not resemble *either* parent.

It all sounds something like John Wyndham's science-fiction classic, *The Midwich Cuckoos*, but the facts are there. In the 1960s, I tried to interest several different editors in an article on this intriguing aspect of the UFO phenomenon, but they all felt it was "too far out," as indeed it is.

It will come as a surprise to many ufologists who are now circulating the hybrid rumor that this concept is *thousands* of years old and is, in fact, an important part of occult and religious lore. The sexual intervention of supernatural entities is mentioned throughout the Bible (in the story of Abraham, for example).

Witches are said to have intercourse with the devil. Gypsies believe that any woman who is seduced by the devil has special powers afterwards, and such women are given very special respect. Numerous black magick rites involve sex practices – sexual submission to the strange entities that materialize during the rites.

In *Oahspe*, the amazing book written by a New York dentist while in a trance back in the 1880s, there are pages of drawings depicting special children with sober faces and deep black eyes, who were supposedly hybrids planted here by some unknown force.

Several modern contactees have seen strange things happen to their families. Their teenaged daughters have staggered home claiming they had been sexually assaulted by space beings. Their wives have disappeared for hours or even days, and returned suffering from amnesia – and pregnant. Several of the early contactees in the 1950s enraged the "scientific ufologists" with their tales of having been required to express their manhood on other planets or while flying around in saucers.

The hybrid concept has a disastrous effect on the ufologists who accept it blindly. They become totally paranoid. They believe that hybrids have infiltrated the highest government circles – that they are controlling the entire world. In the 1960s, Secretary of Defense Robert McNamara was frequently accused by contactees of being a hybrid.

A related aspect is the clone theory. A clone is an exact duplicate of a living organism. Theoretically, a clone can be produced from a single cell of your body. Each cell contains all the necessary biological information to construct a duplicate. Scientists around the world have been working on the process for years. Several modern contactees have told of how they were taken aboard a UFO and a small sample of their skin was scraped from their arm. If we had the technology and know-how, a small sample is all we would need to create an exact duplicate of a person.

As most readers know, exact duplicates of several well-known ufologists have been seen by reliable witnesses. In occult lore, such duplicates are called "doppelgangers." They are an age-old psychic phenomenon. In the 1960s, a doppelganger of New York ufologist James Moseley turned up on a number of occasions. And a doppelganger of yours truly appeared repeatedly in several states, from Long Island, NY to West Virginia to California, while I was actually occupied elsewhere. Were these characters clones, or physical entities made of solid flesh? Or were they psychic projections of some sort?

Several years ago, a young Englishman came to me with some very interesting photographs. He had attended an outdoor rally in Britain, and had taken pictures of the crowd. When he examined the photos later, he was surprised to see two strange-looking men standing in the crowd. They were not together, but were widely separated in the throng. Both were dressed identically in black turtleneck sweaters. Both had very short hair (unusual for that time and for men of their apparent age). The oddest thing of all, though, was that both had *identical* facial characteristics. They looked like twins. They had angular faces, high cheekbones, and thin lips. They really stood out in the photograph.

Similar beings form an integral part of our Men in Black lore. These Men in Black have even attended flying saucer lectures and conventions. In some reports, there have been three of them, all looking exactly alike. Were they clones?

Ufology has become a mixed bag, with all kinds of ancient psychic and occult phenomena stirred in with the evidence of "extraterrestrial" visitants. Today there are many people who have become convinced that they, themselves, *really are* hybrids. A number of contactees – some of them quite well known – started life as orphans, and never learned the identity of their true parents.

Some contactees have lived in terror for years, fearing that they were going to be whisked off to a farm on some other planet and bred like cattle.

Are there really hybrids and clones living among us? Who knows? Perhaps you lost a few minutes of time when you saw a strange object in the sky a few years ago. Maybe there is *another* you out there somewhere on a distant planet, or just on the other side of town.

PROBLEMS OF ETYMOLOGY: UFOLOGY TERMINOLOGY

I once served as science editor at Funk & Wagnalls, writing and editing many of the scientific pieces that appeared in their encyclopedia. I was also geography editor of Funk & Wagnalls' *New College Dictionary*. These publications are still on sale in some parts of the country, although Funk & Wagnalls has undergone a series of mergers and no longer exists as a separate entity.

As a professional lexicographer, it was only natural for me to pay particular attention to UFO terminology when I began serious research in 1966. The paucity of proper terms was an indication of the scholastic poverty of the UFO field. Even the U.S. Air Force had failed to contribute to the language, aside from the inappropriate term "unidentified flying objects" and the phlegmatic "meandering nocturnal lights."

In my earliest articles, I joined Ivan Sanderson in complaining about the term "unidentified flying *objects*." In many cases, we can question if these things are objects at all. They usually float rather than fly and, in innumerable instances, they assume a definite "identity" to the percipient – as if it were a lifeform rather than an object. Charles Fort labeled them OOFs ("objects observed floating"). In *Anomaly #1*, I suggested "aerial anomalies" as a more appropriate substitute.

Most of the popular ufological terms, such as "mothership" (the less matriarchal NICAP called them "parent craft"), are based upon contactee lore and unfounded beliefs about their actual nature. Such terms sound absurd to a newcomer, and are even more absurd when quoted in newspaper and magazine articles. In fact, the very absurdity of the UFO terminology probably escalated the nonsense and ridicule associated with the subject. If you use crackpot terms, you understandably run the risk of being called a crackpot.

Despite all of the alleged UFO research of the past two decades, we found that no one had introduced the accepted medical and scientific terms for the various symptoms and manifestations of the phenomenon.

For example, many witnesses to occult, religious, and UFO manifestations have described a reduction or impairment of their willpower.

In psychiatry, this is known as *patholesia*. "Parergasia" (schizophrenia, regarded as "a disorder of action") might be an appropriate term for the reactions and behavior of many "contactees" (for whom a better label would be "communicants"). In parapsychology, a study that now has a fairly solid academic and scientific footing, the word "percipient" is widely used. When I introduced "percipient" to ufology in 1969, I was amazed that I was accused of having invented the term. (In retrospect, it is natural for people who make up terms to suspect others of making up terms as well.) "Percipient" can be found in any good dictionary; "contactee" cannot.

There are other words that are quite appropriate from a scholarly viewpoint. The Greek term "skiamachia" (or "sciamachy") can be applied to ufology. In philosophy, there are many ideas and terms that could be useful to ufology. As I tried to point out in *Our Haunted Planet*, the will to believe is much greater than the will to understand. It is far easier to accept a half-baked theory than to perform the necessary studies, tests, and experiments to produce qualified understanding. Philosophy has always been concerned with this will to believe. One school of philosophy, phenomenology, founded by Edmund Husserl in the 1800s, is particularly relevant to the study of ufology. Without realizing it, many ufologists have been indulging in what Husserl called "phenomenological reduction."

None of the so-called "theories" outlined in my books were new or original to me. The term "ultraterrestrial" has been around a long time, and is included in most good dictionaries. In my work, I have tried to outline all of the major and minor beliefs of mankind, and to illustrate the kinds of manifestations that inspired those beliefs. When viewed in this larger context, the popular notions of ufology are not unique, nor are the manifestations that are used to support them.

At best, ufology is just another "devil theory" cult. Advocates of devil theories tend to be fanatical, and are often paranoid-schizophrenics. The religion, medicine, and philosophy sections of your local library contain many books describing and defining these things in detail. Ufologists who dig into such literature can suffer the shock of recognition, and abandon ufology in dismay and disappointed disgust. In my own books and articles, I tried to soften this shock somewhat.

Overall, the UFO neologisms are rooted in the psychoses of the ufologists themselves and, to a lesser degree, in the glossology of the mischievous elementals, ultraterrestrials, and schizoid hallucinations. There is an overlapping of quasi-religious terms adopted from other frames of reference. I prepared an extensive glossary of terms for the *Flying Saucer Review* special, "Beyond Condon," but it was not published. An expanded version was deleted from *Operation Trojan Horse*. However, I published many definitions in *Anomaly* and in my articles. Happily, many of the "new" terms I have introduced are coming into wide usage.

Recently, a mineralogist in England complained because I have not defined the term "unidentified flying object" itself. The phrase is, of course, self-definable but, realistically, UFOs can never be defined until we know *exactly* what they actually are.

Clearly, a wide assortment of natural and unnatural phenomena have long been lumped into a single classification. Many (perhaps most) aerial anomalies are mistakes and misinterpretations of perfectly ordinary objects. Others are subjective impressions of observers with psychic ability. Solid objects with machinelike characteristics are seen, but in our close examinations of the witnesses of such "solid" objects, we found they also experienced the symptoms of hypnotic or mediumistic trance. So, are we really being asked to define what are essentially hallucinations?

Legitimate fields of research produce their own vocabulary and introduce new words into the language. The space program, for example, has given us a whole new dictionary of terms. Even science-fiction has enriched the language. If a research field can be judged by the impact of its terminology, what has ufology really contributed?

The best way to attain the respectability so long desired by ufologists is to introduce and use valid medical and scientific terms, and do away with the nonsensical terminology of the 1950s and 1960s. To achieve this, we must first recognize the shocking fact that UFO manifestations and characteristics are not unique, and certainly are not new to scholars in other frames of reference. It would help if ufologists would stop practicing what professional writers call "suspension of belief" (which enables you to accept an unbelievable James Bond movie as believable – at least for two hours or so), and to start practicing suspension of judgment.

PROBLEMS OF METHODOLOGY: UFOS IN 1952

As the "flying saucer flap" of 1952 mounted, the administration and faculty of Ohio Northern University, a small Methodist institution located in Ada, Ohio, set up what they called "Project A: The Investigation of Phenomena." Some 30 members of the faculty of four related colleges – engineering, pharmacy, law, and liberal arts – coordinated their efforts in eight fields in an attempt to study unidentified flying objects.

Chief proponent of the study was Dr. Warren Hickman, dean of the university. He had been with Ohio Northern since 1949, and became dean in 1951. A cum laude graduate of Colgate University, he was chief of the file section for Eisenhower's SHAEF (Supreme Headquarters Allied Expeditionary Force) command in Europe during the war, and was recognized by the Brookings Institution for his competency in foreign affairs. Hickman said: "It is time somebody did something about it. We may find an astral body, army research, atomic reactions, or flights from outer space, but whatever it is, we must find an accurate answer."

The basic objectives of Project "A" centered on four points:

1. To objectively collect data from all possible sources dealing with "flying saucers," and to analyze this data in various departments of the university.

2. To make public the results of research of a private institution unhampered by bureaucratic restrictions.

3. To stimulate and promote objective study of all types of illusory phenomena by individual observers, and to issue reports of the project investigations.

4. To aid in creating more accurate observers for the civilian air defense program.

Procedure was explained as follows: Data on saucer sightings was collected, categorized as to geography, type, time, number of observers, and then was subjected to scientific analysis in eight departments of the university. These departments were physics, mathematics, astronomy, chemistry, psychology, history, electrical and mechanical engineering, and philosophy and religion. The precise methods of "scientific analysis" were not defined.

With the objectives and methods procedure set up, and with the faculty cooperating in the effort, the university set out in the summer of 1952 to solve the mystery. The school received nationwide publicity and, soon, reports began to flow in from every state in the union and from places like Germany, Australia, Canada, and Denmark. The total number of reports received was not revealed.

In March 1953, Project "A" released its first and only report, which revealed that of the many sightings reported to the university, only 54 could be definitely categorized as not having a known natural explanation. Some 20% of the sightings received did not fit explanation by light reflection, cloud formation, ionization, or other natural phenomena.

Most of the sightings examined were in the southwest U.S. during the summer months of July, August, and September of 1952. It is noteworthy that the U.S. Air Force's Project Blue Book claimed to have received 1,900 sightings for that year, with over 300 being classified as "unknowns." Years later, the 1952 total was modified to 1,501, without explanation of the reduction (which achieved a final percentage of 20%, equal to the Project "A" numbers).

Early in 1953, the CIA-sponsored Robertson Panel convened in Washington, D.C. to examine the material collected by Capt. Ruppelt's Project Blue Book teams. That panel decided upon a policy of suppression, and suggested that the public should be "educated" to dismiss the phenomenon. Soon afterwards, Ohio Northern University *also* released *their* solitary report, and then abandoned further research, with a vague announcement that "lack of cooperation" on the part of the press, the public, and the military made it "impossible to continue." This was contrary to earlier statements on how freely the reports were flowing in.

A close study of the Project "A" Report indicates that it was apparently assembled in haste, and it lacked the detailed analysis promised in the preliminary announcements. It did, however, comment on phenomena such as the "falling leaf" motion of some UFOs, and might serve as a crude model for new studies.

PROBLEMS OF DISTORTION AND DISTENTION: THE TIME CYCLE FACTOR

In February 1968, a young man in Adelphi, Maryland allegedly experienced a time distortion while aboard an unidentified flying object. According to his story, he first encountered a UFO around 1:00 a.m. on the morning of December 10, 1967, while driving outside of Washington, D.C. A normal-looking man dressed in coveralls approached him and conversed with him briefly, asking the simple, routine questions so often reported in such initial meetings. This man identified himself as "Vadig."

The young man, a psychology major at a Maryland university, worked evenings as a waiter in a Washington restaurant. He had not mentioned this to "Vadig." Nevertheless, Mr. Vadig appeared at the restaurant in early February, dressed this time in conventional clothing, and invited the student for a ride aboard his craft. The youth was taken by automobile – a 1955 Buick that looked and even smelled new – to an isolated farm area some 30 minutes outside of Washington.

A large, egg-shaped craft on tripod legs was waiting there. The young man was ushered aboard and sealed alone in a compartment containing a contour chair and a large "TV screen." By his reckoning, he was taken on a trip that consumed from four to five hours. Then he was returned to the same spot and driven to his home. This drive also took about 30 minutes. When he entered his apartment and confronted his roommates, he was amazed to discover that *little more than an hour* had actually passed from the time "Vadig" had first picked him up at the restaurant.

Ufologists have been hearing this kind of story for years, often dismissing them as being hallucinatory or the "fiction" of psychotics. Occult literature is also filled with many documented accounts of strange distortions of time and space. In this particular incident, the witness claimed he never lost consciousness and, although he was not wearing a watch, he was painfully aware of the passage of time, because there was nothing for him to do while sealed in the compartment. During two lengthy interviews in March 1968, he was able to provide numerous significant details common to such stories, but never published or publicized.

Actually, the young man described four different meetings with "Vadig," and each time the "spaceman" ended the conversation with the phrase, "I'll see you in time."

Other contactees have told me of similar phrases. Traditionally, the first question the ufonauts ask is: "What time is it?" or "What is your time cycle?" You may recall that "time" questions were asked in some of the alleged contacts of 1957, and in the Gary Wilcox case of 1964.

One notable ufonaut characteristic, as related by numerous contactees, is *their* apparent inability to understand and utilize our standard measurement of time. As such cases pile up in each succeeding flap, it is becoming more and more obvious that a very special time factor exists, and in some instances, the phenomenon seems to be able to manipulate both time and space – at least insofar as the involved witnesses are concerned. This could be the result of some hypnotic technique, of course, but it cold also provide us with an important clue to the overall nature of the phenomenon.

The two most commonly reported time distortion effects (TDE) are:

1. Time compression, as in the Adelphi, Maryland case. The witness undergoes an experience of seemingly long duration, but later discovers that a comparatively short period of real time – Earth time – has passed. Experiments have shown that

seemingly long and involved dreams often occupy only a few seconds or minutes of the sleeper's real time. Therefore, we must examine time-compression experiences from a psychiatric approach as well as a physical approach.

2. Time lapses, in which the witness suffers partial or total amnesia, and is unable to remember how he passed specific periods of time. Several cases have been reported to me in which the witnesses, who were usually in automobiles, saw an approaching object and then suffered a memory lapse. They had no awareness of losing consciousness or otherwise undergoing an unusual experience. Such witnesses complain that it took them two hours or more to drive distances of only a few miles. This type of experience also demands psychiatric examination.

Those who assume that all of these many witnesses are insane, or are liars, are obliged to explain how it is possible for so many widely separated people to report *the same identical details* in their "lies."

The UFO phenomenon is frequently "reflective"; that is, the observed manifestations seem to be deliberately tailored and adjusted to the individual beliefs and mental attitudes of the witnesses. Both the objects and their occupants appear to be able to adopt a multitude of forms, and the contactees are usually given "information" that conforms to their own beliefs or ability to understand. UFO researchers who concentrate on one particular aspect or theory often find themselves inundated with *seemingly* reliable reports that tend to substantiate that theory. My own extensive experiences with this "reflective" factor have led me to carry out several weird experiments, which confirmed that a large part of the reporting data is engineered and deliberately false. The witnesses are not the perpetrators of these hoaxes, but merely the victims. The apparent purpose of all this false data is to create confusion and to divert us from the *real* phenomenon. It has also served to convince the Air Force and the scientific establishment that the phenomenon is nonphysical and, therefore, non-real.

Ufologists are thus confronted with the problem of sorting out the meaningful "hints" and important facts from the mass of totally irrelevant diversionary material. The science-fiction-like manifestations reported by the witnesses are far more important, and deserve far more study, than the often inane "messages" transmitted to them. The elusive and abstract time factor may be far more important to us than a detailed description of the object used in the Maryland incident.

Time and space are steady, inflexible factors in our environment, and it is difficult for us to comprehend any large variances in these measurements. However, assume that a planet exists trapped in a binary star system. Its orbit is such that all sides of the planet are constantly bathed in light. No day/night cycle exists there, and the inhabitants would have no way of measuring time – even years – in their early development. As they developed a technology, it might be possible that they could work out a sophisticated time system quite different from our own, based perhaps on their own life-cycles or even upon the deterioration of radioactive materials. But, by our standards, they would be living in a timeless void. I do not believe there is such a planet, but I am merely using this as an example. (One ufonaut phrase that is repeated by many contactees is: "The same sun shines on us all," indicating that the UFOs share our own planetary system.)

Our first conclusion from the contactee data is that the UFOs originate from a place outside of our time frame. They can enter our environment either at will or by accident, and certain human individuals can be transported somehow across this time bridge. This may involve certain physical changes, which have always been defined in occult and contactee literature as "vibrational" or "frequency" changes. We do not, as yet, have the scientific knowledge necessary for the construction of a workable hypothesis.

In recent years, assorted scientists have toyed with speculations about "anti-matter" and "negative universes." It has even been suggested that a "negative universe" might be moving through time in a direction *opposite* to ours. Their future would be our past, and vice versa. (Dr. Stannard, a physicist at University College, London, has postulated in the scientific journal *Nature* that a parallel universe – with time running in the reverse direction – could indeed exist.)

Recently, a number of unsophisticated, uneducated contactee claimants have astounded me by bringing up and discussing this "reverse time cycle" in lucid and knowing terms. The extraterrestrial theory has dominated the American UFO scene, and very few UFO articles, book, or lecturers have touched upon the old "time traveler" theme. It has very few adherents, if any at all. So it is doubly disconcerting that the contactees could have even considered the theory. You might say that they *had* to be told.

One West Virginia contactee, Woodrow Derenberger, talks knowledgeably about this backward-time factor. This former preacher is not well read, and does not even have a basic knowledge of the moon and solar system. On Wednesday, November 2, 1966, he allegedly encountered a UFO on a highway outside of Parkersburg, West Virginia, and conversed with a man who identified himself as "Indrid Cold." Mr. "Cold" reportedly visited with Derenberger many times after that, and later took him on trips to his planet, "Lanulos." Derenberger's initial "contact" received national press attention, but his story of the follow-up developments has not been published or circulated. I have interviewed him at great length many times, both in West Virginia and in New York. The young witness in Adelphi, Maryland produced details identical to those in Derenberger's still-unpublished story.

"They're time travelers," Derenberger has explained. "One reason they can't stay here too long at a time is because they get younger instead of older. If they stayed here too long, I think they'd go back in years and possibly forget how to manipulate their craft."

It's easy for us to scoff at such outlandish statements, but we should consider the possibility that people like Derenberger may only be passing along their own interpretations of complex information, and that on some occasions, the ufonauts may have tried to communicate valid information by simplifying it in terms that would make some kind of sense to the contactees. You can't really discuss the Einstein theory with an ex-preacher in West Virginia. Derenberger had, he claims, suffered peculiar distortions of time and space during his UFO experiences and he had, reasonably enough, asked for some sort of explanation. He was purportedly told, in simplified terms, that *their* time stream was different from ours, and was somehow running contrary to our own time cycle.

Nearly every contactee is given a set of prophecies or predictions concerned not only with his or her immediate interests and future, but with national affairs as well. Many of these predictions are very precise – pinpointing time, place, and so on with incredible accuracy. I have collected many such predictions and have been impressed with their validity. We have *absolute* proof. Contactees told me, far in advance of the events, of the collapse of the Silver Bridge at Point Pleasant, West Virginia, the murders of Martin Luther King and Robert F. Kennedy, and of innumerable ship disasters, aircraft crashes, and major earthquakes. A small percentage of these predictions missed because the time coordinates were slightly off. Collecting, documenting, and validating such predictions can lead to the development of an important body of evidence.

These predictions also prove something else: that the ufonauts have an intimate knowledge of our future. They may attempt to explain this strange talent to the contactees by claiming that they come from our future and are headed into our past. We cannot determine the validity of this claim without extensive study and research. Until such studies can be made, we must consider the claims a definite possibility.

It is far more likely that "they" originate *outside* of our timeframe. It is also likely that the entities are *not* individuals with separate intelligences and free wills, but are actually cells in a larger whole, controlled by a computerlike intelligence that manipulates them like puppets. Thus *they* do not actually know who they are or what they are, or even where they came from. Like machines, they have only two states: turned on, or turned off.

When you review *all* of the data instead of just those parts that conform to your own theories, it becomes obvious that a careful plan is being followed by the entire phenomenon, and that it is closely patterned after the same techniques of psychological warfare that we, ourselves, employ. Again, we must stress that the phenomenon is *reflective* and that a large part of it is a total hoax being foisted upon us. Were we not being tricked by the distention of time, for example, we might find that all UFO events are interrelated, and that although they may be widely separated according to our time cycle, they might be almost simultaneous events to the ufonauts.

There is not enough room here to outline all of the cases and experiences that have led me to these far-out theories, but the evidence does exist. It has been ignored for too long. There is a great mass of historical documentation going back several centuries, all of it substantiating these conclusions.

Ufology has made the mistake of isolating and studying individual events, rather than correlating those events. We have tried to fit these individual events into our own environmental framework. In other articles, I have noted that UFO events tend to recur year after year, and century after century, in the same locales. It has been noted, for example, that some UFO flaps occur during those months when Mars is closest to the earth. Many ufologists regard this as "proof" that the UFOs come from Mars. Actually, this only proves that certain periods in our time cycle coincide with specific periods of activity in the UFO time cycle.

One of the patterns in the contactee phenomenon is the fact that most of the initial "contacts" of the past three years have all taken place on Wednesdays. This does not necessarily mean that the ufonauts are using our calendar, but rather that our Wednesdays coincide with something in their own time cycle.

If we can break through the barriers of our own consciousness and our own environmental limitations, we might be able to unscramble *their* time cycle by examining all the reports of the past 100 years, particularly in "window" areas where reports consistently recur. We might even be able to construct a "UFO calendar."

Instead of dismissing all contactee reports as "crackpot," we should be sifting through these reports for clues. There is no clinical precedent for the contactee phenomenon in psychiatry. There is no medical explanation. This may be because not enough contactees have been studied by experts, but Woody Derenberger and others *have* been given thorough psychiatric tests, and *passed* them.

At present we have no frame of reference for these events. Only those of us who have had some direct experience with the phenomenon can begin to understand it. A long and tedious road lies ahead. Extensive research is essential, and it must be organized and systematic. I am confident that all the answers already exist, buried within the available material, but we must ferret them out, digest them, and reduce them to some tangible form.

A reflective phenomenon cannot be dealt with in the same way that our military intelligence apparatus determined the nature and origin of the German rockets of World War II.

If it is reflective, then we may be able to learn to exercise some control over it. There is the very chilling possibility that someone on this planet *has already learned to do so.*

CHAPTER 9

THE MAN WHO INVENTED FLYING SAUCERS – *WHOLE EARTH REVIEW*, 1986

North America's "Bigfoot" was nothing more than an Indian legend until a zoologist named Ivan T. Sanderson began collecting contemporary sightings of the creature in the early 1950s, publishing the reports in a series of popular magazine articles. He turned the tall, hairy biped into a household word, just as British author Rupert T. Gould rediscovered sea serpents in the 1930s and, through his radio broadcasts, articles, and books, brought the Loch Ness Monster to the attention of the world. Another writer named Vincent Gaddis originated the Bermuda Triangle mystery in his 1965 book, *Invisible Horizons: Strange Mysteries of the Sea*. Sanderson and Charles Berlitz later added to the Triangle lore, and "rewriting" (plagiarizing) their books became a cottage industry among hack writers in the United States.

Charles Fort put "bread on the table" of generations of science-fiction writers when, in his 1931 book *Lo!*, he assembled the many reports of objects and people strangely transposed in time and place, and coined the term "teleportation." And it took a politician named Ignatius Donnelly to revive lost Atlantis and turn it into a popular subject (again and again and again). Donnelly's book, *Atlantis*, published in 1882, set off a 50-year wave of Atlantean hysteria around the world. Even the characters that materialized at séances during that period claimed to be Atlanteans.

But the man responsible for the most well-known of all such modern myths – flying saucers – has somehow been forgotten. Before the first flying saucer was sighted in 1947, he had already suggested the idea to the American public. Then he converted UFO reports from just "silly season" media tidbits into a real subject, and kept that subject alive during periods of total public disinterest. His name was Raymond A. Palmer.

Born in 1911, Ray Palmer suffered severe injuries that left him dwarfed in stature and partially crippled. He had a difficult childhood because of his infirmities and, like many isolated young men in those pre-television days, he sought escape in "dime novels" – cheap magazines printed on coarse paper, filled with lurid stories churned out by writers who were paid a penny a word. He became an avid science-fiction fan, and during the Great Depression of the 1930s, he was active in the world of "fandom" – a subculture of mimeographed "fanzines" and abundant interpersonal corre-spondence. (Science-fiction fandom still exists and is very well organized, with well-attended annual conventions and lavishly printed fanzines, some of which are even issued weekly.)

In 1930, Palmer sold his first science-fiction story, and in 1933 he created the Jules Verne Prize Club, which gave out annual awards for the best achievements in science-fiction. A facile writer with a robust imagination, Palmer was able to earn many pennies during the dark days of the Depression, undoubtedly buoyed by his mischievous sense of humor – a fortunate development motivated by his unfortunate physical problems. Pain was his constant companion.

In 1938, the Ziff-Davis Publishing Company in Chicago purchased a dying magazine titled *Amazing Stories*. It had been created in 1929 by the inestimable Hugo Gernsback, who is generally acknowledged as the father of modern science-fiction. Gernsback, an electrical engineer, ran a small publishing empire of magazines dealing with radio and technical subjects. (He also founded *Sexology*, a magazine of soft-core pornography *disguised* as science, which enjoyed great success in a somewhat conservative era.) It was his practice to sell – or even give away – a magazine when its circulation began to slip.

Although *Amazing Stories* was one of the first of its kind, its readership was down to a mere 25,000 when Gernsback unloaded it on Ziff-Davis. William B. Ziff decided to hand the editorial reins to Palmer, the young science-fiction buff from Milwaukee, Wisconsin.

At the age of 28, Palmer found his life's work. Expanding the pulp magazine to 200 pages (and as many as 250 pages in some issues), Palmer deliberately tailored it to the tastes of teenage boys. He filled it with nonfiction features and filler items on science and pseudo-science, in addition to the usual formula short stories of BEMs (Bug-Eyed Monsters) and beauteous maidens in distress. Many of the stories were written by Palmer himself, under a variety of pseudonyms such as "Festus Pragnell" and "Thorton Ayre," enabling him to supplement his meager salary by paying himself the usual penny-a-word. His old cronies from fandom also contributed stories to the magazine, with a zeal that far surpassed their talents. In fact, of the dozen or so science magazines then being sold on the newsstands, *Amazing Stories* easily ranks as the very worst of the lot. Its competitors, such as *Startling Stories*, *Thrilling Wonder Stories*, *Planet Stories*, and the venerable *Astounding* (renamed *Analog*) employed skilled, experienced professional writers like Ray Bradbury, Isaac Asimov, and L. Ron Hubbard (who later created Dianetics and founded Scientology).

Amazing Stories was garbage in comparison, and hardcore sci-fi fans tended to sneer at it. I myself was an active sci-fi fan in the 1940s, and published a fanzine called *Lunarite*. Here's a quote from *Lunarite* dated October 26, 1946:

> *Amazing Stories* is still trying to convince everyone that the Bug-Eyed Monsters in the caves run the world. (And I was blaming it on the Democrats!) "Great Gods and Little Termites" was the best tale in this issue. But Shaver, author of "The Land of Kui," ought to give up writing. He's lousy. And the editors of *Amazing Stories* ought to join Sgt. Saturn on the wagon and quit drinking that Xeno, or the Bug-Eyed Monsters in the caves will get them.

I clearly remember the controversy created by the Shaver Mystery, and the great disdain with which the hardcore science-fiction fans viewed it.

Amazing Stories might have limped through the 1940s, largely ignored by everyone, if not for a single incident. In *Cheap Thrills: An Informal History of the Pulp Magazines* by Ron Goulart (Arlington House, New York, 1972), Howard Browne, a television writer who served as Palmer's associate editor in those days, recalled:

> Early in the 1940s, a letter came to us from Dick Shaver purporting to reveal the "truth" about a race of freaks, called "Deros," living under the surface of the earth. Ray Palmer read it and handed it to me for comment. I read a third of it and tossed it in the wastebasket. Ray, who loved to show his editors a trick or two about the business, fished it out of the basket, and ran it in *Amazing Stories*. A flood of mail poured in from readers who insisted every word of it was true, because *they* had been plagued by Deros for years.

Actually, Palmer had accidentally tapped a huge, previously unrecognized audience. Nearly every community has at least one person who complains constantly to the local police that someone – usually a neighbor – is aiming a terrible raygun at their house or apartment. This ray, they claim, is ruining their health, causing their plants to die, turning their bread moldy, making their hair and teeth fall out, and broadcasting voices into their heads.

Psychiatrists are very familiar with these "ray" victims, and relate the problem to paranoid-schizophrenia. For the most part, these paranoiacs are harmless and usually elderly. Occasionally, however, the voices they hear urge them to perform destructive acts, particularly arson. They are a distrustful lot, loners by nature, and very suspicious of everyone, including the government and all figures of authority. In earlier times, they thought they were hearing the voice of God and/or the Devil. Today, they often blame the CIA or space beings for their woes. They naturally gravitate to eccentric causes and organizations that reflect their own fears and insecurities, advocating bizarre political philosophies and reinforcing their peculiar belief systems.

Ray Palmer unintentionally gave thousands of these people focus to their lives. Shaver's long, rambling letter claimed that while he was welding, he heard voices that explained to him how the underground Deros were controlling life on the surface of the earth through the use of fiendish rays. (It is interesting that so many victims of this type of phenomenon were welding or operating electrical equipment such as radios, radar, etc. when they began to hear voices.) Palmer rewrote the letter, making a novelette out of it, and it was published in the March 1945 issue under the title: "I Remember Lemuria – by Richard Shaver."

The Shaver Mystery was born. Somehow the news of Shaver's discovery quickly spread beyond science-fiction circles and people who had never before bought a pulp magazine were rushing to their local newsstands. The demand for *Amazing Stories* far exceeded the supply, and Ziff-Davis had to divert paper supplies (remember, there were still wartime shortages) from other magazines so they could increase the press run of *Amazing Stories*.

"Palmer traveled to Pennsylvania to talk to Shaver," Howard Brown later recalled, "and found him sitting on reams of stuff he'd written about the Deros. He bought every bit of it and contracted for more. I thought it was the sickest crap I'd run into. Palmer ran it and doubled the circulation of *Amazing Stories* within four months."

By the end of 1945, *Amazing Stories* was selling 250,000 copies per month, an amazing circulation for a science-fiction pulp magazine. Palmer sat up late at night, rewriting Shaver's material and writing other short stories about the Deros, under pseudonyms. Thousands of letters poured into the office. Many of them offered supporting "evidence" for the Shaver stories, describing strange objects they had seen in the sky, and strange encounters they had had with alien beings. It seemed that many thousands of people were aware of the existence of some distinctly non-terrestrial group in our midst.

Paranoid fantasies were mixed with tales that had the uncomfortable ring of truth. The "Letters to the Editor" section was the most interesting part of the publication. Here is a typical contribution from the issue for June 1946:

Sirs: I flew my last combat mission on May 26, 1945, when I was shot up over Bassein and ditched my ship in Ramree Roads off Cheduba Island. I was missing five days. I requested leave at Kashmir. I and Capt. (deleted by request) left Srinagar and went to Rudok, then through the Khese Pass to the northern foothills of the Karakoram. We found what we were looking for. We knew what we were searching for. For heaven's sake, drop the whole thing! You are playing with dynamite.

My companion and I fought our way out of a cave with submachine guns. I have two 9" scars on my left arm that came from wounds given me in the cave, when I was 50 feet from an object of some kind, moving in perfect silence. The muscles were nearly ripped out. How? I don't know. My friend has a hole the size of a dime in his right bicep. It was seared inside. How, we don't know. But we both believe we know more about the Shaver Mystery than any other pair. You can imagine my fright when I picked up my first copy of *Amazing Stories* and saw you splashing words about the subject.

The identity of the author of this letter was withheld by request but, later, Palmer revealed his name: Fred Lee Crisman. He had inadvertently described the effects of a laser beam – even though the laser wasn't invented until years later. Apparently Crisman was obsessed with Deros and deathrays long before Kenneth Arnold sighted the "first" UFO in June 1947.

In September 1946, *Amazing Stories* published a short article by W.C. Hefferlin, "Circle-Winged Plane," describing experiments with a circular craft in 1927, in San Francisco. Shaver's (Palmer's) contribution to that issue was a 30,000-word novelette, "Earth Slaves to Space," dealing with spaceships that regularly visited the Earth to kidnap humans and haul them away to some other planet. Other stories described amnesia, an important element in the UFO reports that still lay far in the future, and mysterious men who supposedly served as agents for those unfriendly Deros.

That same year, Palmer decided to put out an all-flying saucer issue of *Amazing Stories*. Instead, the publisher demanded that he drop the whole subject after two men in Air Force uniforms visited the office. Palmer decided to publish a magazine of his own. Enlisting the aid of Curtis Fuller, editor of a flying magazine, and a few other friends, he put out the first issue of *Fate* in the spring of 1948. A digest-sized magazine printed on the cheapest paper, *Fate* was as poorly edited as *Amazing Stories*, and had little impact on the reading public. But it was the only newsstand periodical that carried UFO reports in every issue. The *Amazing Stories* readership supported the early issues wholeheartedly.

In the fall of 1948, the first flying saucer convention was held at the Labor Temple on 14th Street in New York City. Attended by about thirty people, most of whom were clutching the latest issue of *Fate*, the meeting quickly dissolved into a shouting match. Although the flying saucer mystery was only a year old, the side issues of government conspiracy and censorship already dominated the situation because of their strong emotional appeal. The U.S. Air Force had been sullenly silent throughout 1948 while, unbeknownst to the UFO advocates, the boys at Wright-Patterson Air Force Base in Ohio were making a sincere effort to untangle the mystery.

When the Air Force investigation failed to turn up any tangible evidence (even though the investigators "accepted" the extraterrestrial theory) General Hoyt Vandenberg, Chief of the Air Force and former head of the CIA, ordered a negative report to release to the public. The result was Project Grudge, hundreds of pages of irrelevant nonsense that was unveiled around the time *True* magazine printed Keyhoe's *pro*-ET article. Keyhoe took this personally, even though his article was largely a rehash of Fort's book, and Ralph Daigh had decided to go with the extraterrestrial hypothesis because it seemed to be the most commercially acceptable theory (that is, it would sell magazines).

Palmer's relationship with Ziff-Davis was strained now that he was publishing his own magazine. "When I took over from Palmer in 1949," Howard Browne said, "I put an abrupt end to the Shaver Mystery – writing off over 7,000 dollars worth of scripts." Moving to Amherst, Wisconsin, Palmer set up his own printing plant and eventually he printed many of those Shaver stories in his *Hidden Worlds* series.

As it turned out, postwar inflation and the advent of television soon killed the pulp magazine market. In the fall of 1949, hundreds of pulps suddenly ceased publication, putting thousands of writers and editors out of work. *Amazing Stories* has changed hands often since, but is still being published, and is still paying its writers a penny a word. A few of the surviving science-fiction magazines now pay (gasp!) three cents a word. But writing sci-fi still remains a sure-fire way to starve to death.

For some reason known only to himself, Palmer chose not to use his name in *Fate*. Instead, a fictitious "Robert N. Webster" was listed as editor for many years. Palmer established another magazine, *Search*, to compete with *Fate*. *Search* became a catchall for inane letters and occult articles that failed to meet *Fate's* already low standards. Although there was a brief revival of public and press interest in flying saucers following the great wave of the summer of 1952, the subject largely remained in the hands of cultists, cranks, teenagers, and housewives who reproduced newspaper clippings in little mimeographed journals, and looked up to Palmer as their fearless leader.

In June of 1956, a major four-day symposium on UFOs was held in Washington, D.C. It was unquestionably the most important UFO affair of the 1950s, and was attended by leading military men, government officials, and industrialists. Men like William Lear, inventor of the Lear Jet, and assorted generals, admirals, and former CIA heads freely discussed the UFO "problem" with the press. Notably absent were Ray Palmer and Donald Keyhoe. One of the results of the meetings was the founding of the National Investigation Committee on Aerial Phenomena (NICAP) by a physicist named Townsend Brown.

Although the symposium received extensive press coverage at the time, it was subsequently censored out of UFO history by the UFO cultists themselves, primarily because they had not participated in it. When David Michael Jacobs wrote *The UFO Controversy in America*, a book generally regarded as the most complete history of the UFO maze, he chose to completely revise the history of the 1940s and '50s, carefully excising any mention of Palmer, the 1956 symposium, and many of the other important developments during that period.

The American public was aware of only two flying saucer personalities, contactee George Adamski, a lovable rogue with a talent for obtaining publicity, and Donald Keyhoe, a zealot who howled "Coverup!" and was locked in mortal combat with Adamski for newspaper coverage. Since Adamski was the more colorful (he had ridden a saucer to the moon), he was usually awarded more attention. The press gave him the title of "astronomer" (he lived in a house on Mount Palomar where a great telescope was in operation), while Keyhoe attacked him as "the operator of a hamburger stand." Ray Palmer tried to remain aloof of the warring factions, so naturally, some of them turned against him.

The year 1957 was marked by several significant developments. There was another major flying saucer wave. Townsend Brown's NICAP floundered, and Keyhoe took it over. And Ray Palmer launched a new newsstand publication called *Flying Saucers From Other Worlds*. In the early issues, he hinted that he knew some important "secret." After tantalizing his readers for months, he finally revealed that UFOs came from the center of the earth, and the phrase "From Other Worlds" was dropped from the title. His readers were variously enthralled, appalled, and galled by the revelation.

For seven years, from 1957 to 1964, ufology in the United States was in total limbo. This was the "Dark Age." Keyhoe and NICAP were buried in Washington, vainly tilting at windmills and trying to initiate a congressional investigation into the UFO situation. A few hundred UFO believers clustered around Coral Lorenzen's Aerial Phenomena Research Organization (APRO). And about 2,000 teenagers bought *Flying Saucers* from newsstands each month. Palmer devoted much space to UFO clubs, information exchanges, and letters-to-the-editor.

So it was Palmer, and Palmer alone, who kept the subject alive during the Dark Age and lured new youngsters into ufology. He published his strange books about Deros, and ran a mail-order business selling the UFO books that had been published after the various waves of the 1950s. His partners in the *Fate* venture bought him out, so he was able to devote his full time to his UFO enterprises.

Palmer set up a system similar to sci-fi fandom, but with himself as the nucleus. He had come a long way since his early days and the Jules Verne Prize Club. He had been instrumental in inventing a whole system of belief, a frame of reference – the magical world of Shaverism and flying saucers – and he had set himself up as the king of that world.

Shaver – probably with some astonishment – witnessed the things he had been fabricating for years suddenly come to life and become *real* to legions of "ignored" percipients. Once the belief system had been set up, it became self-perpetuating. The people beleaguered by mysterious rays were joined by the wishful thinkers who hoped that living, compassionate beings existed out there beyond the stars. They didn't need any real evidence. The belief itself was enough to sustain them.

When a massive new UFO wave – the biggest one in U.S. history – struck in 1964 and continued unabated until 1968, APRO and NICAP were caught unawares and unprepared to deal with renewed public interest. Palmer increased the press run of *Flying Saucers* and reached out to a new audience.

Then in the 1970s, a second "Dark Age" began. October 1973 produced a flurry of well-publicized reports, but then the doldrums set in. NICAP strangled in its own confusion, dissolving into a puddle of apathy along with scores of lesser UFO organizations. Donald Keyhoe, a very elder statesman, now lives in seclusion in Virginia. Most of the hopeful contactees and UFO investigators of the 1940s and '50s have passed away.

Palmer's *Flying Saucers* quietly self-destructed in 1975, but he continued with *Search* until his death in 1977. Richard Shaver is gone, but the Shaver Mystery still has adherents. The sad truth is that none of this might have come about if Howard Browne hadn't scoffed at that letter in that dingy editorial office so long ago.

John Keel began having paranormal experiences at a young age on his family farm, which led him to the public library and an interest in writing. He was editor of his high school newspaper, and his early writings display the same keen wit he was known for as an adult. Keel closely followed UFO developments for twenty years before he actually began writing on the subject in 1966. Some have compared his writing to that of Mark Twain, whose family was from Point Pleasant, West Virginia. When Keel made his last appearance in Point Pleasant, in 2003, he wore a white suit in honor of Twain (see page 274). This historical sign is located on the old Twain farm next to Lakin Hospital - just south of the Defense Logistics (DLA) facility in Point Pleasant.

CHAPTER 10

T-shirts declaring, "I Traveled the Bermuda Triangle" are now a hot souvenir item in the Bahamas. But sooner or later, there will be T-shirts announcing "I survived New Jersey" and "I got out of Idaho alive."

Why? Because "warp zones," with high accident rates and frequent disappearances, are *not* confined to the famous triangle in the Atlantic. The entire North American countryside is dotted with areas haunted by weird manifestations and strange anomalies. Airplanes have disappeared in the placid skies of New Jersey and the calm, civilized air space of Illinois. Automobiles vanish along midnight roads everywhere. Your chances of disappearing into oblivion while walking your dog in Kentucky are as great as a seaman's chances of being swallowed up in the notorious Bermuda Triangle.

Every community in the country has at least one "Dead Man's Curve" or hazardous stretch of highway, where several accidents occur each year. Most of these places are well known to the local inhabitants, and carefully marked with warning signs. But every state also has a patch of highway, usually a straightaway free from ordinary hazards, that produces several fatal accidents each year, much to the bewilderment of the local authorities.

A few years ago, the late Ivan T. Sanderson was called upon to investigate such a warp zone in New Jersey. We know of similar places in New York and several other states. In West Virginia, we once investigated a strip of straight road where, for no discernible reason, drivers were always veering into a river. Most of them drowned. Those who survived could not explain their actions.

The 10-mile stretch of Interstate 15 between Inkom and McCammon, Idaho, is known locally as a "mystery road," because so many automobiles have suddenly and inexplicably crashed while traveling down it. Two people were killed there in a single month last summer, and there were four accidents within as many days that July.

The Idaho Highway Department and the State Police have been concerned with the number of accidents along this seemingly harmless length of road for several years. Rumble strips designed to shake up sleeping drivers have been installed along with special guardrails, patches of light and dark colored pavement, and other safety devices. The police patrols have been tripled there. Still, the accidents continue.

Six years ago, the police began taking statements from people who happened to witness the accidents. In most cases, the doomed drivers were proceeding normally at moderate speed when, for no apparent reason, they chose to swing off the road, often with fatal results. In one case, a truck carrying two men was followed by a car filled with highway engineers. Suddenly the truck left the road, slammed into some rocks, and flipped over. The two men survived with no idea of what had happened to them. The engineers in the car behind them saw no reason for the accident.

Other survivors of crashes on the mystery road told the same story. One minute they were driving along leisurely; the next, they were off the road and upside down, with no recollection of what had happened. Medical tests of the victims have yielded inconclusive results. The drivers were well rested and healthy. The police even tested for unusual gases in the area, and a wind-speed study was carried out. No explanation for the accidents has been found, and none of the safety measures have worked. Probably the only solution is to build a bypass and close Interstate 15's "haunted 10 miles" forever.

With millions of people traveling our highways each day, it's not unusual that Driving Unknowns (DUNKS) are becoming more and more common. UFO literature now abounds with reports of the strange things that happen to people in automobiles. A majority of our monster and tall, hairy humanoid reports come from solitary motorists, usually those driving alone along country roads late at night.

In the average account, the car comes around a bend and suddenly encounters a landed UFO or a monster shuffling across the road – like an animal seeking the other side. Many of the classic episodes in the annals of ufology began this way. Add to this the growing number of stories from witnesses who innocently stopped to aid what appeared to be a fellow motorist in distress, only to be suddenly confronted by Men In Black, who grimly warn them to keep quiet about something they previously saw. Driving today can be *really* hazardous to your health.

Some people are susceptible to a form of hypnosis when driving, particularly on long trips. They actually lapse into a sort of trance, although they generally remain in complete control of their car. Trees or telephone poles whizzing by along the side of a road can induce such a trance. A barren straightaway where traffic is light, such as a lonely desert road, can have the same effect.

The first thing that is affected is the sense of time, just as the sense of time is distorted in a real hypnotic trance. Prof. Graham Reed, a Canadian psychologist, calls this a "time-gap experience," because the driver can cover many miles safely in this condition. They don't snap out of it until they reach an intersection, a town, or a sudden change in scenery. Then they find they can't recall having driven those miles. They think the trip was remarkably short, until they glance at their watch. While this seems like a genuine DUNK to the driver, it is really not unusual. Investigators often waste much time and paper recording this commonplace experience.

On the other hand, there are many DUNKs and time-gap experiences that cannot be so deftly explained. Idaho's mystery road is too short to induce such trances. Yet from the statements of surviving victims of the phenomenon, it is clear that they were entranced by *something*. Whatever that something was, it interfered with their conscious minds and forced them to drive irrationally.

Several years ago, a British case received considerable publicity when a driver reported that his headlights suddenly seemed to *bend* into a nearby field at a spot where several strange accidents had previously occurred. Light *can* be bent by a powerful gravitational field, but a force strong enough to bend a light beam would certainly be strong enough to be felt by the driver, and it would certainly pull the car itself off the road. We have no reports of bent headlight beams from Idaho.

There are other possible explanations for DUNKs, though. Radiowaves, particularly microwaves such as radar beams, affect the human body and brain in many ways. A radar sweep from an airport or weather station could, when conditions are just right, affect a driver negatively. He might instinctively and unconsciously swerve his car in a futile attempt to get out of the beam. Doctors and radiologists have been aware of this for years, and there are frequent studies made to monitor this electromagnetic pollution caused by the rapid spread of microwave relay towers and radar stations. Some people are so adversely affected by these radiowaves that they become violently ill. Others develop great thirst because the waves dehydrate the body; they literally cook you from the inside out.

Pilots who have survived harrowing experiences in the infamous Bermuda Triangle have reported that their radios and instruments went haywire, and that they felt physically and mentally disoriented – clues that point to electromagnetic pollution. But since there are no relay towers or radar sets out in the Atlantic, what could be the source of these difficulties?

We know that beams of energy on all frequencies constantly bathe the earth from space. Much of this radiation is trapped, or at least weakened, by the Van Allen Belt and the planet's atmosphere. But some of these beams get through intact, and sweep over our planet in much the same way that our radar beams have explored Venus and Mars.

Ancient astrologers were aware of this and they based their science on their fragmentary knowledge of these "rays." Could it be that someone on a distant planet is examining our globe with radar, and that when a human is occasionally caught in one of these probes, he drives his car off a cliff or dives his plane into the ocean?

Many motorists have experienced bizarre distortions of time that can't be explained by psychologists or radiologists, because they have physically traveled great distances in impossibly short periods of time. In a number of well-documented instances, airplanes have also passed through these inexplicable time warps. Such distortions of space can only be accounted for by some direct, mysterious rearranging of our physical, three-dimensional world.

If you draw two dots on a piece of paper, they remain at a fixed distance so long as their reality – the two-dimensional world of the paper – remains static. But if you fold the paper, you can bring the dots closer together. By folding it, you have altered its physical state. Space itself can be folded in upon itself, so that the immediate reality of airplane or car is altered, and the seemingly fixed distance between points A and B is changed. Machines and people caught in these space warps also experience a compression of time.

There is now strong evidence that some UFOs are surrounded by a force-field that exerts a strong influence on the space-time coordinates of our reality. It is not a gravitational pull in the accepted sense of the term, yet it possesses some of the characteristics of gravity. The headlights of that car in England were diverted by such a space-time warp. If it had been stronger, the car and its driver would have probably passed through a spatial distortion, as in so many other cases.

While UFOs usually get the credit for DUNKs, it is possible that these wandering warps are a natural phenomenon, and that the UFOs have learned to utilize them. If our scientists would go out into the field to study this phenomenon, we might also find a way to take advantage of these natural anomalies. We might discover that we can hitchhike on them, and travel from New York to Los Angeles in seconds.

The logical place to begin such research is any one of the hundreds of mysterious roads like Idaho's Interstate 15. Perhaps if we learn why perfectly competent drivers suddenly run of the road, we can also learn how to eliminate roads altogether, and with them jet engines, rockets, and space shuttles.

CHAPTER 11

Tuesday evening, August 16, 1966, began with the relaxed, tepid stillness of midsummer. Rockers and porch swings quietly squeaked on tree-lined streets in America's Midwest, as people fanned themselves with the evening papers. There was no moon, and only a few filmy clouds glided silently overhead, on their way to some place cooler.

At 9:45 p.m. that night, a grandmother named Mrs. Ray Allen was loading her family into a car outside Flandreau, South Dakota. With her were her son, Clifford, her daughter, Mrs. Darlene Herrick, and her small grandson, David. Just as she climbed behind the wheel of the car, Mrs. Allen noticed a bright light hanging low over a nearby cornfield. "It looked like the moon, " she said later, "but we knew it couldn't be."

As she called the others' attention to the light, it began to move slowly, seeming to drift across the field toward the car. There was something frightening about this luminous globe of white light. Young David screamed that a "werewolf" was coming to get them. The women leaped out of the car and, followed by their children, ran into the house, where they alerted Mr. Allen. He stepped outside in time to see a streak of light disappearing into the sky. This was a small incident perhaps but, before another two hours had passed, thousands of people in five states had seen similar lights. Many of them never will forget that night for as long as they live.

Shortly after 10 p.m., Harold and Sophie Pikal of Henning, Minnesota, who were fishing on West Battle Lake (a small body of water almost 200 miles north of Flandreau, SD), saw a large ball of light, surrounded by an eerie mist, suddenly sail out of the night sky and head toward them. Badly frightened, they watched numbly as the light changed from white to red to green, and was joined by another light just like it. "There was a little poof," Mr. Pikal recalled later, "and then both balls grew smaller and smaller, and faded away as they hovered above the sandy beach on the northern part of the lake."

Thirty miles farther north and a half hour later, at about 10:30 p.m., the two Frenzel brothers of Detroit Lakes, Minnesota – who also were fishing on Eagle Lake – spotted an odd light in the sky. It was circular, Lawrence Frenzel said, and colored red, yellow and orange. While they stared in astonishment, it vanished, leaving a peculiar "vapor spot" in the sky, which continued to glow for half an hour. Other witnesses in the area reported seeing the same thing.

At 10:45 p.m., some 60 miles northeast of Eagle Lake, customers at the Erbe Drive-In outside of Cass Lake, Minnesota, gaped at a pink, horseshoe-shaped light that appeared to hang about 200 feet overhead. It turned blue, then white, and gradually grew dimmer, until only a vertical straight streak of white light remained in the sky. Then it, too, slowly melted away.

About the same time, in Hibbing, Minnesota, 75 miles due east of Cass Lake, another group of fascinated people were watching a multicolored object the size of the moon.

"It turned darker in the middle," Patrick McKenzie of Hibbing said, "then took on a horseshoe shape, and then seemed to vaporize."

Terry Backstrom, a *Hibbing Tribune* staffer, said, "It remained in one spot for about half an hour."

Along the border of Canada and Minnesota, more people stood on their porches looking at the night sky. In the vicinity of Warroad, Minnesota, they watched a circular shape surrounded by a green haze. The thing turned red, they agreed, and then became orange, blue and green as it seemed to shrink. Finally it took on the appearance of a large smoke ring and faded from view.

Meanwhile, at 10:30 p.m., Jack Miller of Big Mantrap Lake, Minnesota, was driving along Highway 71, a few miles south of Cass Lake and just north of Walker, Minnesota, when he saw what he later described as a disc-shaped object measuring only two or three feet in diameter, bouncing along just above the treetops. After he passed it, it seemed to follow his car. Alarmed, he raced to the nearest telephone and called Sheriff Bob Potter at Detroit Lakes. Sheriff Potter had a busy night. An hour later, he received more calls from residents in nearby Ponsford, who told him that they were watching a circular object, about three feet in diameter, as it hovered and discharged a bluish flame a few hundred feet up in the air.

At the same time, a luminous, silvery-green object was gliding along, just above treetop level, on Highway 34, south of the town of Walker. This was only 20 miles from Miller's position on Highway 71. According to the excited testimony of two 17-year-old boys, Pat Dermody and Bob Carmody, the object seemed to follow them for a short distance. They watched it uneasily for about four minutes before they turned around and sped back to the Twin Pine Resort, where they picked up Pat's father, John

Dermody. When they returned to the site, the older man said he saw a peculiar vapor and a huge white circle in the sky.

At 11:30 p.m., a group of women traveling the same road reported seeing a large white disc descending below the treetops. County authorities later revealed that several policemen had seen a similar object, in that same spot, 11 days before, on August 5.

Back on the northern border of Minnesota, at 11 p.m., a large group of baffled adults and teenagers studied a large reddish object as it wobbled low over the Community Building in Ranier, near International Falls. They all claimed it was larger than the local water tank. Its red glow faded until there was only a red rim around a dark object. The object itself seemed opaque and "resembled a filmy plastic substance." Several more people phoned the Falls Environmental Services office at 11:15 to report other strange lights flying around the vicinity.

But the most dramatic sighting took place just outside the city of Duluth, Minnesota, earlier in the evening, when a rotating multicolored globe terrified four people who were driving along Lakewood Road. "At first it looked like the moon," the driver, James Luhm, said, "but it seemed to move along with the car."

"I think that 'blob' is going to get us," Luhm remarked jokingly to his passengers. But before his sister Sally and two cousins, Pam and Debby Lind, could laugh, the object started to spin, changed colors and moved swiftly toward them.

"It was bigger than a football field," Luhm declared, "and when it got close to us, the car windows began to steam up."

Luhm pulled into a driveway, turned around, and fled down the road with the "blob" weaving along behind. He stopped at a residence and called the police. The Duluth police already had their hands full. Calls were pouring in from persons reporting smaller objects, green and red, measuring about three feet in diameter, hovering throughout the area.

The same kind of nightmare was taking place across the state border. About 100 miles southeast of Duluth and east of Cameron, Wisconsin, a horrified couple sat and watched a weird oblong shape plummet from the sky and pass over them. "It came closer and closer," the woman said. (They asked newspapers not to use their names.) "In fact, it came so close that my husband stopped the car and turned off the headlights. He broke out in a sweat of fear."

The object first appeared moon-shaped, the woman reported; it changed colors and, as it approached, they could see it was a vague, cigar-shaped thing. Their windows steamed up as it passed. Fifteen other persons in the same area called police to report seeing the object. Miss Linda Nelson and several other women claimed that the thing frightened them by heading straight for them before veering away.

Still another unidentified object boldly patrolled the streets of Racine, Wisconsin, that night, traveling at an altitude of about 100 feet. It was flat and round, according to several witnesses who said they saw it at various times between 8:45 and 11:00 p.m., in different parts of the city. It had a single red light on top and a series of white lights around its perimeter, according to their descriptions.

Wisconsin, however, had only a few isolated cases. Minnesota was blanketed by UFO activity that night. At the Flying Cloud Airport south of Minneapolis, several pilots reported seeing a glowing object actually *land* briefly on the east-west runway, before silently zooming off again.

The men in the control tower at the Minneapolis-St. Paul Airport reported seeing a strange luminous object pass over the city. Twin Cities radio stations recorded over 75 calls that night from persons reporting sightings.

Southwest of Minneapolis and about 80 miles straight east of Flandreau, South Dakota, where it all seemed to start, the Herb Geiger family of Sleepy Eye, Minnesota, saw a moon-shaped object descend through the clouds. "It appeared to be at a height of about 8,000 to 10,000 feet," Mr. Geiger said, "when suddenly the light disappeared and – poof – there was a cloud of vapor remaining, shaped the same as the object. Then it, too, disappeared. We didn't know what to make of it, but we were really stunned for a while."

Thousands of people in Arkansas, all totally unaware of what was happening in Minnesota, were equally stunned that same night as they watched eerie multicolored lights cavorting above their farms, villages, and cities. News commentator John Garner of station KFSA, Fort Smith, Arkansas, took his microphone outdoors for an on-the-spot broadcast with the 1500 people who were standing in the streets and fields staring at the dazzling display of lights.

Sgt. J.W. Gilbreth, Jr., of the Fort Smith Police Department, studied the sky with binoculars. He said, "Four red lights, immobile but seeming to rotate like a police patrol car warning beacon, were spread out in the sky like the points of the corners of a square. One set of red and green lights appeared traveling in straight lines from one of the four red lights, and then on to the others. A blinking white light and, later, a steady white light proceeded in the same manner."

In Paragould, Arkansas, Ken Bock of station KDRS also broadcast his eyewitness description of the freakish lights, which were rotating in a tight circle over that town. The objects would hover briefly, move up and down, and then zoom away again.

A group of lights in triangle formation, and changing from red to green, was viewed by many of the citizens of Forrest City, Arkansas that night. And in Hiwasse, Arkansas, the Rev. Paul Seymore, pastor of the Church of the Nazarene, reported seeing a set of triangular red and green lights that were "definitely attached to an object."

A formation of glowing circular objects paid a courtesy call on the air base at Newport, Arkansas, a number of witnesses revealed. "They were red and green in color," Mrs. Velma Dunavin recalled. "All of a sudden, there was a flash of light across the sky, and the smaller lights got into a wad and disappeared."

Hundreds of sightings were recorded in 13 widely separated areas of Arkansas that unforgettable evening of August 16. Most of the descriptions were in agreement, and some of the bobbing weaving lights remained in view for hours. Many came down fairly close over cities such as Little Rock.

Hundreds of miles from Minnesota and Arkansas, a New Jersey couple told of seeing a cigar-shaped object, red and pulsating, hover just above a high-tension line outside of Butler, NJ, that night. Another couple, Mr. and Mrs. Louis Osborn of East Orange, NJ said they observed two bright lights sweeping across the sky.

What happened on August 16, 1966? Soon after the overwhelming number of UFO reports began to hit the local papers, the usual vague explanations appeared. A weather bureau meteorologist in St. Paul, Minnesota, sagely announced that everyone had been watching the "northern lights." His theory was not very well-received by Minnesoteans, who know the difference between the aurora borealis and funny lights that flit along at treetop level. The Air Force and other authorities in Arkansas were too far south to blame it all on the northern lights, so they announced that everyone had been seeing meteors. (Meteors that hovered, changed course and color, and circled around each other?)

Homer Berry, a retired Air Force Major living in Little Rock, Arkansas, had his own explanation. It was the result of his rainmaking experiments, he announced. Instead of raining water, it had rained chemically inspired UFOs.

However, August 16, 1966, was not actually unique.

On March 30, 1966, hundreds of UFO sightings were reported in the states of New York, New Jersey, Michigan, Iowa, Ohio, California, South Carolina, and Wisconsin. No one yet has determined why so many sightings suddenly took place on a single date, in so many widely scattered areas.

On July 13, 1966, a sudden outbreak of UFO sightings covered the whole state of Nebraska. The official explainers said it was a "meteor." But the meteor did not appear over any of the adjoining states! There were, however, other important sightings that day in far-off Michigan and Illinois.

On July 27, 1966, North Carolina, Idaho, California, and Oklahoma enjoyed a misplaced display of northern lights. It's interesting to note that the majority of these "flap dates," as the ufologists call them, all happened to be Wednesdays. (August 16, however, was a Tuesday.)

Since most of the Minnesota sightings occurred at approximately the same time, and since the Arkansas sightings were occurring simultaneously, it would appear that a great number of these unexplained lights and objects were in our atmosphere on August 16.

There have been "flaps" of equal or greater intensity since that memorable date, but it takes long months of research and sifting to evaluate the reports and organize them into meaningful form.

Apparently three different kinds of phenomenon were in evidence that night. First, there were the small, low-flying objects seen by so many. Second, there were the strange balls of color-changing light seen repeatedly over Minnesota, which simply faded out or vanished with a "poof." Third and last, there were the high-flying formations that playfully traversed the skies of Arkansas. Perhaps all of these were related in some way, but the skeptics point to these differences to support theories of "electrical plasma" and other "natural" explanations.

One skeptic who became convinced was Dennis Tyo, 19, of Duluth, Minnesota. Accompanied by two girls, he was driving along the Rice Lake Road outside of Duluth the following night – August 17 – and was expounding his skepticism of James Luhm's story, which had been published in all the papers that day. They were not far from the area where Luhm and three others said they had been chased by a multicolored flying thing. Suddenly, Tyo's girl friend, Bonnie Mattila, 17, gasped and pointed out a huge, dark, circular object with flashing orange lights. It was moving slowly northeast at a low altitude. The two girls were crying hysterically by the time former skeptic Dennis Tyo called the police at 10:45. "I was scared stiff," he admitted. "It's one of those things that just don't happen!"

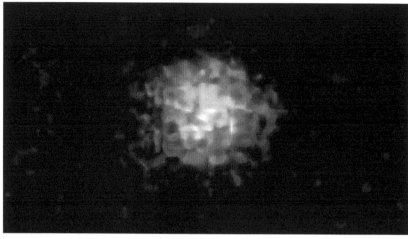

In late August 2011, the editor, Andy Colvin, shot two photos (top and center) of a UFO over the Jim Creek Naval Radio Array in Washington State, which indicate that it shapeshifted from a "ball of light" into a "flying humanoid" in the Mothman vein. Other witnesses have taken similar photos, such as the one publicized in 2013 by UFO moviemaker Paul Kimball (bottom).

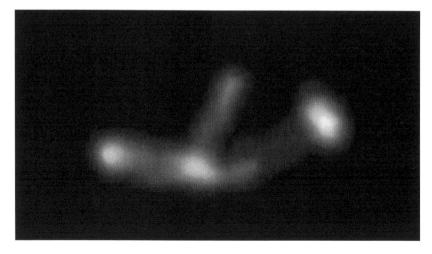

CHAPTER 12

Early in May 1969, four blinding lights descended from the sky over the little island of Allumettes on the Ottawa River, which divides the Canadian provinces of Quebec and Ontario. A farmer named Leo Paul Chaput was sitting in his kitchen with his wife and two of their 10 children at 2 a.m. on the morning of Sunday, May 4th, when they noticed a sudden flash in a field about 400 feet from the house.

They stepped outside, curious at first, and then were terrified as they had to throw their hands to their faces, to protect their eyes from the intense glare of four luminous objects, which they estimated were about 30 feet in diameter and 16 feet high. The things hovered eerily a few feet above the brightly illuminated ground for five or six minutes before sailing off into the darkness. As they departed, Mr. Chaput said he thought he heard a slight noise – something like the chugging of a boat motor. When daylight came, Chaput visited the field and found the ground was burned in four circular patterns 27 feet in diameter, each ring about two feet wide. The grass was still burning in some spots. Two small trees inside of one of the circles were singed and smoldering.

In the weeks that followed, the mysterious visitors returned to the Chaput farm several times, emitting a bright orange light as they passed silently overhead at an estimated altitude of 500 feet. One month later, on June 2nd, 1969, another scorched circle was found on the side of a hill on the John McLaren farm outside Meath, Ontario, only a short distance from the Ottawa River and Allumettes Island. This one was also a two-foot wide ring and was about 30 feet in diameter. It was clearly visible from the living room window of the McLaren farmhouse 200 yards away.

"The circle wasn't there on Sunday, June 1st, because we would have noticed," Mrs. McLaren said. "It must have happened after everyone was asleep, and that was past 1:00 a.m."

What has been burning up the Canadian landscape? In colonial times, these scorched patches were called "fairy circles." The people of Northern Europe blamed "fairies" for creating them, while early scientists dismissed the circles as the work of freak lightning bolts. They have been found on every continent, and are often discovered at spots where witnesses claim to have seen unidentified flying objects land. Usually vegetation in these circles does not grow back for several years. Grazing animals carefully nibble around the edges of the circles, but never step over their boundaries. Various scientists in Canada, France, England, and the U.S. have collected and studied soil and plant samples from these circles, and have been unable to find any chemical or biological reason for the observed effects.

The scorched circles on Allumettes Island and at Meath are only the latest in a long series of puzzling "flying saucer" events that have been stirring up controversy, confusion, and fear in many parts of Canada for several years. Villages all along the Ontario side of the Ottawa River have produced a steady stream of UFO reports, many of which seem to be concentrated around Pembroke, a town with a population of about 17,000, directly opposite Allumettes Island. Pembroke is also a few miles south of the Deep River Nuclear Research Laboratory and the Chalk River Nuclear Power Plant.

Ufologists the world over have long noted that "flying saucer" activity seems to be unusually intense around nuclear installations. The U.S. Air Force publicly confirmed this pattern in the early 1950s, and the late Captain Edward Ruppelt, first chief of the Air Force's UFO-chasing project, Blue Book, commented on the sightings around atomic plants in his authoritative book *Report on Unidentified Flying Objects* (1956).

A Canadian UFO investigator, Mr. Henry McKay, checked into a group of sightings at Deep River on February 7th and Chalk River on February 8th. Apparently some very unusual aerial objects were maneuvering over those strategic sites early in 1969. Residents of the village of Petawawa, sandwiched in between Pembroke and the Chalk River nuclear plant, have seen all kinds of flying lights and strange objects in recent years.

At 3:30 a.m. on the morning of Sunday, July 13th, 1969, Edgar Paquette was driving along a back road from Pembroke to Petawawa, with an unnamed female companion, when the road was suddenly "lit up like day." Then they saw a bright light following close behind them.

"I always thought I had guts, but I was never so scared in my life," Paquette told reporters later. "It seemed to be aimed right at us."

Paquette stopped his car and got out, signaling to the object with a flashlight as it made a low pass. It was, he said, about eight feet in diameter and seemed to have two legs hanging down from it. When it descended to within sixty feet of the ground and began to inch towards the car, Paquette panicked. He sprang back into his vehicle and drove to the nearest house, occupied by Mr. and Mrs. Gerry Chartrand.

"His lady-friend cried hysterically, "My God, have you got a phone?"

They called the police, and two constables and three military policemen responded. "It was really bright," Constable Jack McKay noted. "There wasn't another thing in the sky, and it was dawn before it disappeared."

Constables McKay and Grant Chaplin pursued the object for 38 minutes as it moved southeastward. A cab driver in Pembroke, John Chasson, also reported seeing the same thing, and said it was brighter than a star and appeared oval in shape.

Before the police pursuit began, the object apparently followed Edward Paquette home, where it hovered and was seen by his son, Sam, 14, and his daughter, Gloria Ann, 14. "The four of us drove as far as the gate, and then the light came down at us again," Paquette reported. "It didn't bother us after that, but Gloria Ann had run back into the house, she was so scared."

Eleven days earlier, Constable F.D. Instant had observed a similar UFO near the spot where Paquette's adventure began.

There have been hundred of documented incidents in which "flying saucers" have pursued motorists, often following them all the way home and hovering directly outside their house for several minutes. Reports of this type have come from South America, Europe and Australia, as well as from all over the U.S. and Canada.

The UFOs returned to Allumettes Island on September 3, 1969, when something hovered directly outside the bedroom window of an 18-year-old waitress in the village of Chapeu. Earlier in the evening, Pauline Ouellette, Mike McLean, Robert McLaughlin, and John Stotts had watched a fiery red object cavort about the sky. Soon after Pauline went to her room, she saw an oval-shaped thing hovering about 20 feet off the ground. A small object seemed to emerge from it, and it glided towards her window.

"It was oval-shaped, the same as the larger one, and it had a ring of lights around it," she reported. "It was about four or five feet long and two or three feet deep, with a small antenna coming out the top. It was much too small to have anything human inside. I was scared to death, and when it got within six feet of the window, I ran out of the room and hid in the hallway. I lay down on the floor and stayed there until daybreak. When I went back, about 7 a.m., the thing was gone."

Pembroke is one of the many UFO "windows" in the province of Ontario. There are many other isolated, thinly populated areas where "flying saucer" sightings have been disturbingly consistent. Over in the western part of the province, along Lake Huron, some startling UFO events have been recorded in the vicinity of the Douglas Point nuclear plant. On Thursday, July 3rd, 1969, Robert Thompson and Judy Storgaid reported seeing a star-like object plummet from the sky near Kincardine, only a few miles from Douglas Point. They said it seemed to stop abruptly and flashed red beams of light in various directions. The next night, July 4th, 187 persons phoned a local TV station at nearby Wingham to report a mysterious light. Witnesses in Harriston watched the object for 20 minutes, and said it seemed to have some kind of appendage.

The month before, residents in Kincardine were awakened around 4:30 a.m., Tuesday, June 10th, by a series of loud booms. Mrs. Jack Gardiner went downstairs to check things out in her kitchen, and she was surprised to find her house so brightly illuminated that she didn't need to turn on the lights. When she looked outside, she saw a hovering light larger than a star, but half the size of the moon. It remained for 40 minutes before it disappeared in the northeast, leaving a black vapor trail behind.

Other UFO hot spots in Ontario include Hamilton, London, and Barrie. Sightings around Barrie, Ontario date back to the early 1950s, and include such anomalies as "flying question marks" and bizarre transparent and translucent saucer-shaped and cigar-shaped objects. A typical Hamilton sighting took place early in July 1968, when Constable Walter Jewel reported seeing a hovering egg-shaped object. He watched it for 35 minutes, during which it was a bluish-green. Then it turned to a bright red and disappeared in a westerly direction. In London, Ontario a boy was allegedly burned when he touched a UFO hovering in a field behind a police station in 1966. Authorities later explained the many UFO sightings around London as being caused by lights reflecting from the bellies of geese flying overhead!

Although Canadian UFO events never receive any publicity in the United States, they are as numerous as the sightings in Michigan, West Virginia, and other American UFO hot spots. Interest in the subject is so high that journalist John Magor publishes a slick magazine, *Canadian UFO Report*, in the western province of British Columbia. In the central province of Manitoba, The Canadian Aerial Research Organization (CAPRO), headed by Brian Cannon, tries to keep track of reports, and in the east, Gene Duplantier has published his magazine *Saucers, Space, and Science* for several years, and has conducted radio programs devoted entirely to "flying saucer" reports. These groups and publications are closely allied to American UFO research organizations.

Some of the phenomenal events in Canada seem to be directly related to events in the United States. One of the oddest of these is the "mysterious crater" phenomenon. At 12:37 a.m. on the morning of Friday, September 27th, 1968, a tremendous blast shook the village of Arnprior, Ontario and was heard as far away as Pakenham, Galetta, and Renfrew. Windows were shattered, and a mild panic ensued. The switchboard at the Arnprior Filtration plant lit up like a Christmas tree as hundreds of people called, anxiously inquiring if the plant had blown up.

Two days later, a crater was discovered on the bank of a creek on the property of Stanley Reid. It was eight and a half feet in diameter and four and a half feet deep. Explosives experts visited the spot and were baffled. Two weeks later, a tremendous blast shook Polar Ridge, NY shortly after midnight on November 12th, 1968. A gaping hole was found the next day on the farm of Howard W. Lacey. To add to the mystery, there had been identical incidents on the Lacey farm in 1966, and again in 1967 (*also* on November 12th). No one could account for the sudden appearance of the craters. It may be significant that Polar Ridge, NY is 183 miles south of Arnprior, Ontario, in a straight line.

Inexplicable explosions are merely one of the many side effects of the UFO phenomenon. Waves of unbearable heat also accompany the appearances of the objects. In September 1968, a family in a farmhouse in Melfort, Saskatoon heard a high-pitched sound overhead. As the frequency of the pitch rose, the temperature inside the house also skyrocketed, and the terrified family fled into their cellar. A neighbor reported seeing a strange luminous object hovering near the house, and another farmer reported seeing three UFOs in the area. This heat effect has been frequently reported, and could be a form of *inductopyrexia* caused by the induction effect of magnetism. (Magnetic induction ovens broil meat from the inside-out with magnetic waves.)

A variation of this magnetic effect often paralyzes the flow of electrons in electrical circuits, causing telephones and power systems to fail and automobiles to stall. In its milder form, this effect produces static on radios and "snow" on television sets. This EM (electromagnetic) effect is constantly being reported all over the world. Canada has been no exception. Mr. Ben Briggs of Hudson Bay, Saskatoon, reported that his auto headlights dimmed and went out completely on the evening of October 24th, 1968, as he watched a large orange object slide across the sky. After the object disappeared, his headlights came back on. His engine did not quit.

There have been many major and minor power failures in UFO "flap" areas. The lights go out simultaneously with the appearances of mysterious objects. Utility companies usually don't even try to explain these occurrences. They simply announce that the cause of these failures "is not known."

Montreal, Quebec lies a few miles to the southeast of the UFO hotspot at Pembroke, Ontario. The Montreal sector has also produced hundreds of amazing UFO reports in the last few years, including numerous UFO landings and bizarre creature sightings.

Throughout 1968, a "flying saucer" wave encompassed the mountainous regions southeast of Montreal. More than 60 objects were reported by 250 persons in the municipalities of Thetford Mines, Black Lake, Coleraine, Disraeli, Vimy Ridge, St. Ferdinande de' Halifax, Ste-Julie, St-Adrien, and St-Robert in August 1968. The duration of the sightings ranged from five minutes to three hours. Near the village of Asbestos, 15 white UFOs were seen by 20 persons and two agents of the Surete. The UFOs came up slowly along the side of Vimy Ridge, twisting around the trees and valleys as if they were under intelligent control.

But the strangest stories of the "flap" came from the town of Drummondville, located a few miles northeast of Montreal. According to the *Sherbook LaTribune* of October 9, 1968, a family was watching TV early in October, when the wife shouted to her husband in another part of the house, "Paul, hurry, look!" He rushed outside and saw a rectangular green object in the sky. It seemed to be illuminated from behind. His wife said she had seen something similar before in the same place. After a few minutes, the object became brighter and greener, and then a saucer-shaped form, with a yellow-orange light encircling it, came out of a cloud.

The husband and his brother-in-law got into a car and drove in the direction of the objects, taking the route to St-Georges. The saucer inclined itself to the right, they said, and changed position, disappearing behind a cloud that then turned green. The men continued driving and soon a "truly dazzling ball of yellow-orange came out of a cloud." The men stopped and were joined by some boys as they walked across fields towards the lights. The lights soon became so blindingly bright that they paused, unable to see through the glare.

Meanwhile, back at the house, the wife and her sister were able to watch the objects. Both women claimed that they actually saw two human-like figures glide out of the saucer *and walk in midair*. Finally, the lights slowly drifted off in the direction of Windsor, Quebec and vanished. In Drummondville, eight witnesses testified they had seen a UFO occupant who walked stiffly like a robot.

Incredible though it may seem, reports of little green men are commonplace in UFO stories all over the world. Back in 1955, Captain Robert White, then Pentagon spokesman for Project Blue Book, told the press, "In the past three years, I've heard all kinds of descriptions of ufonauts, but the most frequent are of little, green, luminous, smelly types. People keep insisting that they've seen little green men."

"Flying saucer" activities persisted along the "UFO belt" stretching between Pembroke and Montreal throughout 1969. Canada's National Research Council continued to collect and puzzle over the endless reports. Quantities of "angel hair" (a filmy white cellulose substance) were spewed out of UFOs in several areas and carefully studied by scientists. In November 1968, a mysterious chunk of almost pure zinc dropped out of the sky into Wesley Reid's driveway in Cannifton, Ontario, and he turned it over to the government. It appeared to be laced with crystals of pure glass. No one could explain it. Meteorites are usually composed of iron, not zinc.

Coincidences abound in the study of UFOs, and so no one was too surprised when Montreal and a large part of Quebec suffered a sudden power failure at noon on November 8, 1969. "The cause was not immediately known," the newspapers reported. Lights all along the St. Lawrence River were out for about an hour and forty minutes, and most of the communities named above were included in the blackout. If the Quebec power failure had occurred twenty-four hours later, it would have happened on the fourth anniversary of the massive northeastern power blackout of November 9, 1965. And then we would have had a coincidence really worth pondering.

CHAPTER 13

THE FLYING SAUCER SUBCULTURE – *THE JOURNAL OF POPULAR CULTURE*, SPRING 1975

Until 1966, unidentified flying objects (UFOs), more popularly known as "flying saucers," were ridiculed by the press, scoffed at by the scientific community, and regarded as an unprofitable fringe subject by the major publishers. The UFO literature preceding 1966 consisted largely of semi-literate, privately published statements of belief authored in large part by hobbyists, neurotic and paranoid personalities, and individuals (known as "contactees") claiming direct contact with the pilots of flying saucers. Scientists, journalists and scholars drawn to the subject in the mid-1960s found there was virtually no acceptable scientific or literary research material available, despite twenty years of furor and controversy.

"An unidentified flying object," according to Dr. Edward U. Condon's definition, is "the stimulus for a report made by one or more individuals of something seen in the sky (or an object thought to be capable of flight, but seen when landed on the earth), which the observer could not identify as having ordinary natural origin, and which seemed to him sufficiently puzzling that he undertook to make a report of it to police, to government officials, to the press, or perhaps to a representative of a private organization devoted to the study of such objects."

There have been periodic worldwide waves – or "flaps" – of UFO sightings throughout history. In other ages, these aerial apparitions were often regarded as religious phenomena. The witnesses were acclaimed as prophets or denounced as victims of – or accomplices to – the devil. The modern phase began in 1896-97, when large "dirigibles" of unknown origin appeared throughout the United States. Two decades earlier, a farmer named John Martin reported seeing a large circular object pass overhead near Dennison, Texas, on January 24, 1878. He described it as resembling a "saucer." However, the term "flying saucer" did not come into popular usage until the summer of 1947, when there was a sudden outbreak of sightings throughout North America. Kenneth Arnold, a private pilot, employed the term while describing to reporters what he had allegedly seen near Mt. Rainier, Washington, on June 24, 1947.

Flying saucer *literature* can be divided into three important periods, each lagging a year or two behind a major flap. The first was 1950, following the flap of 1947. The second was 1955-56, following the sighting wave of 1952. The third and final period was 1966-69, following the great wave of 1964-67.

The 1950 period produced the extraterrestrial frame of reference – the belief that these apparitions were visitors from outer space. The 1955-56 period advanced this extraterrestrial hypothesis (ETH), adding the testimony of contactees to the literature, and creating a new theme: the allegation of a governmental conspiracy, instrumented by the United States Air Force, to suppress "the truth." This conspiracy became the central concern of the UFO hobbyists for many years after. The principal creators of the lore of the 1950s were: Donald E. Keyhoe, a retired Marine Corps pilot who became the major spokesman for American Ufology; Frank Scully, a columnist for *Variety*; Frank Edwards, a radio newscaster; Morris K. Jessup, an astrophysicist; and George Adamski, an early contactee.

The 1966-69 period marked a gradual return to rationality as a new generation of scientists and journalists examined the UFO lore, rejected much of it, and produced a more valid body of literature. The major contributors to the "New Ufology" of the 1960s were: Vincent Gaddis, a professional writer; Dr. Jacques Vallee, a computer specialist; Ivan T. Sanderson, zoologist; John Fuller, a columnist for *Saturday Review*; and Eugene Olson, a writer using the name of "Brad Steiger." The British journal, *Flying Saucer Review*, was also instrumental in bringing about important changes in the overall approach to the subject.

Ironically, the flying saucer myth is being nullified by the increasing availability of reliable case histories and valid technical information, and the growing acceptance of the subject as a matter worthy of study by scientists, psychiatrists, and sociologists. This acceptance was the major goal of the UFO organizations and believers through all the hard years of ridicule – 1947-66. But now that respectability is at hand, the believers find themselves excluded.

The scope of the UFO phenomenon is unbelievable to newcomers to the field. Thousands of sightings are recorded annually, in every country on earth. Dr. David Saunders, a psychologist with the University of Colorado, has thus far programmed 50,000 documented sightings for computerization. Dr. Jacques Vallee has also produced statistics on thousands of sightings in France, Spain, and the United States. For many years, the flying saucer cultists labored awkwardly to prove the reliability of such sightings, rather than to attempt to determine what, if anything, the witnesses had actually seen, and what were the real stimuli.

The very few social scientists who have made admittedly superficial studies of the problem have innocently confused the UFO believers with the UFO witnesses. Buckner (1965) studied one small group of West Coast believers and concluded that the subject attracted the elderly, the lonely, and the philosophically disorientated. Meerloo (1968) equated belief in flying saucers with "the need for miracles." Warren (1970) also confused the UFO sighter with the UFO believer.

Actually, flying saucer witnesses come from all age groups and all levels of society. Condon (1969) found that only about 10 percent report their sightings to anyone, the fear of publicity and subsequent ridicule being the reason most often cited by non-reporting witnesses. To some witnesses, the experience is an intensely personal one, like an occult or religious experience, and they do not even discuss it with their own family.

The hardcore flying saucer cultist, on the other hand, is a very special personality who has thus far escaped close scrutiny by the scientific community. Contrary to Buckner's findings, a poll of 250 hardcore American "ufologists" in 1969 determined their median age to be 31. Teenagers and housewives constitute the most active groups, collecting clippings of sightings and issuing amateur newsletters and magazines, usually mimeographed. The classic search for identity plays an important role. The teenaged ufologist is most often isolated on a farm, or otherwise separated from his peers, because of his eccentric personality. The house-wives are often suffering from marital problems (the divorce rate among female ufologists is high), or are the type of personality who busies herself with all kinds of community and social affairs, merely adding ufology to her list of escapist activities.

Ufology provides an "ego trip" for those who establish themselves as the local UFO "expert" and thus brighten an otherwise ignored and undistin-guished life. They are eager to lecture before local clubs, appear on local radio and television, and give out newspaper interviews. When they are heavily and publicly ridiculed – which is often – they accept this as part of the great conspiracy against the truth.

In contrast to the innumerable witnesses, the ufological population is extremely small. During each major flap period, dozens of UFO newsletters and magazines appeared. Their average circulation is forty; their average lifespan is 18 months. The largest UFO magazine in the United States, Ray Palmer's *Flying Saucers*, was founded in 1957 and, even with newsstand distribution, only reached a circulation of 14,000 during a peak year of interest – 1967. Today it has a paid circulation of 2,000. The Aerial Phenomena Research Organization (APRO), founded by Mrs. Coral Lorenzen in 1952, had a total membership of only 800 when the wave of the 1960s began. Although dozens of small UFO journals blossomed momentarily in the 1966-69 period, only a handful have survived. Only two, Missouri's *Skylook*, published by Mrs. Norma Short, and the *Ohio UFO Bulletin*, published by Mrs. Bonita Roman, have managed to retain a circulation of more than 100.

Hardcore ufology can be divided into three main groups. The first group, the "super-hardcore," consists of about fifty people, most of them in their late teens or early twenties. They publish the newsletters, contribute articles to each other's publications, attend the conventions, and make the most noise. The second group is the "hardcore," which subscribe to the publications of the first group and generally support them. The third and largest group are the "pure believers." They buy the books, attend the lectures, and cluster around the various contactees.

Altogether, hardcore ufology numbers less than 5,000 people in the United States. Interestingly, the hardcore believer has never seen a UFO (Hynek, 1972), tends to be overly skeptical of "non-UFO" phenomena (such as Bigfoot or the Loch Ness monster), and has an extremely suspicious nature, perhaps because he/she has created an imaginary self-image and constructed the necessary lies to maintain it. Thus they tend to believe that everyone else shares these personality flaws. They often project or transfer their own problems to the UFO witnesses they interview. Many sincere percipients and contactees have been branded liars by UFO enthusiasts who thought they detected *their own* behavioral problems in them.

Scientism dominates the UFO movement. The study of myths, religion, and occult phenomena, being generally unacceptable to the scientific establishment, is even more unacceptable – even odious – to the aspiring pseudo-scientists of ufology. Their view is totally materialistic. Very few have the ability to deal with abstractions. Many laboriously study astronomy, but few are interested in – or can deal with – philosophy.

The two types of distinguishable personalities present at UFO conventions and club meetings are the obsessive-compulsive and the paranoid-schizophrenic.

In order to be able to understand the flying saucer literature itself, and the underlying trends, we must reconcile ourselves with the above cruel facts. The flying saucer myth could not have come into being, and could not have perpetuated itself without the involvement of such personalities.

In the 1920s, a failed novelist, Charles Fort, compiled a book of scientific anomalies that he collected by patiently sifting through old newspapers and journals. He was intrigued with the endless accounts of frogs raining from the sky, objects observed floating in the air (OOFs), and the mysterious disappearances of objects and people (he coined the word "teleportation"). No one wanted to publish his *The Book of the Damned* until his friend, Theodore Deiser, informed publisher Horace Liveright that if he didn't publish Fort, he (Dreiser) would take his next novel elsewhere.

So, Charles Fort became the father of ufology. Before his death in 1932, he had published four books blending carefully documented "erratics" with a tongue-in-cheek attack against the scientific establishment. His books are still in print in paperback, and the International Fortean Organization (INFO) carries on his name as the successor to the Fortean Society, founded by novelists Tiffany Thayer and Ben Hecht. INFO members, about 2,000 worldwide, are interested in a wide variety of phenomenon, not just UFOs. Several leading Forteans are, in fact, "anti-UFO."

When the big UFO flap of 1947 erupted, reporters had no sources to turn to. The U.S. Air Force shrugged in ignorance and dismay, and assigned the Air Technical Intelligence Command (ATIC) to investigate. Tiffany Thayer gleefully filled the pages of *Doubt*, his Fortean magazine, with sightings, coupled with his own peculiar political beliefs (he thought just about everything was a governmental conspiracy of some sort). The national magazines commissioned writers to "get to the bottom of the mystery," and Charles Fort became the man of the hour. His books were the only ones that collected together the OOF sightings of the nineteenth century.

Major Donald E. Keyhoe digested Fort, talked with witnesses, and produced "Flying Saucers are Real" for *True* Magazine. His conclusion was one Fort disagreed with: UFOs were extraterrestrial.

H.G. Wells' 1898 novel, *The War of the Worlds*, had suddenly crossed the borderline that separates fiction from reality. To Keyhoe, and thousands of others, flying saucers were very real. Their reported maneuvers seemed to prove their superiority to any known earthly aircraft, therefore they had to come from some other planet.

There was an interesting and significant prelude to the 1947 flap. In 1944, a science-fiction magazine, *Amazing Stories*, edited by Ray Palmer, published a story titled "I Remember Lemuria" by Richard Shaver. Shaver had rehashed an old theme, the underground "Secret Commonwealth" – a "fairy" belief of the Middle Ages. H.G. Wells had employed this same theme himself in *The Time Machine* (1895) with the ugly, evil underground-dwelling Morlocks, who feast upon the gentle, surface-dwelling Eloi. A.A. Merritt used the same theme in *The Moon Pool* (1933). It was a science-fiction cliché. Shaver described his adventures in the caverns of the Dero ("detrimental robots"). He claimed the evil Dero were running the world by controlling the minds of men, through insidious rays projected from their caves.

Palmer was amazed when he was buried under thousands of letters from people claiming that they, too, had had experiences with the Dero, and that Shaver was telling the truth. Actually, many of them were expressing the recognizable symptoms of paranoid-schizophrenia, while others were recounting the classic manifestations of demonology. Palmer ghosted several more Dero stories, the Shaver Mystery was brought into being, and the circulation of *Amazing Stories* skyrocketed, outstripping all its competitors.

In 1948, a disagreement with his publisher over an all-UFO issue led Palmer to leave *Amazing Stories* and become the co-founder, with Curtis Fuller, of *Fate* magazine. Early issues of *Fate* were largely devoted to flying saucers, but in the interest of survival, it soon broadened to encompass all aspects of Fortean and paranormal phenomena. Palmer later withdrew from *Fate* and established a publishing house in Amherst, Wisconsin. In 1957, he launched *Flying Saucers* magazine, advocating the Hollow Earth Theory – a spin-off of Shaverism that contends the earth is hollow and flying saucers come from holes in the poles.

This Hollow Earth concept has been around a long time. In 1818, a man named Symmes almost persuaded Congress to grant him funds for an "expedition" to the center of the earth. A vast subsidiary literature has been built around the theme, and until recently there was even a newsletter, *The Hollow Hassle*, devoted to the subject. The most widely read work of this genre, *The Hollow Earth*, written by one "Dr. Raymond Bernard," was published in 1963. It presented flimsy, often deliberately falsified evidence for the holes at the poles.

Flying saucer reports caused concern when they first appeared, because official circles feared they could represent some new development by the Soviet Union. ATIC reportedly prepared a top-secret "Estimate of the Situation" in 1948, concluding that the UFOs had to be extraterrestrial. Air Force Chief of Staff General Hoyt Vandenberg rejected the estimate, and ordered all copies burned, pointing out to ATIC that the Air Force could not issue such a conclusion without overwhelming evidence to support it. Such evidence did not exist. In response to Vandenberg, ATIC reversed itself and prepared Project Grudge (1949), a 366-page treatment of the subject dismissing UFOs as mistakes, atmospheric and astronomical phenomena, and hoaxes, establishing the guidelines for the official Air Force policy for the next twenty years.

Thayer and Keyhoe viewed Project Grudge as confirmation of their belief that an official conspiracy to downgrade UFO reports existed. Keyhoe expanded his *True* article, and it was published as *The Flying Saucers are Real* in 1950. The earth has been under observation by beings from another planet for at least two centuries, according to Keyhoe, and this observation was stepped up after the atomic explosions in 1945.

In England, science writer Gerald Heard produced *The Riddle of Flying Saucers: Is Another World Watching* (1950), also stressing the extraterrestrial hypothesis.

But the big UFO book of 1950 came from an unexpected source. Frank Scully of *Variety* published *Behind the Flying Saucers*, claiming that a UFO had crashed in the southwest, and that the USAF had recovered the bodies of tiny alien beings from the wreckage. The book was based upon speculation, hearsay, the testimony of contactees, and the allegations of a mysterious "Dr. Gee." Scully's sources were soon exposed as unreliable by other reporters. "Dr. Gee" turned out to be nothing more than a television repairman, and Scully eventually apologized publicly. However, the USAF still receives letters asking if it is true that pickled Martians are hidden away in a jar at some Air Force base.

Although Keyhoe, Scully, Thayer and others had campaigned vigorously for the ETH, opinion polls conducted in 1950 found that fewer than five percent of the population thought flying saucers were coming from another planet. Most felt the objects were a secret weapon of some sort.

Astronomers, physicists, and anthropologists were universally negative about the ETH in 1950. It was doubtful, they said in unison, that life could exist elsewhere at all. Space travel seemed to be the unrealistic dream of science-fiction writers. General Eisenhower, while serving as Chief of Staff, ordered the Army to curtail its research with captured German rockets. Rocket weapons were an "impractical dream," he declared.

ATIC abandoned their UFO research after the publication of Project Grudge. Flying saucers seemed to be officially dead. Sidney Shalett wrote a two-part series for *The Saturday Evening Post* (April 1949), presenting the Air Force case: "If there is a scrap of bonafide evidence to support the notion that our inventive geniuses, or any potential enemy, on this or any other planet, is spewing saucers over America, the Air Force has been unable to locate it."

Aside from a few cranks, people seeking impossible causes, and a spattering of impressionable teenagers and housewives lacking the education to question Scully's speculations and Keyhoe's sophistry, flying saucers were not taken seriously. The whole thing appeared to be a "fad" that would soon go away. The subject's only scientific spokesman was Germany's Professor Herman Oberth, the rocket pioneer, who issued occasional positive statements about the ETH and urged a broader investigation into UFOs.

But the flying saucers did not go away. There were so many sightings that, in 1951, the Pentagon ordered resumption of UFO investigations. ATIC set up Project Blue Book, headed by Captain Edward Ruppelt. To offset the harsh criticisms of the small but vociferous UFO coterie, Ruppelt cooperated with Keyhoe and others, feeding them new cases from the Air Force files.

There were national headlines in the summer of 1952, when formations of mysterious lights cavorted over Washington, D.C. for two straight weeks. They were picked up by radar at all the airports, observed by people in the city's streets, and pursued by military planes. The Pentagon staged press conferences to explain the apparitions away as "air inversions" and natural phenomena. A new generation of housewives and teenagers cranked up their mimeographs and founded short-lived investigation groups.

Concurrent with the 1952 flap, Hollywood entered a flying saucer cycle. Beginning with *The Thing*, filmmakers angered the UFO buffs by peopling space with hostile beings. (Since the UFOs had never bombed New York, they were obviously well-intentioned, according to the ufologists' logic.) One routine opus, *Earth versus the Flying Saucers*, listed Major Keyhoe as consultant. The best of the films produced during that cycle was *The Day the Earth Stood Still*, in which a flying saucer served as a main set. Actor Michael Rennie resembled very closely the stately Venusians described by contactees.

As the sightings poured in from all over the world, New York editors and writers mobilized for a new assault on the public senses. Palmer's "Hollow Earth" seemed too far out, even for the sensationalists, so most of the one-shot magazines, comic books, and quicky paperbacks of the period settled for the ETH. If there were flying saucers, they *had* to come from outer space. In effect, Madison Avenue was unwittingly joining Keyhoe and his colleagues, as propagandists for an idea that had seemed totally absurd only five years before. There was still no hard evidence of any kind to support the ETH (there never would be), but the mounting sightings certainly indicated that some kind of phenomenon did exist.

Arthur C. Clarke, the famed science-fiction writer, focused his attention on the phenomenon in the early 1950s. In *The Journal of the British Interplanetary Society*, May 1953, Clarke questioned the physicality of the objects, noting their observed behavior defied all the laws of physics. They seemed to race through the atmosphere at supersonic speeds without causing booms. They performed right angle turns at high speeds. They appeared and disappeared as suddenly as ghosts. Clarke could not accept the notion of extraterrestrial visitants who would travel millions of miles only to ignore us and avoid formal contact. So he looked deeper, into psychic phenomena, philosophy and theology, and published his findings in *Childhood's End* (1953), a remarkable novel that is still ahead of its time. It would take ufology two decades to catch up with him. His novel is still almost completely unknown to the hardcore UFO enthusiasts.

Science-fiction writers and fans had lampooned the UFO subject since the appearance of Shaver, and so were regarded as the arch-enemies of ufology.

Another arch-enemy was the Harvard astronomer, Dr. Donald Menzel. An active advisor to the Air Force, Menzel dismissed UFOs as mirages, reflections, and air inversions in *Flying Saucers* (1953). Because this was one of the first works on the subject by a genuine scientist, Menzel received considerable publicity, and his theories were frequently quoted thereafter. The UFO magazines viewed him with extreme distaste, ranking him with another astronomer and "Air Force explainer," Dr. J. Allen Hynek. To add to the insult, Dr. Menzel's hobby was writing *science-fiction* under various pseudonyms.

Major Keyhoe countered Menzel with *Flying Saucers From Outer Space* (1953), a book based in large part on UFO sightings from the USAF's official files. Captain Ruppelt, Al Chop, and other members of Project Blue Book had quietly become ETH enthusiasts and publicly endorsed Keyhoe's books.

Early in 1953, a blue-ribbon panel of leading scientists was convened by the Central Intelligence Agency in Washington to review the evidence collected by Project Blue Book. Ruppelt tried to promote ETH, but his evidence was flimsy, and the panel remained unconvinced. Noting that the handling of UFO reports was consuming too much time and money, and threatened to create disastrous confusion if enemy aircraft should one day appear, the panel suggested tightening security on Air Force UFO information, and publicly downgrading the subject. Later, an order was even issued to all USAF personnel, forbidding them to discuss UFO reports with the press or civilians. Keyhoe's major sources of information were suddenly cut off.

The Dark Age of ufology thus began.

Tiffany Thayer's suspicions had been confirmed. The USAF was "out to get" ufologists and Forteans. New UFO sightings were hastily explained as meteors and air inversions. Project Blue Book became nothing more than a slapstick public relations effort. The annual UFO statistics issued by the Air Force were ludicrous; the columns of figures were not even added correctly, and the numbers of sightings allegedly reported to the Air Force in previous years were mysteriously altered in each new statement.

The growing band of UFO hobbyists were convinced that the flying saucer mystery harbored some terrible secret, and that the government would stop at nothing to keep that secret from becoming public. In 1952, Albert K. Bender of Bridgeport, Connecticut founded a correspondence club (which is really what all the UFO organizations are) called the "International Flying Saucer Bureau." It is significant that Bender also had another hobby: the study of black magic. Within a year, Bender was behaving strangely, telling friends he was onto "the secret," and hinting that government agents were trying to shut down his bureau. In November 1953, he did just that, and refused to have anything to do with the subject from that time on. He fell completely silent, and would not discuss his problems with even his closest associates.

Reports of similar cases turned up as far away as New Zealand. Many UFO enthusiasts became convinced the government was tapping their phones, tampering with their mail, and even trailing them in ominous black Cadillacs. Gray Barker, a West Virginia researcher, collected enough anecdotes of this sort to publish a book, *They Knew Too Much About Flying Saucers* (1956), thus setting in motion the main ufological diversion of 1953-66 – speculations about the official "conspiracy of silence."

Major Keyhoe contributed to the darkening atmosphere with *The Flying Saucer Conspiracy* (1955), and newscaster Frank Edwards claimed he had been fired from his job with the Mutual Broadcasting System because he "talked too much about flying saucers." In *My First 10,000,000 Sponsors* (1956), Edwards asserted he had later been offered a high paying job with the Pentagon, supposedly to assure his silence.

Not unexpectedly, this conspiracy-orientation altered the basic character of American ufology by appealing to persons with paranoid leanings and extreme political views. Instead of investigating flying saucers, they turned to investigating each other. Who in their midst was really an Air Force agent? They were suspicious of everyone. Members of Major Keyhoe's NICAP became bitterly antagonistic towards each other.

Dr. Leon Davidson, a man who had played an active role in early atomic research, became involved with UFOs in the early 1950s, and eventually concluded that the whole thing was a Cold War hoax created by the CIA.

The more rational people in the UFO field dropped out in dismay and disgust, leaving the movement to the cranks, publicity seekers, and paranoiacs. The UFO magazines of the later 1950s took on a discombobulated character, blending right-wing politics with rumors and vicious slander. It was ufology's darkest hour.

American research was paralyzed from the outset because of the shortage of qualified investigators and researchers, the lack of leadership, and the total absence of methodology. Even while the cries of official censorship were growing, there was a sudden explosion of new and worthwhile information. Captain Edward Ruppelt produced the first important breakthrough by publishing the inside story of Project Blue Book. His *The Report on Unidentified Flying Objects* (1956) was a blockbuster filled with previously unrevealed Air Force UFO cases, and refreshing insights into the overall problem. The book still ranks as one of the best on the subject.

For its part, the USAF released *Project Blue Book Report 14* in 1955. This was a statistical study of thousands of UFO sightings, prepared for the Air Force by the Battelle Memorial Institute, a "think tank" in Columbus, Ohio. Through some rather questionable mathematical techniques involving probabilities, etc., it attempted to support the USAF's negative UFO stance. Actually, it was the first statistical study of the subject and, as such, remained unique for ten years. The UFO enthusiasts were too caught up in conspiracies to attempt any statistical studies of their own.

Morris K. Jessup, a trained astrophysicist, became a ufological superstar with the publication of *The Case for the UFO* (1957). This book covered a wide range of Fortean phenomena, loosely linking all of it with flying saucers, and including various archaeological and anthropological mysteries. He suggested, for example, that the great stone structures of the ancient world might have been erected through the use of levitating rays wielded by flying saucers.

Soon after the paperback edition of *The Case for the UFO* appeared, a dog-eared copy arrived by mail at the Office of Naval Research (ONR) in Washington. It was profusely annotated in different colored inks by different hands. The notes commented on Jessup's findings, and some of the comments were quite remarkable. Officers at ONR showed the book to Jessup, but he dismissed it as some kind of joke. However, ONR took it so seriously that a naval subcontractor, the Varo Corporation of Garland, Texas, retyped the entire book and printed it in a very limited offset edition, with the annotations in different colored ink. Copies of this "Varo Edition" were classified and distributed to a few dozen scientists and naval officers. Although the Varo book's existence became a legend among UFO enthusiasts, very few were ever privileged to see a copy.

Jessup also became one of the first ufologists to examine the religious implications of the phenomena. In *UFO and the Bible* (1956) he became one of the first bold enough to suggest that religious manifestations might have a direct relationship with flying saucers.

In 1959, Jessup committed suicide, an event darkly viewed by the paranoid UFO cultists. Some felt he had been liquidated by government agents. Jessup and *The Varo Edition* became another ufological legend.

Other important books of the 1955-56 period included *Space, Gravity, and the Flying Saucers* by Leonard G. Cramp, with speculations on their technology; *Flying Saucers on the Attack* by Harold T. Wilkins, the first book to collect together anecdotes of hostile actions by UFO; and *You Do Take It With You* by *Coronet* magazine columnist R. Dewitt Miller. Miller's oddly titled entry was one of the most important books of this period, because it saw the links between mysticism, psychic phenomena, and UFOs.

David Flick published an article in *Library Journal* (February 1, 1955) condemning librarians who wasted tax dollars on flying saucer books "whose purpose seems to satisfy a jaded taste for the bizarre and the sensational." Flying saucers had become more a problem for the librarian than for the scientist.

The following categories for UFO literature had now developed:

1. Anecdotal "seed catalogs" describing the endless sightings.

2. Studies of the official conspiracy of silence and attacks against the USAF.

3. Theories and speculations about the origin and purpose(s) of UFO.

4. Contactee stories.

With the exception of Menzel and the official Blue Book reports, there was no scientific literature.

Enoch's legendary excursions to other worlds in 4,000 B.C. rank him as the first known contactee. Emmanuel Swedenborg, the Swedish mathematician (1688-1772), had years of experience in the twilight word of space travelers and angelic messengers, and wrote a number of books detailing life on other worlds. But eventually, he realized he was the victim of some kind of cosmic con game, and denounced his strange friends as untrustworthy fabricators.

Legends of the "Sky People" can be found in isolated cultures throughout the world, purportedly based upon the stories of those who had direct contact with them. Such contacts are an integral part of many religions. The Hopi Indians for example, believe they were guided northwards from Central America by the "Kachina people," who ride about in luminous objects. The Bible not only devotes several lines to Ezekiel's famous "wheel," but also describes several other UFO sightings and encounters with UFO occupants (ufonauts) as well. Swarms of strange lights are supposed to have appeared in the sky the night Joseph Smith unearthed the metal plates containing the text of *The Book of Mormon.*

Modern ufology began when William Denton of Massachusetts received visitors from Venus in the 1860s. His contacts were largely telepathic or astral-projection experiences, but his books sold well, and he was in great demand as a lecturer.

In the 1890s, a girl named Helene Smith entertained Martians in Geneva, Switzerland, and had so many psychic adventures that she became the subject of an extensive study by Theodore Fluornoy, one of the great parapsychologists of the day.

Denizens of other planets frequently materialized at séances during the spiritualism craze of the 1800s and the 1920s. Then, beginning in 1946, a West Coast parapsychologist, Dr. Meade Layne, made "contact" with the space people through a spirit medium. By 1950, he had accumulated many hours of recorded conversations with entities who described life on other worlds, and fully explained the UFO mystery to Layne's satisfaction. In essence, they merely repeated the same data that had been coming through mediums for thousands of years — that another dimension existed, and that UFOs were not coming from some other planet, but were based in another space-time continuum. Dr. Layne's privately published pamphlet, *Flying Discs: The Ether Ship Mystery and Its Solution* (1950) was not greeted with enthusiasm by the UFO believers, but it was more literate and, in many ways, more rational than some of the material being generated by the ETH advocates.

Between 1947 and 1950, there were vague rumors of UFO landings and contacts. Dr. Jacques Vallee later catalogued 923 landings between the years 1868 and 1968. For some indefinable reason, even the hardiest UFO believers could not accept the plausibility of UFO *landings.* They energetically accepted the existence of flying saucers as tangible space machines, but they rejected landings and alleged contacts off-handedly, bitterly attacking those people who claimed contact.

Contactees could usually not find a hearing, so many of them resorted to paying for the cost of their publications themselves. Scores of pamphlets and books were flooding the narrow, limited hardcore UFO market by 1956, such as William Ferguson's *A Message from Outer Space*, based upon his conversations with an angel named Khauga; *Men in the Flying Saucers Identified* by W.V. Grant (who believed anti-Christ demons were at the controls); *Roundtrip to Hell in a Flying Saucer* by Cecil Michael, who in 1952, reportedly visited the planet Hell in his astral body aboard a flying saucer; and *The Saucers Speak* by George Hunt Williamson. Williamson was a self-styled anthropologist whose *Secret Places of the Lion* (1959) became a perennial favorite with the hardcore. He documented instances of early extraterrestrial visitations with ancient civilizations and American Indians. In the early 1960s, he went off on an expedition to South America and disappeared, permanently and enigmatically.

The 1955-56 period finally brought some of the contactees into the limelight. British contactee Cedric Allingham's *Flying Saucers from Mars*, a description of his encounters with Martians, sold well in a trade book both in England and the U.S. Daniel Fry's *The White Sands Incident* told how he was taken for a ride in a saucer that landed near White Sands Proving Grounds, New Mexico on July 4th, 1950.

But a charismatic Californian named George Adamski became the best-known and most controversial of this new breed. Adamski claimed repeated contacts with UFOs and Venusians near Mount Palomar. He produced several spectacular UFO photos as proof of his adventures, and on a number of occasions other people were allegedly present when he chatted with Venusians. One of these witnesses was George Hunt Williamson. Adamski's *Inside the Spaceships* (1955) enjoyed modest sales for years, inciting the wrath of the "scientific ufologists" with its preposterous account of a ride to the moon (where Adamski noted rivers and trees).

Another early moon traveler was a sign painter named Howard Menger. He claimed flying saucers landed regularly on his farm near High Bridge, New Jersey, in 1955-57. He brought back some rocks that he called "moon potatoes." His appearances on the Long John Nebel radio program in New York turned him into a celebrity. His book *From Outer Space to You* (1959) repeated the sophomoric philosophy of the supernatural entities, and was followed by a phonograph record of "outer space music" picked out by Menger on a piano.

Within a few short years, we heard about scores of planets. According to the contactees, we were not only being visited by Martians and Venusians, but also by the citizens of Zomdic, Korendor, Aenstria, Clarion, and countless other places unknown to us. Keeping track of these visitors was akin to the medieval attempts to catalog all the known angels and demons.

The emergence of the contactees produced a backlash of ridicule that nearly sank the already floundering ship of ufology. Professional writers and major publishers avoided flying saucers between 1956 and 1965, with only a few notable exceptions. Major Keyhoe's *Flying Saucers: Top Secret* (1960) detailed NICAP's futile battle to win a congressional investigation into Air Force censorship and secrecy. Colonel Lawrence J. Tacker, a former USAF public information officer assigned to Project Blue Book, countered with *Flying Saucers and the U.S. Air Force* (1960), another explanation of the Air Force's negative position. Dr. Menzel, with a co-author named Lyle G. Boyd, tried again in *The World of Flying Saucers* (1963).

The subject was doggedly kept alive by *Fate*, Frank Edwards, and by Ray Palmer's *Flying Saucers* magazine, which had fitful newsstand distribution. The UFO believers splintered into a dozen warring factions. Some swung to Dr. Layne's interdimensional theory, some accepted Palmer's Hollow Earth. Others gathered around the various contactees. Lesser cults overlapped into the psychic field. Major Keyhoe became the center of a personality cult that was altogether as fanatical as the group that followed Adamski.

Considering the general tone and content of the UFO literature – now almost totally paranoid and insane – it was not surprising that the flying saucer cultist population diminished to fewer than 3,000 people during the long lull. Gray Barker and Ray Palmer continued to publish contactee pamphlets and books throughout the period, rarely selling more than 2,000 copies of any single title. But two important, privately printed UFO books did finally appear. Mrs. Coral E. Lorenzen of APRO published *The Great Flying Saucer Hoax* (1962), advocating the ETH and stressing the seeming hostility of the UFOs. And Richard Hall, assistant director of NICAP, compiled 746 UFO sightings in *The UFO Evidence* (1964), the first real attempt by a hobbyist to isolate and analyze the many fascinating aspects of the subject. However, the book was poorly organized, unabashedly biased and non-objective, and the enormous quantity of material was not indexed.

Flying saucer sightings returned to the headlines in March 1966, although a huge flap had been building steadily since 1964. Author John Fuller visited Exeter, NH in 1965 to investigate a series of sightings there for *Look* magazine. The result was *Incident at Exeter* (1966), a rational look at the subject, even though the prevalent anti-Air Force paranoia was reflected in the work. It enjoyed healthy sales, but was overshadowed by Frank Edwards' *Flying Saucers: Serious Business*, which appeared about the same time.

Six weeks after Edwards sat down at his typewriter, his book was on the shelves, riding the peak of the 1966 wave. It sold over 50,000 copies in hardcover, and created a stampede among publishers, even though it was filled with errors of fact. Dated UFO books from the 1950s were hastily reissued, and publishers competed to buy the previously obscure contactee books and crank pamphlets. Hack writers waded through Fort, Ruppelt, NICAP's *The UFO Evidence*, and *Project Blue Book Report 14*, rewriting them into paperback potboilers that argued for the extraterrestrial hypothesis and condemned the Air Force.

Thirty flying saucer titles were listed by *Paperbound Books in Print* in 1967. Typically, the UFO believers were taken by surprise by this sudden boom, and had very little in the way of substantial data to offer the professional writers, newsmen, and television producers suddenly pounding on their doors. The only available "experts" seemed to be Dr. Menzel and Donald Keyhoe.

Unfortunately, the few worthwhile books were buried in the sea of trash. Jacques Vallee's *Anatomy of a Phenomenon* had quietly appeared in 1965, ahead of its time. It analyzed UFO sightings scientifically and statistically. Long-time Fortean Vincent Gaddis contributed *Mysterious Lights and Fires* (1967), which offered a sensible synthesis of UFO and electromagnetic phenomena. English author John F. Michell's *The Flying Saucer Vision* dealt effectively with UFOs as a modern myth, examining its origins and speculating on its ultimate influence. Ivan T. Sanderson, an authority on animals, attempted to define the complex situation and suggest guidelines for future research in *Uninvited Visitors* (1967).

In Iowa, a young college teacher named Eugene Olson began to supplement his income by grinding out paperbacks of cases borrowed from the UFO magazines. But he was soon investigating new cases on his own, and was emerging as an important writer in the UFO and occult fields, under the name "Brad Steiger." A copy of the legendary *Varo Edition* fell into his hands, and he published excerpts in *New UFO Breakthrough* (1968).

An editor for *Aviation Week & Space Technology*, Philip J. Klass, joined the shrinking ranks of UFO critics with *UFOs: Identified* (1968). He theorized that most UFOs were "natural plasmas of ionized air," a concept that had been considered by the USAF, in 1948, and rejected as untenable.

Public outcry over the great wave of 1966 led the USAF to grant Colorado University $500,000 to set up an investigative project headed by Dr. Edward U. Condon. Personality conflicts caused the whole project to collapse inwardly early in 1968. The final report of the group was issued in late 1969, stressing an anti-ETH conclusion. It was hastily assembled by people who had not worked on the original project, and consisted largely of padding. Bantam Books optimistically printed 200,000 copies of the 900-page book, but succeeded in selling only a small fraction of the total. The U.S. Air Force closed down Project Blue Book in December 1969, and the flying saucer era seemed to be at an end.

While American ufologists were divided, busily investigating the USAF and each other throughout the 1950s, ufology was making progress in other parts of the world. An early editor of *Flying Saucer Review*, Brinsley Le Poer Trench, examined the historical material in depth and subsequently produced a series of important books on the early myths, including *The Sky People* (1960), *Men Among Mankind* (1963) and, most recently, *The Eternal Subject* (1973). In the latter work, he demonstrates how many of the effects and manifestations of the UFO phenomenon are similar to, or identical to, the well-known manifestations of psychic phenomena.

France's Aime' Michel, a professional writer and an authority on psychic phenomena, studied the French sightings and landings of 1952-54, and discovered the routes of the objects followed straight lines for great distances. He termed the phenomenon "Orthoteny," and published *Flying Saucers and the Straight-Line Mystery* (1956), an important research work.

England's John Michell has been making a study of leys, a very ancient grid of trails or tracks that join Great Britain's megalithic monuments. In the course of his research, he found that the ancient Chinese also established such grids, supposedly along the paths followed by strange aerial objects in ancient times. His findings were recently published under the misleading title *The View Over Atlantis* (1969).

Even the Loch Ness monster is getting into the act. British author F.W. Holiday, an expert on Nessie, has carefully researched the dragon legends of England and re-examined the mysterious archaeological structures of Great Britain, in an attempt to reconcile reality with myth. He notes that discs were almost always included in the many dragon carvings of the British Isles. In his book *The Dragon and the Disc* (1973), he states: "Man's most ancient religion, that of the dragon and the disc, was therefore not based primarily on mystical utterances and nonsensical dogmas cooked up by bunches of priests for their own political ends, but on actual observable phenomena."

Captain Ivar Mackay, a British parapsychologist and former chairman of the British UFO Research Association, has compiled dozens of effects and manifestations that occur in psychic phenomena, and which are also common in flying saucer reports. These include conjunctivitis, lacunar amnesia, failure of mechanical and electrical apparatus, apportation, teleportation, levitation telepathy, materializations, etc. Apparently all of these phenomena have a common cause, regardless of the frame of reference in which they occur.

In *Passport to Magonia* (1969), Dr. Jacques Vallee reviewed the fairy lore of Europe and compared the stories with modern UFO reports. "Is it reasonable," he asks, "to draw a parallel between religious apparitions, the fairy faith, the reports of dwarflike beings with supernatural powers, the airship tales in the United States in the last century, and the present stories of UFO landings? I would strongly agree that it is for one simple reason: the mechanisms that have generated these various beliefs are identical.

The latest books published in the United States are actually dealing with material explored by the Europeans fifteen years ago. Raymond W. Drake, an Englishman, and Paul Misraki of France, suggested, along with Trench, that ancient religious and occult events had been influenced by the UFO phenomenon in some way. But this concept did not again gain popular currency in the U.S. until 1970, when the spectacularly successful *Chariots of the Gods*, by a Swiss amateur archaeologist, Erich Von Daniken, was published. It has spawned a number of imitations, such as Eric Norman's *God's and Devils from Outer Space* (1973). Eccentric books that only a few years ago would have been restricted to mimeographed pamphlets, with very limited distribution, are suddenly on newsstands (e.g., *God Drives a Flying Saucer* by R.L. Dione).

Arthur C. Clarke's 1953 theology is slowly becoming a part of the American UFO scene.

While NICAP and the American "scientific ufologists" were battling the contactees in their struggle to attain responsibility and a congressional investigation, European investigators were closely observing the "contact" situation. Charles Bowen and Gordon Creighton of *Flying Saucer Review* realized, like Dr. Vallee, that many of the manifestations were demonological rather than interplanetary. When, for example, Albert K. Bender finally published his story in *Flying Saucers and the Three Men* (1960), he described the same kinds of problems often experienced by practitioners of witchcraft and occultism. His "government agents" were phantasms, but few American ufologists had the background to recognize the symptoms. They denounced him as a liar trying to make a buck with an outrageous story.

Contactees remained in disgrace in the U.S. until 1966, when John Fuller published the story of Betty and Barney Hill, a couple who had suffered lacunar amnesia while on a trip in 1961. Later, when hypnotized by a psychiatrist, they recalled being taken aboard a UFO and being examined medically by a group of little men. A condensed version of the story was printed in *Look* and given wide circulation, encouraging many "silent" contactees to come forward with their own stories.

The major contribution in solving the contactee phenomenon did not come from professional scientists, psychologists, or psychiatrists, however, Author Brad Steiger spent several years investigating people who had experienced "revelation" through conversations with angels, demons, and "spacemen." He found that the messages conveyed by these entities were always the same, no matter what frame of reference was being used. While Vallee could only speculate on this mechanism, Steiger took the first step towards proving it in *Revelation: The Divine Fire* (1973), which, despite its title, is probably the most important book to come out of the entire American flying saucer scene. Needless to say, the hardcore American ET believers have ignored Vallee, Steiger, Michell, Creighton, et al.

Ufology has been a propaganda movement rather than a scientific movement. The ufologists began stumping for a myth in the late 1940s, before the sighting evidence was empirical. Additional myths were gradually developed and absorbed into the main premise (the ETH), while the mounting correlations between UFO and psychic phenomena were ignored or even suppressed by the ET believers – not by the USAF or CIA.

The flying saucer myth did have a number of indirect effects on American science and culture, however. All of the talk about extraterrestrial life not only influenced Hollywood, but led a number of scientists to reconsider the long-held scientific view that life could not – and did not – exist elsewhere in the universe. Radio astronomy was growing in importance, and when the Soviet Sputnik went into orbit in 1957, a cultural shock resulted.

The officially stated purpose of the U.S. manned space program was the search for life beyond earth. Millions were funneled to scientists and institutions for a strange new pursuit called "exobiology" – the study of extraterrestrial life. Without samples of any kind, or even without the slightest proof that planets existed in other star systems, this was a very difficult study, indeed. But a massive scientific literature on exobiology quickly appeared. To the UFO believers' disgust, this literature carefully avoided any substantive discussion of flying saucers. Some of the exobiologists, like Dr. Carl Sagan, did not hesitate, however, to exploit the UFO mythology when it served their purposes. Sagan was active as an advisor to Project Blue Book, and a participant in the numerous flying saucer symposiums of the late 1960s.

That the UFO propagandists had done their job well was proven by a 1966 Gallup poll, which found that 48% of those polled believed flying saucers were real. And a poll conducted for the Colorado project found that 69% believed the government was suppressing UFO information. A whopping 70% thought that intelligent life could – or does – exist elsewhere in the universe.

On another level, several generations of teenagers had grown up believing in UFOs, the ETH, and governmental conspiracy. If the government could lie about flying saucers, then it could lie about anything. The UFO propagandists of the 1950s undoubtedly contributed to the growing credibility gap between the government and the people. The impressionable teenagers carried into adulthood the distorted attitudes of the UFO movement. Dr. Condon commented strongly on this: "We feel that children are educationally harmed by absorbing unsound and erroneous material as if it were scientifically well-founded. Such study is harmful not merely because of the erroneous nature of the material itself, but also because such study retards the development of a critical faculty with regard to scientific evidence, which to some degree ought to be part of the education of every American."

Much of the UFO literature, particularly the contactee literature, is pure propaganda of the type long circulated by the entities described by RAF Air Marshal Sir Victor Goddard as "illusion-prone spirits" who framed theses "to propagate some special phantasm to indulge an inveterate and continuing technological urge toward materialistic progress."

The great UFO wave of the 1960s had a visible effect on the youth subculture. The use of hallucinatory drugs often produced visions remarkably similar to the visions of the contactees. The recognizable propaganda of those "illusion-prone spirits" appeared in the lyrics of popular songs, in endless articles and poems in "underground" newspapers, and even in comic books.

The "Woodstock Nation" went on a cosmic trip that dwarfed the adventures of Adamski and Menger. During the peak years, UFO lecturers were in great demand on college campuses, often extracting large fees to spread the gospel of the space people. James Moseley, publisher of *Saucer News* (now defunct); Dr. J. Allen Hynek, the skeptic who turned believer in 1966; Stanton Friedman, nuclear engineer turned full-time UFO lecturer; and several others were active on the college circuit by the end of the 1960s.

Dr. James McDonald, a meteorologist and ET enthusiast, also lectured widely before groups of scientists and journalists until his death by suicide in 1971.

Major Keyhoe is now retired, but both NICAP and APRO continue to publish newsletters for their steadily diminishing memberships. The Midwest UFO Network (MUFON) now dominates the American scene after defecting from APRO and regrouping around Dr. Hynek, who is becoming the center of a new personality cult. His book, *The UFO Experience* (1972), was a disappointing rehash of classic cases, and a bitter attack on the ill-fated Colorado University project.

The 25-year search for tangible physical evidence of the ETH continues. MUFON's latest project (in 1973) is the exhumation of a 75-year-old grave in Aurora, Texas which, according to an old and questionable newspaper clipping, allegedly contains the body of a little man killed when his flying saucer crashed into a windmill.

American ufology has always been about ten years behind European research. Dr. Hynek frequently alludes to his "Invisible College" of American scientists working on the problem, but they have produced no studies or literature to date. Instead the involvement of Hynek, McDonald, Condon, and others stimulated feuds and controversies far surpassing the teacup tempests of the UFO enthusiasts in earlier years. However, a number of folklorists, psychologists, and social scientists have entered the field quietly and independently, and may eventually produce a new body of literature free of nonsense.

The shift from causes and beliefs to history, mythology, philosophy, and theology is already apparent in the post-1969 literature, but these subjects lack popular appeal, and are beyond the intellectual range of the average UFO cultists. In any case, the ranks of the cultists are rapidly thinning. Many have become discouraged or disenchanted, because a quarter-century of sightings has produced no significant results. Others have moved on to psychic and religious organizations – the search for self and the nature of reality. Some have simply grown up.

We have set the course for a new ufology devoted to understanding the mechanisms of belief, rather than perpetuating the beliefs generated by those mechanisms. But this could be another futile path, looping back to the ancient philosophical questions, trying to define or redefine reality and discern man's true purpose.

The Mothman Statue (left) in Point Pleasant, West Virginia bears a similarity to the image of Mothman painted by Frank Frazetta, which adorned the cover of Keel's Mothman Prophecies reprint in the 1990s (see page 205). The Japanese "Mothman," the Garuda "Karasu Tengu" (right), sports more birdlike wings and facial characteristics. If seen at night with glowing eyes, it would be easy for witnesses to miss details of the creature's neck, nose, or mouth.

CHAPTER 14

On April 13, 1897, Mr. and Mrs. George Parks were walking across a field outside Pennfield, Michigan when a brightly illuminated object, emitting a low humming sound, suddenly appeared at an altitude of about 100 feet. As the object hurtled past the astonished couple, something dropped from it and buried itself in the ground nearby. Mr. Parks dug the thing up and found that it was "a large wheel made of aluminum, about three feet in diameter, and shaped like a turbine." According to *The Detroit Evening News* for April 15, 1897, the strange wheel was publicly displayed by Mr. Parks as a "memento" of the "airship," which was seen all over the United States that year.

Seventy-one years later, on the afternoon of January 19, 1968, a red-hot disc plunged from the sky in Corona, NY and implanted itself in a basement door. When it cooled, the object – about three feet in diameter – was found to be made of aluminum. Officials of the Federal Aeronautics Administration (FAA) retrieved the object and said that apparently it was the "brake disc from a passing airplane." When I made inquiries and pointed out that if a brake disc has fallen, then the wheel itself had to fall and the plane certainly would have had a difficult, if not totally disastrous, landing, the FAA officials made no further comment. Since the disc was red-hot and could not be touched for several minutes, it must have fallen from a considerable height, or it must have been heated before it dropped.

Actually, metal discs have been falling from the sky since time immemorial. All kinds of assorted debris and metallic garbage have been spewed from unidentified flying objects, often before scores or even hundreds of witnesses. Nearly all of this debris has been proven to consist of mundane earthly materials such as aluminum, chromium, and magnesium. Enthusiastic researchers all over the world have collected and analyzed such substances in the hope that they would furnish physical evidence of the extraterrestrial origin of "flying saucers." When such tests have verified the rather ordinary composition of these substances, the UFO researchers seem either to have played down the results, or suppressed them altogether.

The popular theory is that the UFOs are the product of an "advanced technology" from outer space. Therefore, the objects must be composed of unknown and unidentifiable materials. While there have been occasional rumors of finds of unidentifiable metals, these remain – with a few exceptions – mere rumors. All of the substances that have been collected and actually analyzed have been disappointingly ordinary.

The well-known author and researcher Ivan T. Sanderson has collected quantities of such materials over the years – most of it charred bits of metal, common "slag" similar to the routine waste products of many industrial processes, and other mundane fragments. Mr. Sanderson also has uncovered extensive documentation detailing all manner of strange materials that have fallen throughout history. This list includes such objects as stone pillars, stone and metal wheels, showers of molten metal, and of course the frogs, fish, blood, etc., that so intrigued the late Charles Fort.

In 1824 "little symmetric objects of metal" plummeted from the sky near Orenburg, Russia, according to Dr. Nandor Fodor's *Haunted People*. A few months later, more fell in the very same area. Small metal objects have been raining periodically in specific regions for centuries. Sanderson has in his collection some tiny projectiles that have, at various times and with some frequency, hurtled to Earth in a single field in Pennsylvania. They appear to be small metallic cylinders, and their purpose or function is a mystery.

Every UFO-phile is familiar with the controversial "Maury Island Hoax" of 1947, when a group of donut-shaped objects allegedly belched a vast quantity of "slag" onto a boat in Puget Sound. The fact that analysis of this material showed it to be composed of calcium, aluminum, silicon, iron, zinc, and other earthly elements contributed to the generally accepted conclusion that the whole affair was a hoax. However, this kind of "slag" has been coming from our skies for at least a century, and no one ever has figured out where it comes from.

Slag rained on Darmstadt, Germany, on June 7, 1846. Charles Fort lists many inexplicable "slag falls" from the 19th century. Meteorites always are a readily identifiable metal or stone, so we can rule out a natural cause for the more sophisticated substances. We can only conclude that somebody or something is dumping garbage on us quite deliberately.

When a wildly gyrating metal disc appeared over the city of Campinas, Brazil, on December 14, 1954, hundreds of witnesses reported that it dribbled a stream of "silvery liquid" into the streets. Government scientists collected some of this stuff, and Dr. Risvaldo Maffei later announced that it was almost pure tin. The ET buffs nudged each other knowingly when they heard this news. Obviously it was another "government whitewash," they said, even though the Brazilian government in those days maintained an honest public position towards the UFO phenomenon. Tin hardly supports the extraterrestrial thesis; therefore, in the minds of the "true believers," the case could not be taken seriously.

Silicon substances frequently have been found at alleged UFO landing sites. Sometimes it is mixed with aluminum or other materials to form an odd purplish liquid. Such liquids have been found at landing sites in New York State (Newark Valley, 1964; Cherry Creek, 1965), in Erie, Pennsylvania in 1966, and in dozens of other places. The egg-shaped object that police officer Lonnie Zamora said landed outside Socorro, New Mexico, on April 24, 1964, left behind a metallic material on some rocks. It proved to be silicon (although the Air Force continues to call it "silica," which is common sand). This received little mention in UFO publications. After all, everybody knows that silicon is a simple plastic material that no self-respecting "advanced technology from outer space" would bother with.

On December 2, 1967, patrolman Herbert Schirmer of Ashland, Nebraska, reportedly encountered a grounded UFO on a deserted road a half-mile outside that city. Investigators later found a small, dime-shaped piece of metal at the spot where Officer Schirmer had seen the object. Analysis proved it was made of silicon and iron.

Mysterious exploding UFOs are a historical fact. At 5 a.m. on the morning of June 12, 1790, a glowing sphere whistled out of the sky and settled on a hilltop near Alencon, France. As the amazed villagers gathered, a door of the object opened, and a man in tight-fitting clothes stepped out. He mumbled something incomprehensible and ran into some nearby woods. A few minutes later, the object silently exploded, leaving nothing but a few granules of metallic dust. A search failed to locate the "man."

In April 1960, a whistling orange object reportedly landed outside of the village of Baira, Mozambique, in East Africa. The hundreds of witnesses claimed that a group of "tiny men" sprang from the thing and ran into the forest just as the object exploded.

There were several reports of exploding UFOs over Sweden during the Scandinavian "flap" of 1946. Charles Fort also recounts several exploding UFO cases from the 1800s.

More recently, researcher Michael Campione investigated an interesting sighting near Lions Lake, New Jersey, on August 18, 1966. The witnesses claimed they watched a UFO spray a stream of red-hot liquid toward the ground. They picked up a piece of this substance while it was still flaming.

It was as light as a feather, Mr. Campione reports, and the witnesses felt no heat whatever from the flames. When the substance cooled, it "became a solid, yet discolored, honey-combed, aluminum-like casting" with a strong sulfuric smell. Gradually, it dwindled until it was no larger than a pea. It was never analyzed. (Chemical and spectrographic analysis can cost thousands of dollars, depending on the thoroughness of the tests.)

So, we seem to be dealing with two kinds of substances: one very ordinary, the other highly unstable.

Witnesses in Texas, Md., claim to have watched a shiny disc explode in the air in June 1965. Pieces of it were recovered and examined at the Goddard Space Flight Center on behalf of NICAP. It proved to be ordinary ferrochromium.

Another exploding UFO, this one at Ubatuba, Brazil, in 1957, left behind particles that later were analyzed by APRO and turned out to be magnesium of unusually high purity.

Great quantities of tiny strips of aluminum, with traces of magnesium and silicon, now are being found all over the world. Thousands of people in Chosi City, Japan, reported seeing a circular flying object eject a flood of these strips above their city on September 7, 1956. Piles of it have been found in West Virginia, Michigan, and many other places during UFO "flaps." It frequently is found laid out in neatly ordered patterns on the ground where witnesses have seen UFOs hovering. Quantities of it turned up in a burning field outside Gastonia, NC in 1966, simultaneously with low-level UFO sightings.

I spent a lot of time investigating these cases in 1967. These tiny strips are almost identical to the "chaff" dispensed by high-flying planes to jam radar. However, the "outer space grass," as it is commonly called, is about 99 percent aluminum, while Air Force "chaff" is aluminum-coated fiberglass. "Outerspace grass" is found in clumps or patterns. Air Force "chaff" is specially made so that it won't stick together, and it is packaged loosely and fired through special chutes designed to disperse it over a very large area.

Mysterious hollow metal spheres also have been dropping out of the skies over our planet. Three such spheres were found on the Australian desert in 1963. They were about 14 inches in diameter and had a shiny polished surface. Australian scientists were baffled.

On April 30, 1963, Mr. Allen Fairhall, the Minister of Supply, appeared before the Australian House of Representatives and announced that all effort to open the spheres had failed. The objects were reportedly turned over to the United States Air Force and that was the end of them.

Other metal spheres have dropped from the sky near Monterrey, Mexico (Feb. 7, 1967) and Conway, Arkansas (Nov. 1967). The Mexican ball was identified as titanium, the one in Arkansas as stainless steel. Others have been found in Argentina and Africa. They are not parts of rockets or space satellites, according to the authorities who have examined them. It would not be possible for a piece of a rocket to go through reentry and land intact – as these things have done. In July 1968, similar spheres were found in Nepal.

During my UFO-investigating wanderings of the past two years, I frequently have been shown slag, "outer space grass," and chunks of metal resembling aluminum that have been collected by witnesses at UFO sites. When you review the clippings and UFO literature of the past two decades, you find that literally thousands of these artifacts have been dumped by our mysterious visitors. But since none of these substances offers "proof" of the extraterrestrial thesis, most UFO researchers and their organizations betray an appalling tendency to ignore them.

If all of these "falls" had been methodically collected and their origins documented, we would now have an impressive body of physical evidence that "flying saucers" do exist. The UFO researchers seem to deliberately overlook the material that could supply them with the most important proof of all: proof that unidentified flying objects are physical objects either constructed of, or utilizing, *known* alloys and substances: tin from Brazil, silicon from New York, Nebraska, and New Mexico, and aluminum from Japan, Michigan and West Virginia.

Impressive correlations can be drawn from these incidents. The substances from scattered points can be collected, compared, weighed in the hand, and slammed down in front of skeptical congressmen. We know that there *are* "flying saucers" from the evidence of their garbage!

Even Charles Fort noted from his study of the 19th century "falls" that these things uncannily happened repeatedly in the same areas, year after year. This holds true in many modern cases. The UFOs seem to return time and again to dump their garbage in favored spots. Pennfield, Michigan lies in the "UFO belt" that stretches from Ann Arbor in the east to Benton Harbor in the western part of the state. The UFO activity in West Virginia is historic, and has been almost continuous since 1966.

Perhaps the Maury Island affair wasn't a hoax after all. Perhaps it was just the first time that anybody really caught the UFOs in the process of dumping their garbage. And maybe "they" didn't want us to know, and *that* might explain all of the peculiar machinations that took place when Kenneth Arnold investigated the case.

The documentation is overwhelming. Our skies are filled with junk – and always have been – since Roman times. All of this debris has to originate somewhere.

Perhaps somewhere on this planet there is a hidden industrial complex, and the waste products from that complex have to be hauled off and dumped somewhere. So, it is being dumped right in the ufologists' backyard, but they have been too busy poring over their astronomy books to notice. When a reliable witness hands them a piece of silicon or aluminum, they cry "hoax," throw the scrap of metal into the wastebasket, and happily announce that they have exposed another fiendish attempt to discredit the "flying saucers." But who really has been fooling whom?

In 2014, a "smoke ring UFO" (top) was photographed in England, reopening debate about such "mysterious" rings. In 1968, a similar ring was photographed over Fort Belvoir, Virginia (bottom). While they appear unearthly, their explanation is most definitely "natural," for they are indeed smoke rings (not ETs). But their mechanism is of interest, because if smoke can coalesce in this fashion, think of the "living" saucer-shapes that may form, naturally, from the intermingling of magnetism, cosmic rays, photons, and other high-energy sources, both synthetic and natural.

CHAPTER 15

On Wednesday, October 5, 1960, a formation of unidentified flying objects was picked up on the sophisticated computerized radar screens of an early warning station at Thule, Greenland. Its exact course was quickly charted. It appeared to be heading toward North America from the direction of the Soviet Union. Within minutes, the red telephones at Strategic Air Command headquarters in Omaha, Nebraska, were jangling, and the well-trained crews of SAC were galloping to the their planes at airfields all over the world. Atomic-bomb-laden B-52s already in the air were circling tensely, their crews waiting for the final signal to head for predetermined targets deep within the Soviet Union.

SAC headquarters broadcast an anxious signal to Thule for further confirmation. There was no answer. Generals chewed on their cigars nervously. Had Thule already been hit?

Suddenly, the mysterious blips on the radar screens changed course and disappeared. Later it was learned that "an iceberg had cut the submarine cable" connecting Thule to the United States. It was a very odd coincidence that the "iceberg" chose that precise time to strike. But the mystery of unidentified flying objects is filled with remarkable and seemingly unrelated coincidences.

World War III did not start that day. But it might have. Weeks later, when news of the enigmatic radar signals leaked out, three Labor Party members of the British House of Commons, Mr. Emrys-Hughes, Mrs. Hart, and Mr. Swingler, stood up and demanded an explanation. The U.S. Air Force replied that the radar signals had actually bounced off the moon and had been misinterpreted. The story appeared in *The Guardian*, a leading newspaper in Manchester, England, on November 30, and a week later it was buried on page 71 of *The New York Times*.

Could modern military radar really convert the moon into a formation of flying saucers? I have excellent reasons for doubting it. In May, 1967, I toured a secret radar installation in New Jersey at the Air Force's own invitation, and I was extremely impressed by the complexity and efficiency of the equipment there. By pressing a few buttons, the radar operators can not only instantly detect every aircraft within range, but giant computers also provide complete and instant information on the speed, altitude, direction, and ETA (estimated time of arrival) of each plane. Even the plane's flight number appears on the radar screen! Unknown objects can be immediately picked out in the maze of air traffic, and a routine procedure is followed to identify them quickly. If these procedures fail, jet fighters are scrambled to take a look. It is improbable, if not impossible altogether, for the moon or any other distant celestial object to fool this elaborate system.

There have been frequent radar sightings of UFOs for the past twenty years, not only on military radar, but also on the sets of weather bureaus and airports. Often in these cases, ground witnesses have also reported seeing the objects visually. When the Federal Aviation Agency tower at the Greensboro-High Point Airport in Greensboro, North Carolina picked up an unidentified flying object early on the morning of July 27, 1966, several police officers in the High Point-Randolph County area also reported seeing unidentifiable objects buzzing the vicinity. They said the objects appeared to be at an altitude of 500 feet. They described them as being round, brilliant red-green, and appeared to be emitting flashes of light.

The government's official position toward flying saucers has been totally negative since 1953, although a great deal of attention has been paid to the subject behind the scenes. Obviously, any phenomenon that could accidentally trigger World War III has to be taken seriously.

An extensive flying saucer "flap" broke in March 1966. The Secretary of Defense, Robert S. McNamara, had been well briefed by the Air Force before the subject was interjected into a hearing of the House Foreign Affairs Committee on March 30, 1966. Representative Cornelius E. Gallagher of New Jersey, a state where scores of UFO sightings had been reported that month, asked Secretary McNamara if he thought there was "anything at all" to the flying saucer mystery.

"I think not," McNamara replied, "I have talked to the Secretary of the Air Force and the Air Force Director of Research and Engineering, and neither of them places any credence in the reports we have received to date."

When I first decided to look into these matters, in March 1966, I subscribed to several newspaper-clipping services, and I was stunned by the results. I often received as many as 150 clippings for a single day! My immediate reaction, of course, was one of disbelief. I thought that all of the newspapers in the country had thrown objectivity out the window and were participating in some kind of gigantic put-on. It seemed impossible that so many unidentified things were flying around our sacred skies without being seriously noticed by both the military and the scientific community.

It became apparent that the only way to properly investigate this situation was to travel to the various flap areas personally and interview the witnesses in depth, applying the standard journalistic techniques that I had learned from being a reporter and writer for two long decades. So, in the spring of 1966, I began a long series of treks that eventually took me through twenty states, where I interviewed thousands of people, hundreds of them in depth.

As I traveled, I naturally visited local newspapers and spent time with the editors and reporters who had been handling the UFO reports in their area. They were all competent newsmen, many with years of experience behind them. When I met the witnesses whose stories they had written and published, I realized what a skillful and objective job they had done. So I developed a new respect for the clippings that were pouring into my mailbox. Most newspaper stories were reliable sources for basic information.

The witnesses, I concluded, have been giving honest descriptions of what they have seen, and their local newspapers have been giving objective accounts of what they reported.

The nature and the meaning of what they saw is another matter. And the answer could not be found in newspaper clippings. However, it was possible that those clippings could supply some broad data about the overall phenomenon. None of the UFO organizations had made any effort at all to extract such data. The U.S. Air Force had tried in the early 1950s, but had supposedly given up in despair. So, my next job was to translate the seemingly random clippings and reports of investigated cases into some form of statistical information.

More than 10,000 clippings and reports reached me in 1966 (in contrast with the 1,060 reports allegedly received by the Air Force during that same period). I had checked out many of these cases personally, and had become convinced of their validity.

Throughout 1967, I devoted my spare time to sorting this great mass of material, categorizing it, and boiling it down into valid statistical form. It was an enormous job, and I had to do it alone. I threw out most of the "lights in the sky" types of reports and concentrated on the Type I cases (sightings of low-level objects observed and reported by reliable witnesses). I obtained astronomical data on meteors, etc., for the year, and from the National Aeronautics and Space Administration, I obtained information on all of the year's rocket launches. By checking the UFO reports against this data, I was able to sift out the possible or probable misinterpretations that were bound to occur.

My first interest was to uncover whatever patterns or cycles might exist in the flap dates. I ended up with two files: one containing the Type I sightings (730 in all, or 7.3 percent of the total); and the other, the best of the Type II sightings (high-altitude objects performing in a controlled manner and distinct from normal aircraft and natural phenomena).

There were 2,600 reports in the second group. Thus I was working 33.3 percent of the total. (Radio and television surveys work on a far smaller sampling, claiming that a survey of 1,500 television viewers represents the viewing habits of the whole country.)

As soon as I had organized the sightings by dates, the first significant pattern became apparent. This was that sightings tended to collect around specific days of the week. Wednesday had the greatest number of sightings, and these were usually reported between the hours of 8 to 11 p.m. Of the sampling used, half of one percent were not dated.

If the UFO phenomenon had a purely psychological basis, then there should be more sightings on Saturday night when more people are out of doors, traveling to and from places of entertainment, etc. Instead, we find that the greatest number of sightings is reported on Wednesday, and that they slowly taper off through the rest of the week. The lowest number occurs on Tuesday. This inexplicable "Wednesday phenomenon" proved very valid, and was repeated throughout 1967 and 1968.

This does not mean that flying saucers are out in force every Wednesday night. But when there is a large flap, it nearly always takes place on Wednesday.

By carefully studying the geographical locations of the reported sightings during these flaps, we come upon another puzzling factor. The reports seemed to cluster within the boundaries of specific states. For example, during the flap of August 16, there were hundreds of sightings in Arkansas. These seemed to be concentrated into two belts that ran the length of the state from north to south. Yet we did not receive a single report from the neighboring states of Oklahoma, Mississippi, Tennessee, or Louisiana that night. Minnesota and Wisconsin, both far to the north of Arkansas, participated in that same flap. But the majority of the sightings seemed to be concentrated in Minnesota, and the UFOs seemed to confine their activities within the political boundaries of that state, too. Random sightings were also reported in distant New Jersey that night, and a few sightings were reported in South Dakota, right on the border with Minnesota.

Certainly if the UFOs were meteors or other natural phenomena, they would also be reported in adjoining states. Cross-state sightings are not as common as the skeptics would like to believe. In addition, the objects often linger for hours in one area. At Fort Smith, Arkansas, newsman John Garner took his KFSA microphone into the streets and broadcast a description of the strange multicolored lights that cavorted over the city for hours, as great crowds of people watched.

In my studies of several other flaps, I have discovered this same baffling geographical factor. If the UFOs are actually machines of some sort, their pilots seem to be familiar not only with our calendar, but also with the political boundaries of our states. They not only concentrate their activities on Wednesday nights, they also carefully explore our states methodically, from border to border.

Does this sound like the work of Martians or extraterrestrial strangers? Or does it sound like the work of someone who is using our maps and our calendars and may, therefore, know a great deal about us, even though we know little about "them?"

The skeptics try to explain away the published UFO stories by saying that mass hysteria builds up in flap areas, and that everyone starts "seeing things" once a few reports have been published. This is patently untrue. Nearly all the published reports of flap dates appear on the same day. There is no time lag, no building up of reports. Random individuals in widely separated areas all apparently see unidentifiable objects on the same night, and dutifully report their observations to their local police or newspapers, seldom realizing that anyone else has seen something that night. The next day, the newspapers in several areas, or even several different states, carry the reports. The flap has come and gone in a single day. Even then, people reading *The Arkansas Gazette* never learn that other papers in other states were filled with UFO accounts on that same day.

Most UFO buffs, who depend upon one another for clippings, are never aware of the full extent of the flap. With the exception of the North American Newspaper Alliance, no news service assigns men to keep track of these things and tabulate them. So while an occasional sighting may be sent out by a wire service, data on the overall situation is simply not available.

In March and April of 1967, the published UFO sightings outstripped all previous years. I received more than 2,000 clippings and reports in

March alone, and was able to investigate many them at firsthand. Yet the major news media ignored this flap, perhaps because none of the editors realized it was happening. Instead of the mythical censorship so lovingly expounded in some cultist circles, we have a lack of communication and a complete lack of research. The indifference so long fostered by the official government position has come to public frutiion.

The biggest flap in March of 1967 occurred on a Wednesday – March 8. Let's review briefly some of the sightings reported on that day:

1. Minnesota: "A strange object in the sky hovering above our homes here is giving some of us folks the shivers. It's so mysterious that we can almost work our imagination into seeing it drop green men from outer space into our backyard. This brilliant light moves with a gliding motion, sometimes just hovering, and sometimes moving with utmost speed. It appears each night at 8 o'clock and stays for about one hour before it fades away." (Floodwood, Minnesota, *Rural Forum*, March 9, 1967.)

2. Michigan: "Police said they received eight reports that a UFO hovered over Liggett School about 8 p.m. Wednesday." The Air Force and Grosse Point Woods police were investigating reports of a "burning orange oval" that had been photographed by two persons that week. "There was definitely something out there," said Major Raymond Nyls, Selfridge Air Force Base operations officer. "Too many people saw it." (Detroit, Michigan *Free Press*, March 11, 1967.)

3. Oklahoma: At 8:45 p.m. on Wednesday night, Mrs. Homer Smith stepped unto her back porch and "was astounded to see a twirling object with colored lights" going over Ninth Street and headed south. She called her ten-year-old son, and he saw it, too. She said the UFO was traveling and twirling so fast that it was difficult to count the lights on it, but they were colored, and what she believed to be the rear of the ship had what looked like "spits of fire coming from it." (Henryetta, Oklahoma, *Daily Free Lance*, March 19, 1967.)

4. Arkansas: Mrs. Ned Warnock of Brinkley, Arkansas, viewed an object from her kitchen window that night. "It was a reddish orange," she said. "And it changed to a silver-white color just before it took off. It was round and pretty large. It was real low, but gained height and speed as it took off. It was moving too fast for a star." She alerted her neighbors, Mr. And Mrs.

J.H. Folkerts, and they also saw the object. (Clarendon, Arkansas, *The Monroe County Sun*, March 16, 1967.)

5. Maryland: Two residents and a police officer observed an object that appeared circular, with "a shiny gold bottom." When it hovered, the top glowed red. It flew an oval-shaped path, going back and forth from Fort Meade to Laurel three times before taking off. (Laurel, Maryland, *Prince George's County News*, March 16, 1967.)

6. Montana: Mrs. Richard Haagland of Stevensville, Montana, reported to the Missoula County Sheriff's office that he had seen a circular flying object that "dropped three balls of fire before disappearing" at 8:20 p.m. Wednesday night. (Missoula, Montana, *Missoulian-Sentinel*, March 9, 1967.)

7. Montana: "Many people have seen unidentified flying objects in the Ekalaka, Lame Jones, and Willard areas. The report is that they seem to hover about a mile from the ground, 'fly' up and down, or in any direction that seems to pleasure them. They are lit up with red and green lights, and are apt to be seen in the early night. The report to the *Times* office by Mrs. Harry Hanson, of Willard, relates that Stanley Ketchum has seen them at what seems to be a closer range than most, and makes them literally disappear into thin air." (Baker, Montana, *Fallon County Times*, March 9, 1967.)

8. Missouri: Mr. J. Sloan Muir of Caledonia, Missouri, observed a flashing light from his kitchen window at 7:15 p.m. last Wednesday and called his wife. They said it was "a shiny, metal, oblong globe, shaped something like a watermelon. Around the perimeter were many beautiful multicolored lights – green and red mostly, but also white, blue, and yellow, running into orange." They estimated that it was about 35 feet long and said they watched it for 15 or 20 minutes before it flew out of sight. (Bardstown, Kentucky, *Kentucky Standard*, March 16, 1967.)

9. Missouri: "In the past two and one half weeks, 75 to 100 persons have reported sightings in the Osage Beach and Linn Creek areas." (Versailles, Missouri, *Versailles Leader-Statesman*, March 16, 1967.)

10. Missouri: Mrs. Phyllis Rowles of Bunceton, Missouri, reported seeing a multicolored object at 8 p.m. Wednesday.

She described it as having flashing blue, green, and white lights. It hovered for two hours, moving in an up-and-down motion. Many others in the area had similar sightings, including Leo Case, a newsman for station KRMS. (Boonville, Missouri, *Daily News*, March 9, 1967.)

11. Illinois: Mr. and Mrs. Lonnie Davis were driving on Route 30 around noon when "they saw a beam of light come from a wide-open area south of them." They stopped and observed a strange object for three or four minutes. "It was very brilliant," Mrs. David said. "It cast a red and blue color, and was circle-shaped. It seemed to come toward us, but gained height until it went back of a small cloud. We watched for about ten minutes more, but it never appeared again." Ronald Kolberg of Aurora, Illinois, said he and other residents of his neighborhood "have noticed an unusual light in the sky west of their area every night for a few months." (Aurora, Illinois, *Beacon-News*, March 9, 1967.)

12. Illinois: Several witnesses in Pontiac, Illinois, reported sightings to the state police on Wednesday. They said a white light flashed occasionally with a less frequent red light and a periodic green light. The object appeared between 10 p.m. and midnight, and moved up and down slowly. "More than a dozen people have seen the object this week." (Pontiac, Illinois, *Leader*, March 10, 1967.)

13. Illinois: Knox County Deputy Sheriff Frank Courson and 20 other persons watched a pulsating white and red circular object for several hours on Wednesday night. The object resembled an upside-down bowl and appeared to be about 2,000 feet off the ground. Deputy Courson added that a similar object crossed over his car Monday as he drove along Interstate 74 near Galesburg, Illinois, but he "was scared to tell anyone about it then." There were also reports of UFO sightings Wednesday night in Warren and Henry counties, west of Galesburg. (Associated Press story, widely circulated, March 10, 1967.)

14. Illinois: State police and scores of others watched UFOs near Flanagan, Illinois, on Wednesday night. A state trooper named Kennedy said he had followed the object to U.S. 51, where he met two Woodford County deputies who had been watching it approach Minonk from the east. The object

was a brilliant bluish-white and red. (Bloomington, Illinois, *Pantagraph*, March 10, 1967.)

15. Illinois: "Flying saucer reports, one of them from a veteran policeman and pilot, flooded the Knox Country sheriff's office in Galesburg Thursday. Dozens of similar reports poured into police departments in Moline, Illinois." (Chicago, Illinois, *News*, March 9, 1967.)

16. Iowa: "On Wednesday, Thursday, and Friday nights of last week, unidentified flying objects were reported by several persons, including Dr. and Mrs. W.G. Tietz, Connie Dagit, and her younger brother, Jack Chadwick, and John Kiwala. The UFOs west of Eldora were all reported at approximately the same time nightly, at about 8:30 p.m. UFOs have also been reported in the Steamboat Rock area." (Eldora, Iowa, *Herald-Ledger*, March 14, 1967.)

17. Iowa: A "saucer-shaped blue light" was observed Wednesday night hovering above Dam 18 north of Burlington, Iowa. Deputy Sheriff Homer Dickson said he thought it might have been a "reflection of a spotlight on the ice." Wednesday's sighting was the latest of several reported in the Burlington area the past two weeks. (Burlington, Iowa, newspaper. Name obliterated. March 9, 1967.)

18. Iowa: Mrs. L. E. Koppenhaver reported seeing "a big red ball" sailing over her house at 9:45 p.m. Wednesday. "You know how the setting sun gets a red glow on it?" she said. "Well, that was what this thing looked like. Only this object was very mobile, moving almost out of sight, the bright glow diminishing to a small light. I've seen satellites before, but this was nothing like them. It moved so fast and maneuvered so quickly." Her father, Walter Engstrom, said he also saw the same object. (Boone, Iowa, *News-Republican*, March 10, 1967.)

19. Kansas: Mr. Jake Jansonius of Prairie View, Kansas was driving home about 10 p.m. Wednesday night "when the sky lit up and a bright blue object of some kind appeared." While he was watching it, it shot straight up in the air, and half of it turned fiery red as "three blazing tails reached toward the ground." It moved to the west and then dropped down, out of his line of vision. He drove a short distance when "the sky lit up poof in one big flash, and immediately ahead of me the saucer-shaped object began to spread apart – one half still

blue, the other fiery red. As the distance widened between the two parts, a connecting band that appeared to be about one and a half feet thick formed. While I watched, the object broke up and disappeared in a flash." (Phillipsburg, Kansas, *Review*, March 16, 1967.)

20. Kansas: Several police officers in Marion, Kansas, watched an unidentified flying object Wednesday night between 8 and 8:30 p.m. Marion police dispatcher Sterling Frame and others viewed it through binoculars and stated it changed color: red, green, and yellow. "They all agree they saw it. There's no question about that." (Marion, Kansas, *Marion County Record*, March 9, 1967.)

21. Kansas: "Around nine o'clock Wednesday night, several Towanda youths were parked along the road northwest of town when they observed revolving red, white, and blue lights flashing in the sky above the Wilson field in the vicinity of a city water well." The boys fetched City Marshal Virgil Osborne, and he went with them to the area and viewed the lights himself. Osborne said, "The trees along the river were lighted up from the reflection as the mysterious object moved over them." A line of cars led by Osborne followed the object as it continued its course, without changing direction or altitude, until it was out of sight. (Whitewater, Kansas, *Independent*, March 9, 1967.)

22. Kansas: Sheriff G.L. Sullivan and Police Chief Al Kisner watched a hovering object for more than an hour on Wednesday evening near Goodland, Kansas. They said the thing resembled a sphere from 12 to 14 feet long, with an object attached to the bottom that appeared to be about 12 feet in diameter. There were three lights on it – red, green, and amber. A Goodland policeman, Ron Weehunt, reported seeing an oval-shaped, domed object about 50 feet long that same evening. He said it flew over the city at moderate speed and appeared at an altitude of 1,000 to 1,500 feet. (Norton, Kansas, *Telegram*, March 14, 1967.)

These twenty-two reports are a mere sampling, but they provide an idea of what happened on a single Wednesday night in March 1967. This was not an exceptional flap. It was, in fact, a rather ordinary one, and none of these incidents is of special interest. There were *74* flap dates in 1966, many of them much larger than that of March 8, 1967.

The flap of March 8 seemed to be largely concentrated in the states of Kansas and Illinois. In fact, much of the UFO activity in recent years has been focused on the Midwestern states, and a simple pattern seems to have emerged. Less densely populated areas had a higher ratio of sightings than heavily populated sections.

The Air Force discovered this odd fact back in the late 1940s. If this were a purely psychological phenomenon, then there should be more reports in the more densely populated areas. Instead, the reverse had been true. The objects still apparently prefer remote sectors such as hill country, deserts, forested areas, swamplands, and places where the risk of being observed is the least. As you will note from the sample cases mentioned previously, the majority of the sightings were made between 7:30 and 9:30 p.m. But throughout rural America, most of the population is at home and planted in front of the TV sets at that hour, particularly on weekday nights.

In other studies, we have determined that the majority of the reported *landings* occur very *late* at night, in very isolated locales, where the chances of being observed are very slight. In most farming areas, the people are early risers, and therefore most of the population is in bed before 10 p.m. It is after 10 p.m. that the unidentified flying objects cut loose. When they do happen to be observed on the ground, it is either by accident or design. And usually they take off the moment they have been discovered, or they inexplicably disappear into thin air!

Already we can arrive at one disturbing conclusion based upon these basic factors of behavior. If these lights are actually machines operated by intelligent entities, they obviously don't want to be caught. They come in the dead of night, operating in areas where the risks of being observed are slight. They pick the middle of the week for their peak activities, and they confine themselves rather methodically to the political boundaries of specific states at specific times. All of this smacks uneasily of a covert military operation, a secret buildup in remote areas.

Unfortunately, it is not all this simple. The first major UFO flap in the Midwest took place in 1897. There's something else going on here. If secrecy is "their" goal, then both our newspaper wire services and our government have happily been obliging them. What are the reasons? And, more important, what are the pitfalls? If strange unidentified flying machines are operating freely in our midst, I wonder if we can really accept what Secretary of Defense McNamara told the House Committee on Foreign Affairs on March 30, 1966: "I think that every report so far has been investigated," he said. "And in every instance we have found a more reasonable explanation than an object from outer space or a potential threat to our security."

The newspaper of March 9, 1967 quoted Dr. J. Allen Hynek as dismissing a number of the March 8 sightings as being "the planet Venus." But I worry about the report of two Erie, Pennsylvania, policemen, William Rutledge and Donald Peck, who said they watched a strange light over Lake Erie for two hours on Wednesday, August 3, 1966. It appeared as a bright light when they first noticed it at 4:45 a.m. It moved east, they said, stopped, turned red, and disappeared. A moment later it reappeared and was now a bluish white.

They watched it until 6:55 a.m. As the sun came up and dawn flooded the sky, the object ceased to be a mere light. It became a definite silvery object, possibly metallic, and then headed north and disappeared.

Could all of these strange lights in the night sky *also* be silver metallic objects when viewed in daylight? If so, then we can forget about all of the theories of swamp gas, meteors, plasma, and natural phenomena that have been bandied about by the skeptics for the past twenty years.

On August 7, 2009, this "Mothman" crop circle (the size of several football stadiums) appeared in Goes, Holland. While most blame "ETs" for such "authentic" (non-hoaxed) circles, their source may be terrestrial (satellite-based), since their symbologies are invariably "human" in nature.

CHAPTER 16

The American public is not telling the Air Force the truth about flying saucers. Over 10,000 sightings of unidentified flying objects were reported in detail in newspapers from coast to coast during 1966, but only a meager 1,060 were reported directly to the Air Force. The majority of that 10% who bothered to inform the Air Force were sent a form to be filled out; that form constituted the Air Force's "investigation" of their sighting. If they failed to fill in a basic question, such as the state of the weather at the time of the sighting, the Air Force shelved the whole report in their "insufficient" file.

One such witness, Charles Paulus of Maple Shade, New Jersey, not only carefully filled out all of the questions on the Air Force form, but he included drawings, maps, and other data that he thought was pertinent to his sighting. Three other witnesses had been with him on the night of October 30, 1966, when he saw a gigantic, brilliantly illuminated, metallic disk hovering a couple of hundred feet in the air directly above an RCA computer plant in Cherry Hill, NJ. Two hundred other people in that densely populated area claimed that they saw the same object, or a similar one, before, during, or after the quartet's sighting. Paulus tediously rounded up newspaper clippings, names and addresses of other witnesses, and other corroborative data.

The Air Force's "Project Blue Book" responded to this mass of material with a short letter declaring that it was "insufficient," implying that the case did not deserve further study.

That night, October 30th, was a "flap" period, a time when there was a sudden outbreak of sightings all over the country. While Paulus and his friends were staring in disbelief at the high object (they estimated that it was 340 feet long and 140 feet high) hovering in the dark New Jersey sky, hundreds of other people in New York State, Oklahoma, Nebraska, Pennsylvania, and Kentucky were gaping in wonder at equally mysterious aerial intruders. All of them were dead certain of what they were seeing. If you dared to suggest that they were looking at clouds of swamp gas or meteors, they would laugh in your face.

They, and millions of others, now believe that they have briefly glimpsed solid machines under intelligent control. For twenty years, the Air Force and the scientific establishment have tried to ignore the ever-growing mass of UFO sightings, perhaps in the hope that they would eventually go away, but more likely because the existence of non-manmade aerial vehicles was improbable. Then, when civilian UFO researchers emerged in the late 1940s, they gave the Establishment a perfect "out." Enthusiastic pseudo-scientists began to rave about "spaceships" and "extraterrestrial visitors," and these premature conclusions were unpalatable to the public.

To believe in "flying saucers" was to believe in "little green men" from outer space, and that was patently ridiculous. Leading scientists and astronomers pooh-poohed the notion that life "as we know it" could exist elsewhere in the universe. They stubbornly adhered to this belief until the mid-1950s, when a gradual change in thinking began to occur. By 1960, the very men who had been scoffing at the possibility of "extraterrestrial" life only a few years before were now leaping on a new bandwagon. And, in 1962, NASA formally announced that the "purpose" of our space program was "the search for extraterrestrial life."

Throughout that period, a seemingly well-organized campaign began in the press, stressing the possibility of "extraterrestrial life" with almost monthly statements by various learned scientists and astronomers. Today, even leading churchmen and theologians are blandly admitting that Man is probably not alone in the Universe. We have had to adjust, almost overnight, to the sudden realization that there may be literally billions of planets and millions of inhabited worlds besides our own puny little ball of mud and water.

But actual "flying saucers" remain ridiculous – except to the people who have seen them. And, as the ET buffs keep chanting, UFO witnesses include pilots, police officers, senators and congressmen, clergymen, ambassadors, generals and admirals, astronomers, engineers, ad nauseum. All of these people are obviously screwballs and crackpots. How can you see something that couldn't possibly be there?

These non-existent objects not only perform frequently for "lunatics" in every country on the face of the earth, but they follow definite flight patterns and schedules.

This author tediously collected, through expensive clipping services, thousands of published UFO reports in 1966, and prepared a thorough statistical analysis of the many factors involved. We found that the sightings tended to group around certain "flap dates," no matter what their geographical location. Since the general press and major news media ignore most UFO reports, it is highly unlikely that the people in Minnesota, for example, ever knew that while they were viewing odd lights in the sky, the same kinds of lights were chasing automobiles in Massachusetts and following boats in the English Channel.

On March 30th, 1966, local newspapers gave the details of extensive sightings in Michigan, South Carolina, Iowa, Wisconsin, New Jersey, Ohio, California, and New York. But only the Michigan sightings received any national notice at all. Among the other important "flap dates" of 1966 were July 13th (UFOs reported over Nebraska, Kansas, Michigan, Illinois) and July 27th (North and South Carolina, Idaho, Oklahoma, California, Michigan, Illinois, Montana).

On the night of August 16th alone, there were hundreds of sightings in five states: Minnesota, Arkansas, South Dakota, New Jersey, and Wisconsin. Project Blue Book later said that this flap was caused by the launching of a rocket in northern Canada, which ejected a "barium cloud" into the upper atmosphere. Unfortunately, the data does not fit this explanation. Panic-stricken drivers in three states reported low-level approaches to their autos that night. In some cases, the UFOs remained in view for hours in front of thousands of people (barium cloud experiments last for only a few minutes) in several cities in Arkansas. Many of the things reported were identical to the massive reports of the summer of 1947 (when 500 sightings were recorded in a single two-week period), which, of course, occurred long before we had really gotten into the rocket-launching business.

A study of the 1966 flaps reveals several surprising patterns. Over 20% of all the 1966 sightings took place on Wednesday evenings, while only 7% were recorded on Tuesdays. This puzzling "Wednesday phenomenon" has continued into 1967. The majority of all sightings seem to occur shortly after sunset and shortly before dawn, but daylight reports are no longer rare. The bulk of the "touchdown" (landing) reports seem to be concentrated around the hours of 2 a.m. and 4 a.m., a time when most of the population is counting sheep. (There were hundreds of little-publicized landing reports in 1966-67.)

Things quieted down in December of 1966, although there was a small flap in a few isolated localities throughout that month. But during the third week of January 1967, all hell broke loose. Major sightings involving thousands of people erupted in twenty states, hitting a peak on January 16th. The Air Force dusted off its "barium cloud" explanation again. And sure enough, a "barium cloud" rocket *had* been launched from Florida at 4 a.m. that morning. Most of the sightings of that date took place hours before, however. The "barium cloud" supposedly could only be seen within a 300-mile radius, and most of the UFO reports came in from states in the north and Midwest.

The March-April 1967 "flap" was so big that we must have launched hundreds of "barium cloud" rockets, almost on an hourly basis. The author has collected over 1,200 published UFO reports for the month of March alone, exceeding the total number of reports received by the U.S. Air Force for the entire year of 1966. All kinds of unusual phenomenon were reported, ranging from giant reddish spheres hovering directly over Philadelphia and Atlantic City, to tiny 6-inch disks buzzing farmers in Oregon and Nebraska. As usual, the UFOs played their mysterious game of chasing automobiles and, as usual, there were a number of local power failures in the wake of well-qualified "flying saucer" sightings by bewildered police officers and other reliable witnesses.

Staggered by the unbelievable quantity of sightings being recorded in small daily and weekly newspapers throughout the country, we made a tour of twenty states to find out for ourselves if all of this was really happening. We quickly discovered that only a small proportion of sightings were even being reported and, in many areas, the newspapers were becoming very selective and only publishing "the most interesting ones." We also found that newspapers in many sections were ignoring the phenomenon altogether.

In West Virginia, for example, we stopped in the little town of Sistersville. The last published UFO report from there was in 1897! "We've been seeing these things for months," Mr. Robert Wright, a leading Sistersville attorney, declared. "In fact, since last summer they've been showing up here almost every Wednesday, like clockwork. Everybody's been watching them, but not everybody likes to talk about them. Now we're so well organized that when somebody spots of them passing over, they just grab the phone – we're all on party lines here – and yells 'UFO east,' or 'UFO west,' or whatever direction it's going in, and everybody runs out and watches."

In Point Pleasant, West Virginia, the UFOs seemed to be following a regular schedule, passing over the outlying McClintic Wildlife Preserve every night at 8:30. Everyone, including the entire police force and county sheriff's department, had been watching the low-flying luminous globes. In April 1967, the author saw so many unexplainable objects in the skies over West Virginia that he actually lost count. Yet we rarely found anyone who had actually bothered to contact the Air Force's Project Blue Book and report a sighting.

Half an hour from New York City, in any direction, UFO sightings became commonplace. They busied themselves off Long Island throughout the summer of 1967, and they spent a lot of time around the reservoirs in northern New Jersey and the Catskill Mountains. In late June, a massive flap engulfed Europe from Italy to England. South America, always a hotbed for "flying saucer" stories, exploded in a new frenzy of sightings that spread from Antarctica to the Caribbean. It was no longer a matter of keeping track of random clippings. Now all we could do was number the flood of new reports and try to keep a vague check on the scope of the phenomenon. The individual "cases" no longer seemed to matter. The same descriptions were coming in from every part of the world. If this was some form of mass hysteria, then it was time to build a fence around the whole planet. Everybody was flipping out!

The more incredible thing about this massive flap – the biggest in recorded history – was the manner in which it was slighted by the major news media. Wire service stories on local sightings rarely went beyond the borders of the states in which they occurred. The major TV and radio networks avoided the subject, and the big city dailies in areas where sightings were few, such as New York, continued with the pretense that "flying saucers" didn't exist.

Meanwhile, millions of people were discovering – somewhat to their horror – that they could expect no help or advice from the Air Force or the government. Farmers who wanted to find out what had landed in their fields and left a big circular burn mark, learned that the bloated Washington payroll included no experts on this mind-numbing phenomenon. In a random few cases, Air Force investigators would make token visits to "flap" areas, mumble something about weather balloons or misinterpretations of the planet Venus, and dash away, leaving an angered and bewildered citizenry.

If even 1% of all these thousands of reports are true, then our space is being invaded by large numbers of unlicensed aerial vehicles that are blatantly ignoring all of our aircraft regulations and zoning laws. What's even worse, our expensively maintained and superbly equipped Air Force seems totally helpless and unable to do anything about it.

There are now hundreds of reports of these things landing on highways from Africa to Oklahoma. Ask any private pilot, and they will tell you that there's a law against that. There are also scores of reports in which these circular metal machines are said to have set down briefly in private fields and even in people's backyards. And, brother, we have several laws prohibiting that kind of flying! The UFOs also seem to be fond of hedge-hopping, even over towns and villages, and that is hardly legal. What's worse, they have frequently been reported buzzing – or even landing on top of – schools from Lima, Peru to Boston, Massachusetts to Melbourne, Australia. And, of course, when they have nothing better to do, they chase automobiles all over the world, scaring drivers half to death.

But maybe if we keep calling these things "swamp gas," they'll get insulted and go away.

How long has this been going on? Perhaps a good deal longer than we would like to believe. England had a UFO flap back in the 1830s. They began to show up – or at least be noticed – in the United States around 1860. In 1897, there was a worldwide flap with many landings reported. Strangely enough, the UFO activity back then seemed to be centered in areas where it is still going strong: Australia, Nebraska, Arkansas, Illinois, Virginia, Oklahoma, etc. Researchers are only just beginning to wade into old newspaper files throughout the country to re-examine the reports of that distant period.

Africa had a flap in the early 1900s. The first "little men" stories came out of the 1897 flap but, by 1914, "little men" were being reported in Venezuela and Canada. Then in 1922, another huge flap engulfed the world. Washington responded to the complaints of the citizens of North Carolina by sending a geologist who raised their ire by reporting that everyone there was only seeing "locomotive headlights."

In 1930 "mystery airplanes" were causing a lot of concern in Scandinavia, and unidentified "dirigibles" were baffling the people of West Virginia, in the area around Point Pleasant. Gleaming flying disks were reported over Ethiopia, in 1937, when Mussolini's troops marched in. Those "little men" even popped up in Estonia in 1939!

Throughout the Second World War, thousands of servicemen saw strange flying disks and weird inexplicable lights on every front. Fighter pilots called them "Foo Fighters." In New England, where a large flap took place in 1940, newspapers referred to them as "mystery planes," as did the newspapers in Florida in 1945. In 1946, over 2,000 reports of "ghost rockets" were recorded in Sweden. By early 1947, they were being seen throughout the United States again, but it was not until June 1947 that pilot Kenneth Arnold's historic report of nine saucer-shaped objects over Mount Rainier turned the subject into headlines.

We have had many years to seriously study the problem and find out what these things are, and what they are doing here. Unfortunately, we have not done so. In the meantime, each year has brought larger flaps, and the reported behavior of the objects has been bolder and bolder. Where once they only whizzed over at high altitude, they are now descending, hovering, and even landing.

More and more stories of attempted kidnappings are now coming to light. In many widespread rural areas, we have been told stories of dogs and cattle vanishing after UFOs were sighted over farms and pastures. There are now too many of these stories for us to laugh at, or discount, any longer.

Since we seem to be contending with some kind of science-fiction nightmare, perhaps we should be prepared to listen to stories that sound like science-fiction. Perhaps we should heed tales like the one told by Beau Shertzer, 21, who was driving a Red Cross bloodmobile along Route 2 in West Virginia on March 5, 1967, when, according to his account, a large luminous object descended over his vehicle and lowered two prongs, one on either side, as if it were going to pick up the bloodmobile. Shertzer stepped on the gas in terror while his passenger, a nurse, went into hysterics. They were sure that the object was trying to pick up their truck, they said. Fortunately, some traffic appeared from the other direction and the object shot upwards when the headlights hit it.

Much of the UFO situation is so bizarre and unbelievable that you must experience it firsthand. You must sit around the kitchen tables of America and hear honest, ordinary citizens relate their incredible stories. And you must hear hundreds of these stories in many different places, so that you can see for yourself how much the details match. The author has lived for weeks in the heart of flap territories. We have talked to thousands of people from all walks of life and interviewed them in depth, trying to trip them up, searching for logical earthly explanations of what they claim to have experienced. Our conclusion: there is no logical, earthly explanation.

Another remarkable thing about this business is why no responsible reporter has investigated it during these past twenty years. It was not until John Fuller's visit to Exeter, NH in 1965 that the subject was taken out of the hands of the bumbling amateur UFO buffs and studied by a trained, professional journalist.

The Air Force's Project Bluebook is primarily a public relations effort and their "investigations" have been perfunctory. They have most often offered ill-suited explanations, making some astonishingly stupid blunders along the way. (Air Force officers have personally lied to me directly on a number of occasions, and I've caught them at it.) They have antagonized whole states with their lame "answers," and they have deliberately muddled the issue with unnecessary secrecy and outright incompetency.

Why? Is the government afraid of panic, as many have suggested? Is the

Air Force stuck with a badly planned policy, as others claim? When UFO activity is popping all over, why do they maintain a head-in-the-sand position?

The hard facts are simple, yet weirdly complex. There is no "mystery" to the "flying saucers." The "mystery" was created by that knot of fanatics who seized upon the subject in 1947, and who have dominated it ever since. By employing loud mouths and weak minds, they managed to create a curtain of absurdity around the most serious problem of our times. If they had kept silent, and if the press had not heaped so much ridicule on the subject in the early days, we would have learned more, and learned it faster. Serious scientists and journalists would not have been frightened away from the problem because of "guilt by association." Ordinary citizens with disturbing experiences to tell would have been listened to. Gradually, the UFO phenomenon would have been taken seriously and studied carefully by qualified scientists, instead of by boobs and teenagers. The enormity of the situation would have been understood sooner.

As pointed out earlier, the first idiotic stumbling block was created by the fanatics' insistence that the UFOs were "extraterrestrial." This is impossible to prove. What's more, there is absolutely no observational data to support it. While all of our astronauts have seen unidentified objects in the upper reaches of our atmosphere, no astronaut or astronomer has ever seen a UFO entering or leaving the vicinity of Earth. How are these thousands of objects slipping unnoticed into our atmosphere?

There is a damned obvious answer. They aren't.

Hard research indicates that these objects have been observed frequently throughout mankind's long history. Since 1897, they have been observed almost constantly, and in the same areas. For example, an abortive UFO study carried out by Ohio Northern University in 1952 revealed that most of the sightings for that year were concentrated in the same areas in Texas, Ohio, Arizona, Nebraska, etc. – where they were concentrated in 1966.

Are they flying in from Mars or Andromeda every year to visit the very same rather dull and thinly populated spots? Or are they somehow coming from undiscovered bases in these remote areas? Could it be possible that from 1860 on, a number of cleverly concealed bases were established throughout the world? Could such bases have *always* existed?

Maybe we have always been unknowingly sharing our planet with a group of beings who prefer to have nothing to do with us, or who are participating in some unknown plan of cosmic scope and importance. That is, they will reveal themselves to us at a proper time in our history. Perhaps the sharp increase in UFO activity indicates that that time is drawing near.

This may sound like a crackpot theory, but the known facts support it more easily than they support the "extraterrestrial" fantasy. Perhaps we have been misleading ourselves all these years, and have been floundering in a morass of deceiving speculations. We have hired astronomers to study things in the sky – in the atmosphere – and we have asked physicists to figure out what makes these things go. And in twenty years of study (as of 1957, the Air Force had spent $200,000,000 on such studies) they have not managed to come up with a single plausible answer. Instead, we have been handed a barrage of "swamp gas" and "weather balloon" explanations. Thousands of people have been told they were crazy or were hallucinating. Millions have been told they were mistaken.

And all this time, the UFOs appear to have been quietly expanding their "bases," sweeping over Earth in preparation for the last stage of their plan, whatever it might be. If their ultimate intent is a hostile one, then we have been betrayed. Man is no longer alone on his own planet!

Somewhere in the remote, almost inaccessible back hills of West Virginia, there may be a vast underground headquarters populated by strange beings that have been there since 1897, or even longer. There may be dozens, or hundreds, of similar "bases" throughout the United States and throughout the world. And, if these aliens do come from outer space, slipping in unnoticed in some unfathomable fashion, they might be only the vanguard.

All of the intensive UFO activity may be concerned with the distribution of personnel and material, and the establishment of more "bases." And these "bases" may be making ready for the arrival of the "main force." We could wake up one morning and find every city in the world encircled by strange craft. Then, all of the skeptics, doubters, and explainers would finally learn the "truth" about flying saucers.

This "hostility thesis" is now gaining support from serious ufologists in every country. Many believe that the Air Forces of the world have been cleverly deceived all these years, and that our governments will be caught completely off-guard when the UFOs enter their final stage of operations: overt contact.

But there is another totally unpublicized aspect to the situation, which might indicate that there is some hope for us. Everywhere we have traveled, we have discovered "silent contactees" – ordinary people who claim that they have actually been approached by the UFO entities. All of their stories are basically the same, and none of these stories have been published. If these people are telling the truth, we may be facing a situation more complex than any of the amateur UFO buffs have ever imagined.

From 1947 on, a number of vociferous and rather misguided souls have ranted about being contacted by tall, handsome blonds from "Venus" and other worlds. They have supplied a stench to the whole contactee situation, and their antics have caused the "silent contactees" to withdraw. Though it may be impossible for you to believe, the latter group can now be numbered in the thousands. They don't go on TV or radio. They don't write profitable books about their trips in "flying saucers." They don't join UFO clubs. In fact, one startling characteristic of all "silent contactees" is that they have little or no interest in the UFO phenomenon at all!

These "silent contactees" are apparently carefully selected, long before they are approached directly. A long and well-planned pattern of approach is followed. In case after case, we have heard the same identical details of events leading up to the final face-to-face contact. The "aliens" test them in several unusual ways before finally confronting them. According to testimony and documentation now in my files, only about 1% of all those selected ever become full fledged "contactees." Some of the others go running to the police in alarm. Some have mental crack-ups, and a few commit suicide.

Whatever "truths" are passed on to them must have tremendous emotional impact. Those who are strong enough to sustain continued contacts become engulfed in a serious of events so amazing that often they never reveal the details to their spouses. They find themselves living a secret "double life," being called upon at all hours to perform bizarre tasks for the UFO occupants, and becoming engaged in such improbable experiences that they fear for their sanity. Those "silent contactees" we uncovered have the same story to tell, however, and these consistencies have caused us to take a long look at the whole situation.

If the UFOs are operating as openly and as constantly as they seem to be, and if they have now established "bases" of some kind around the world, extensive "contacts" with isolated terrestrials might be a very logical step in preparing for large and more open contact with us. Many of the "silent contactees' claim to have undergone thorough physical examinations, and hours of involved questioning and interrogation aboard the UFOs. This would also be a logical procedure for any "alien" race making a systematic study of our planet and its peoples. The time has come for us to take such stories seriously, and to investigate them in depth.

Unlike the earlier, well-publicized "contactees," this new quiet crop seems to consist of emotionally stable people with fine reputations in their communities. Yet they speak in hushed tones of "telepathy" and other things that also appeared in the "crackpot" stories of previous years.

For example, the Reverend Anthony De Polo, assistant pastor of the Bethel Assembly of God Church in Boardman, Ohio, is a college teacher with three degrees in psychology and philosophy. At 1:30 a.m. on the morning of July 18, 1967, he claims that a strange whining sound awoke him and caused him to get out of bed and look outside his house. There, he says, he saw the figure of a man in some kind of a "space suit and helmet" standing in the driveway. This figure was surrounded by a strange luminosity and held one arm upraised, apparently in a gesture of peace.

Reverend De Polo stepped outside, unafraid, and received a definite mental message, "You have nothing to fear. I will not harm you; and I know you will not harm me." He started toward the figure, but it suddenly faded out and vanished. In the aftermath of this curious story, over 200 people in the immediate area came forward, all claiming to have seen a luminous circular object hovering in the vicinity at the same time as the Reverend's "contact."

Reverend De Polo is only one of the thousands who have reported seeing luminous figures in spacesuits that appeared and disappeared like ghosts. Very few of these stories have been widely circulated, but now they are coming from all parts of the world. France had a rash of such visitations in 1954. Hundreds of such cases have been recorded in South America, Australia, England and other widely scattered countries. The smoke has been around for a long time. Our job is now to find the fire.

The "truth" about the flying saucer "mystery" has always been there if anyone cared to look for it. Let's stop arguing about whether or not they exist. The evidence is massive and incontrovertible. Let's stop wondering what makes them fly. They do fly; they fly all the time. Let's find out what they are really doing here, and what they plan to do in the future. We've wasted twenty years. Let's not waste another twenty haggling over inconsequential, trumped-up theories and explanations.

Somewhere in the universe, a clock is ticking.

CHAPTER 17

People are always asking me how far back in ancient times UFOs visited the earth, and if they were manned by some form of humanoid.

Well, they have found caves in Siberia, China, and Africa that indicate cavemen saw objects in the sky. The paintings usually show a circular object with a man-shaped thing standing on it, larger than the people standing on the ground. Also, here in the U.S., we have what are called "petroglyphs" – carvings or paintings made by the Indians on the sides of cliffs – all over the country. Some of them are so strikingly similar to UFO photographs that "flying saucers" just might have been what the Indians were recording. The Native Americans used their own language in these petroglyphs, and there are notations on some of them in the West, such as: "This is the valley of the Little People."

There are Indian legends like this going as far back as one can trace them, and Eskimo legends, too. The Eskimos believe they were flown to the far north in some sort of machines ("metal birds"), which is as good as an explanation as any as to how they got up there in the first place. In China, there are all kinds of legends going back 5,000 years – the dragon legends. Apparently, they were talking about what we now call UFOs. The dragons were described as "brilliant lights in the sky." They followed regular routes throughout China, and it was considered lucky to own real estate along these "dragon routes." In England and Ireland, of course, these things go way back in history. They have found *more* cave paintings in France, too, so there's every indication that flying saucers *were* here before man. When man began to see them, he naturally thought these sightings were important enough to portray them in paintings.

In Japan, there is popular legend that the Japanese people dropped out of the sky. To this day, they have parks in Japan that are dedicated to flying saucers. They believe that the original Emperor of Japan came from the sky, just as the people of South America believe their ancient king came from the sky. There are similar legends in Africa. They believe their original kings came from the sky, too, much as the pharaohs of Egypt, and so on. But there is no real evidence that we are descended from extraterrestrial planetary systems. There are people who believe we originally came from Venus – that Venus was the Garden of Eden.

There are all kinds of beliefs that are simply not based on any kind of evidence, and yet a lot of people accept them. They seem to be legends that some imaginative person created long ago, and passed down to his children until they became accepted as "fact." The historical material indicates that these beings from the sky deliberately conveyed the impression that they were gods – that they "owned" the earth as well as the people on it. It was not an interpretation "of the people"; their acceptance was coerced by these so-called "gods" (who sound a lot like colonialists).

The problem of the origin of the human race intrigues me. I've studied evolution a great deal, and frankly, in my opinion, evolution doesn't work. People just need philosophies to believe in. Of course, over time, a lot of these philosophies have been modernized, or simplified, by various scholars writing popular books. The teachings of Buddha were really very complex. Buddha didn't claim that he had talked to a spaceman, but he *did* experience overnight illumination. The other great philosophers of the ancient past were also dealing with rather complex ideas at that time; we have simplified them by translating them into books. (There is little direct, person-to-person philosophic training now.)

In 1954, I was living in Egypt when I saw my first UFO, while visiting the Aswan Dam. It was bright and sunny in the middle of the day, and I saw a metallic object hovering about 500 feet above the dam. It seemed to be in two parts. The outer part, the rim, was rotating, while the inner part was stationary. It was a classic saucer. There were no portholes in it, but it definitely *seemed* metallic, and it was close enough that I got a good look at it. But I wasn't carrying a camera. It only stayed less than a minute, and then it shot out of sight in a few seconds. There were a lot of people there, and each one gave a different estimate of the size and altitude. It's almost impossible to judge such things if you don't know any of the actual dimensions.

There's no way witnesses can prove their stories today, any more than I can prove I saw this thing in 1954. But there are many reliable witnesses – airline pilots, astronomers, scientists, military personnel, etc. These people are educated, and certainly wouldn't make up these stories, which tend to undermine their positions of authority. There are skeptics everywhere, waiting to pounce on them. There are professional skeptics for everything. There are now "skeptics" (lobbyists) saying that we shouldn't try to control air pollution, because it will adjust itself "on its own." I don't take such skeptics seriously, especially when there is money involved. Over the years, many UFO skeptics have suddenly experienced sightings themselves, and that usually shuts them up pretty good.

I have talked with literally thousands of people in the last few years who have seen these things. They are from all walks of life. I'm interested in what common, ordinary people see. The average person would normally be extremely skeptical of a flying saucer, but these sightings seem to change their mind. A lot of people are gradually switching over to the theory that there is an interdimensional aspect involved here – that the UFOs are not necessarily from outer space, but may be from another dimension.

There are "window" areas all over this earth, where strange occurrences go on year after year, century after century – things like the haunting of houses, and the appearing and disappearing of animals. It's a permanent condition of the planet. We get strange reports all the time – usually with a minimum of attention in the newspapers – and UFOs fall into this category. They are seen in these same window areas. To simplify it, suppose there were another world made out of an atomic structure different from ours, yet existing in the same space as ours. When conditions are right – we don't know what these conditions might be, but they seem prevalent in certain locations – strange beings and animals from this other world may be able to get over into our world. It's an overlapping of two worlds. We can't perceive the other world, but it exists, and is as real to them as our world is to us. Apparently they can enter and leave our world at will, while we can't do the same with theirs. It sounds completely absurd, yet we're gradually building up empirical evidence that this may be the answer. And if it is the answer, we can never definitely prove it, or do anything about it, until we can learn to go over into their world.

This theory is becoming very popular nowadays, but the extraterrestrial theory has always been the most popular one. But professional researchers can't seem to find any real evidence to support it. It's all pure speculation. While it's very possible there could be life on other planets and in other galaxies, there is no evidence that that life is coming here to see us. Certainly if such life existed and did attempt to come all the way to Earth, they wouldn't behave in a fashion in which UFOs and their occupants are known to behave. They wouldn't be as elusive and aloof – deliberately keeping their presence unknown, and deceiving us.

Maybe our UFOs want something from us. Ancient Chinese philosophy maintains that the human soul is "moon food." One of the popular beliefs in all religions is that the human soul is a target – that there are those who feast on the human soul. That would certainly be considered to be hostile.

NASA published a booklet a few years ago in which they catalogued some 500 of these strange lunar sightings. All kinds of things have been seen on the moon. They remain unexplained to this day, including sightings by astronauts, who have photographed many things on the moon that have not been publicized. Every time they went up on a mission, they saw and photographed unusual objects trailing them out in space or on the moon itself. NASA claims the men were seeing some kind of spots in front of their eyes. They published an absurd technical paper saying that cosmic rays had somehow leaked into the space cabin and affected their eyes.

Speaking of seeing things, in 1952 there was a report in *The New York Times* that a UFO had landed in New York's Central Park, near Harlem. The area was roped-off by police and government officials. People were told not to say a thing about it. There was only one small byline in the paper – no ballyhoo at all. A female witness turned up in New York a year or two ago. She claimed she had lived in that section of Central Park West at the time, and immediately after it happened, military men came around, from door to door, warning everyone to stay in their homes and not to admit any strangers. Of course, we just have her testimony for this; it does sound a little bit like something out *The War of the Worlds.* I've never heard anything else about it, or about anything like it.

I've talked to many people who claim to have been taken to other planets in spaceships. These people seem to be suffering from a kind of hallucinatory experience that was quite common in the Middle Ages. In literature about fairies and leprechauns, there are striking parallels between fairies and UFOs. Woody Derenberger went through a series of games with Indrid Cold of the planet Lanulos, who waylaid Woody on the highway by blocking the way with his spaceship. NASA paid for Woody and his family to come to Cape Kennedy, where they spent a week interrogating Woody. At the end, they showed him a "star map" and said, "This is where Lanulos is." He couldn't even tell what they were pointing at on the complicated map.

After this original contact, Indrid Cold came to his farm many times to see Woody. He invited Woody to "Lanulos," and so they got into a flying saucer and went there. One of the things that struck Woody was that everyone there was *nude.* This served to authenticate his story somewhat for me, because if he were making the whole thing up, why would he make up details like that, which would only serve to discredit him?

Then I found an old book, published in the 1920s, which described some of the same things Woody had mentioned. He, of course, had never heard of this book; it's very rare. For example, Woody described some very high towers on the outskirts of these Lanulosian cities – very special towers with black spheres on top. In this book from the 1920s, there is a similar description, although it is supposedly set on Mars. We find in story after story that there are certain little details that match. We've heard about every planet in the solar system and galaxy, and it would seem that everybody has the power of space flight – except us. That gives rise to the popular UFO legend that there is an intergalactic council, and that the UFOs are here because they are getting ready to enlist us into it, once we find a way to be peaceful and live in "harmony" with the rest of the universe.

We've been trying to communicate with outer space. We've set up radio telescopes all over this planet. Even countries that can't really afford them are building huge ones – places like Argentina and Israel. You wonder just what the value of these telescopes is. They are very expensive toys. A few years ago, we had Project Ozma in West Virginia, during which we broadcast signals into space in hopes that somebody out there might be listening. There have been many stories of strange signals picked up from space. In most cases, these have proven to be what we now call "pulsars," which are stars that are broadcasting a signal at a specific wavelength, with a specific time lapse between each signal. It seems to be a natural phenomenon rather than an organized, intelligent signal.

A lot of contactees have described the insides of the spaceships to me. Again, there are certain details that match. For example, people always describe how the door seems to melt right into the wall after it is closed; another is that there is a TV screen on which colors are flashing. The UFO occupants watch the readouts with interest. It is always described as being sourceless – no lightbulbs or anything. The light just seems to come from the walls. I've heard this many times.

Throughout the long history of the UFO phenomena, we have a long list of mysterious spacemen that all look alike – swarthy men of small stature with Oriental features. You can trace this description way back, and it still crops up in modern UFO stories. In the case of the 1896 airships, we had a man who was slight in stature, with an Oriental cast to his features, who turned up in the office of a famous attorney in San Francisco, claiming to be the inventor of this marvelous new dirigible-like airship. A couple of weeks later, people all over California were seeing strange dirigibles. So, the attorney naturally enough said, "Well, yes, I know all about this. The man who invented it came to see me," and so on. To make a long story short, the man disappeared, and the actual dirigibles weren't flown overtly until several years later. It seems like another ruse to provide a frame of reference for the objects. Throughout the 1920s and '30s, we had a long chain of events, all of which seemed tailored to conform to a frame of reference for that period.

The real evidence for UFOs is statistical. We now have literally hundreds of thousands of these sightings from every country on the face of the earth, going back hundreds of years. We can reduce all of this to statistical analysis and "fact." For example, the highest percentage of sightings occur on Wednesdays, at 10:30 p.m., on the 24th of the month. Those with Native American heritage see more of these than anybody else.

There have been quite a few cases where the UFO witnesses have suffered amnesia and other medical effects. They see a flying saucer and, the next thing they know, it is three hours later and they can't account for the intervening time. In recent years, there have been a number of deaths caused by flying saucers, apparently because of radiation from the object. There have been two or three cases in South America recently, in which the witness closest to the object died almost immediately, of leukemia or some other disease that is caused by radiation. We do try to warn people as gently as possible that if they ever should be lucky or unlucky enough to see a saucer close-up, they should be very cautious and not rush up to it saying, "Welcome to Earth." Because you never know what is going to pop out of the hatch.

The popular belief among ET buffs is they are threatened into silence. But I found out in talking to many of them that, as you dig deeper, the subject gets more and more complicated. You find yourself studying philosophy and religion, and it is difficult to explain it to anybody. Most of these buffs give up simply because they cannot put it into words. As a professional writer, I've tried to do it, but it is very difficult. I've really tried to explore the philosophical and theological aspects of it, in addition to the statistical side.

ESP and psychic phenomena are very common in contactee cases involving telepathic messages from the UFO occupants. The ufonauts have passed along prophecies and predictions to witnesses that have proven to be completely true – right on the nose. Here in the U.S., there are a number of UFO contactees appearing on radio and television, and the majority of their prophecies seem to come true in some form.

All kinds of speculations are possible with UFOs. Judging from their general behavior, there is a possibility that, if they are real machines, they're hostile to us. They could be following a plan of hostility that might take five thousand of our years to complete, but would only be a moment to them. In the UFO cases, we find a number of instances of *deliberate* hostility on the part of the UFOs, which is worrisome.

The U.S. Air Force has now lost over *fifty* men in pursuit of these things; these are only the fifty that the Air Force admits to. We don't know how many others there were. We don't even know whether these plane crashes were accidental or if the UFOs shot them down. All we do know is that there are definitely fifty men who have been killed by flying saucers, or because of flying saucers. We have their names.

We are having a huge UFO flap right now. It started in August of 1970, with an enormous wave of sightings in Prescott, Arizona, which then spread to the Midwest; now it's in New York and California. We've learned to watch specific areas, since the UFOs always seem to turn up in the same places. For instance, every time there is a UFO flap, there are always new appearances over Eldora, Iowa.

I've been working on an interesting story that I heard about: thousands of people in New York City saw a low-flying UFO as it hovered over an outdoor concert in Central Park. It was casting a bright searchlight into the park. We see the searchlight feature in many UFO stories. I'm trying to track down a number of people who saw this thing. The concert was interrupted while everyone stared at the thing. None of the local papers or media mentioned it.

We are generally getting this whole thing down to a science. Within the next five years, we will probably have found out more about flying saucers than we have learned in the last 5000 years. We are beginning to use computers now. Even if we don't solve the mystery, at least we will understand it better. People are becoming more "space conscious" these days. Although I have talked to people who believe our moon landing was a hoax, everyone seems to becoming more conscious of the fact that the earth is just one little mudball swinging around in space, and that there are a lot of other things out there, too.

CLOSE ENCOUNTERS OF THE RELIGIOUS KIND

The long, suspenseful wait has ended. A major flying saucer movie has finally arrived, and it promises to create a new climate for the UFO subject. Despite some rather harsh reviews by the more knowledgeable film critics who resent the weak script and poor characterizations, *Close Encounters of the Third Kind* has struck a responsive chord in America's young people, and they are forming long lines at the box office in New York and Los Angeles, the first cities to present the film.

When Columbia Pictures spent a staggering $14,000,000 to make the movie, they were gambling on the talents of a 29-year-old director, Steven Spielberg, who had written and produced Jaws, a big moneymaker about a man-eating shark. Would UFOs have the same universal appeal as a hungry fish? The cynics thought not. The sophisticated film critics left preview screenings holding their collective noses. They labeled the film "poor science fiction" and compared it to the cheap flying saucer movies of the 1950s. It lacked, they said, the wit and "fun" of *Star Wars*, a science fantasy that has earned millions this year.

They all ignored (or were unaware of) one very important fact: *Close Encounters* is the climax of 30 years of wonder, speculation, and propaganda. An entire generation has grown up hearing about, and believing in, extraterrestrial visitants, and they are ready for a film shorn of the usual science-fiction trappings – one that deals with UFO sightings realistically, and concentrates on how the UFO experience affects the witnesses.

To this generation, *Close Encounters* is more than just a trip to the movies. It is a religious-like experience. It is confirmation of personal beliefs. Thanks to a very loud soundtrack and some truly spectacular special effects, the film engulfs the mind, transcends all logic, and offers something very close to the Second Coming of Christ. Audiences, most of whom are under thirty, leave the theater silent, a glazed look in their eyes. They have been stunned – as stunned as any real-life UFO percipient – because they have been cleverly manipulated by the filmmaker's art.

Columbia Pictures is spending millions advertising and promoting *Close Encounters*, so I won't try to summarize the whole film here. It begins with a sandstorm, the wind howling so loudly that the audience is obliged to lean forward and strain to hear what the actors are saying. Thus they are made tense from the very opening scene – an old trick devised by Alfred Hitchcock many years ago.

The first distinguishable words are: "Are we the first?"

The soundtrack is unrelenting. Even domestic scenes are staged in near hysteria, amidst blaring television sets, ringing phones, and screaming arguments. At some points, you want to cover your ears and cringe in your seat, just as Spielberg intended.

When the saucers appear, the special effects are so well done you almost feel as if you are witnessing a real UFO event instead of just celluloid make-believe. And when a gigantic "mothership" finally descends in the climactic scenes, the effect is awesome. (We also receive a brief, less than awesome, glimpse of Dr. J. Allen Hynek towards the end of the picture.) Screeching electronic music and high-pitched blasts of beeping and wailing contribute to the assault on your nerves. The film literally wears you out.

By leaving almost every question unanswered (Spielberg never even approaches the question, "Where are they from?"), and by steadfastly refusing to fill in the many holes in the slipshod script, the audience leaves with a thousand questions in their minds. Perhaps in the hands of a lesser talent, this picture would have been an unmitigated disaster, and there would have been riots at the box-office as the victims demanded their money back. Instead, they leave strangely satisfied. Spielberg has been honest. He has not attempted to provide an answer. He hasn't even spelled out all of the questions. His main goal is to awe, to attack the senses, and to provide an *experience* rather than mere entertainment. He succeeds.

The picture must gross an unbelievable $45,000,000 before Columbia breaks even. Judging from the success of its first few days, we can estimate that it will probably finally earn around $200,000,000 worldwide. (*Jaws* has thus far earned $185,000,000.) In these days of economic blight, such figures are mind-boggling. The New York press and trade journals like *Variety*, the weekly "bible" of show business, have been preoccupied with the numbers involved. *The Wall Street Journal* was enchanted to note that Columbia's stock rose from $7 per share to nearly $20 per share after the film was released. In fact, Wall Street speculators made over $100,000,000 juggling Columbia's stock *before* the picture even opened. In America, big bucks automatically brings respect. Ironically, money is finally making flying saucers respectable. The news media are no longer joking about UFOs.

There were many snickers when Columbia Pictures announced that it would demand an advance payment of $150,000 from any theater owner who wanted to show *Close Encounters*. This was an unheard of "guarantee," and it seemed unlikely that many theaters would be willing to gamble such a sum against possible earnings. But with the picture now making over a quarter-million dollars per week, playing in only two theaters, the owners are enthusiastically paying in advance.

Dr. J. Allen Hynek acted as special advisor to the film and, of course, the title was lifted from material in his book, *The UFO Experience*. In the past, Hollywood has paid as much as $200,000 just for a title, and *then* written a film to match it (e.g., *Everything You Ever Wanted to Know About Sex*, *The Naked City*, etc.). Hynek has also actively helped promote the film by appearing on radio and television, having been promised widespread publicity for his Center for UFO Studies in Illinois. This kind of involvement for a movie with this kind of budget would normally have called for a minimum payment of $250,000. The New York press rumored that Hynek was being paid only $20,000, or less than ten percent of the norm. Actually, he has received only $1,700 from the producers. When you realize the time and effort Hynek has put into the project, no one can accuse him of profiteering. Instead, he has been exploited by the moviemakers.

There are already indications that *Close Encounters* will out-gross every other movie ever made. The audience will be young, and they will understand all of the hidden ramifications of the film – ramifications that may elude older, more skeptical adults. It is already on its way to becoming a cult film, like *2001: A Space Odyssey*. People who have seen UFOs, and they now number in the millions, will certainly stand in line to see it. People who have never seen a UFO, but have always wanted to – and they also number in the many millions – will also get in line. The picture will make UFOs totally real to millions all over the world. Ufology will never be the same again.

The next big UFO wave will probably attain greater notice than any previous one, all because of this movie. Already, the normally staid anti-UFO New York press is giving space to local UFO sightings. The New York *Daily News*, the largest American newspaper, gave front-page coverage to some recent sightings on Staten Island, under the heading: "UFOs: Close Encounters of the Local Kind" (November 27, 1977). Sightings are beginning to increase in the United States, following the mini-waves in northern Europe and elsewhere in 1977. You don't need a crystal ball to predict a new American wave in the months ahead. *Close Encounters* will naturally ride the crest of that wave. At least six other films with UFO themes are in production to ride the tail of that wave. So 1978 will be the year of the flying saucers.

Those of us who have been concerned about the true nature and intent of UFOs must regard this popularization and exploitation of the UFO lore with some alarm. Hollywood has chosen only a small part of the whole problem for the glamour treatment, and *Close Encounters* assures its audiences that the ufonauts are really friendly, super-intelligent creatures sympathetic to the human condition. We know this has seldom been the case in real-life UFO encounters. The film is a propaganda masterpiece, not only in getting the public to accept UFOs, but leading them to accept the benevolence of the "extraterrestrial" ufonauts. (In the closing sequence, the spindly ufonaut twists his almost featureless face into what passes for a smile. The effect is electric. Audiences respond to it as if they are receiving godly grace.)

This film whitewashes the abject horror of those who have experienced real close encounters, and their agonizing suffering afterwards. People leaving the theater find themselves gazing at the sky wistfully, hoping it will happen to *them*, convinced that the advent of the flying saucers is somehow a religious event – mankind meeting the gods. Future percipients will undoubtedly color their experiences unconsciously to match the film.

For years, the truest believers amongst us have waited patiently for some spectacular UFO event, like a landing on the White House lawn. Though frequently predicted, the event has never occurred. Now Hollywood has done it by creating the landing for us, and by presenting it to the entire world, dressed up in impressive cinematic trickery. Future ufology will be divided into two parts: BCE (Before *Close Encounters*), and ACE (After *Close Encounters*). It will be very interesting to see what strange new games the UFOs play in the post-*Close Encounters* era.

Perhaps the most iconic image of Mothman was the one painted by Frank Frazetta for the Illuminet Press reprint of The Mothman Prophecies. *While the wings could have been more batlike for some fans, the body of Frazetta's Mothman matches witness descriptions, and was a model for the Mothman Statue in Point Pleasant (see page 165).*

CHAPTER 18

Among the many deliberately neglected factors hidden within the mass of UFO sighting data is the apparent ability of the objects to change color, size, and shape while remaining in full view of the observers. A disproportionate percentage – at least three-fourths of the overall sighting reports – describe these unusual, *non-mechanical* characteristics. UFO researchers have tended to ignore these "eccentric" sightings, or have tried to dismiss them as natural phenomena of some kind.

During my first "flap" studies of 1966, I began to divide reports into two main categories: "hard" sightings of apparently metallic objects with discernible physical features such as fins, portholes, domes, and super-structures, and so on; and "soft" sightings of transparent or translucent objects seemingly capable of altering their size and shape dramatically. I placed the almost countless sightings of "lights in the sky" in the "soft" category. It quickly became evident that the "soft" sightings represented the *real* phenomenon, while the "hard" objects seemed to play some kind of diversionary role, often appearing at low level to pursue – or be pursued by – police cars and airplanes.

For twenty years, the ufologists have concentrated on the relatively rare "hard" sightings, regarding them as proof that manufactured machines were the main phenomenon. Having decided that these machines were largely circular flying craft, they were obliged to explain away the lights in the sky and "soft" objects as effects produced by the electrical ionization of the air – byproducts of some little-understood technological development. Theories of this type were developed by qualified engineers and scientists, and do seem valid until you examine all of the data closely and at length.

One of the many troublesome negative factors is the *fact* that although thousands of UFO photos have been taken in the past twenty years, only a dozen or so taken in different parts of the world depict *identical* objects. If the objects were more uniform in design (and origin), there would now be hundreds of identical pictures. Thus, on the strength of the pictorial evidence alone, we can conclude that a wide, almost endless, variety of objects is involved.

When one reviews the great mass of descriptions published in the past two decades, one is also obliged to concede that an impossibly wide variation exists in the descriptions. Again, the ufologists and their publications have concentrated largely on those descriptions of circular, domed objects and assume that they represent the whole. Actually, such objects form only a small part (5 to 10 percent) of the overall sightings.

There is also a very large percentage of "bastard" sightings – very peculiar objects in the form of rectangles, cubes, donuts, and even question-marks. Such sightings have been common throughout the years, but have been slighted by the ufologists, because they failed to conform to the more "acceptable" saucer design.

Any truly objective study of the UFO phenomenon must necessarily include a study of all the objects sighted, not just those objects that seem to support a particular theory. Perhaps the ufologists instinctively recognized that the "soft" and "bastard" sightings weakened the extraterrestrial thesis and their main "cause" – to prove that UFOs were the product of a superior intelligence from an advanced interplanetary civilization.

The U.S. Air Force, on the other hand, did make an effort to study all of the sighting reports in the early 1950s. *Project Blue Book Report 14* contained 240 charts, graphs, and tables breaking down the known and unknown reports into many categories. If you study the report carefully, you will see some of the reasons for the official conclusions. The sightings were too numerous and too frequent to be the work of a single technological source. The descriptions, including those of the coveted "reliable" witnesses, were too varied to support the notion that they were simply and purely manufactured machines. An attempt to develop a "model UFO" from the descriptions in 434 "unknown" cases met with failure. There was no single basic uniformity in these reports. Therefore, either every object was individually constructed and utilized only once, or *none of the objects really existed at all.*

Would even a "superior technology" on some distant planet go through the trouble of manufacturing a complex flying machine and then send that machine millions of miles to our planet to maneuver briefly one time – and one time only – over a farmhouse in Georgia? Certainly, once such a machine had been transferred to this planet, it would be used many times in many places, and eventually we would receive identical descriptions of it – and identical photographs – from several different points.

Instead, we have almost as many different descriptions as different witnesses. In my field trips, I have carefully weighed the psychological factors. I have found groups of six or ten witnesses who all described the same identical details of a given object in a given area. But ten or twenty miles away, another group of witnesses would describe a seemingly different object, even though the timing of their sightings dovetailed. I have been told about tiny "flying buzzsaws" hovering over strip mines, and gigantic, multi-windowed spheres hovering above power plants. Yet I have not discovered identical objects hovering over *different* power plants or strip mines.

On the other hand, the many thousands of "soft" sightings are very uniform. Witnesses in Nebraska describe essentially the same phenomena as witnesses in Maine or Manitoba. How many times have you read about groups of tiny, bright lights, all apparently under intelligent control, suddenly converging to form one big light, which then flies off? Or, frequently, the process is reversed, and one big light will suddenly split into several small ones, with each one flying off on an independent, controlled course. These cases are usually mentioned once in the UFO publications and then forgotten.

Most authors of ufological books focus only on the "most interesting" cases (i.e., the "hard sightings"), and use them to build a case for "extraterrestrial" visitants. This means that most of the available UFO literature is biased, non-objective, and possibly completely erroneous.

The "lights in the sky" and "soft" sightings don't seem to tell us very much about our friends from outer space, so we try to forget them. But they comprise 76% of the 2000 independent sighting reports I examined for my special article, "The Flap Phenomenon in the United States" (also known as "Beyond Condon"). Obviously, the "soft" category constitutes the main phenomenon, and deserves the most study.

Are there really thousands of different physical objects, of different sizes and shapes, entering our solar system and flitting around our skies, as the ET buffs would like to believe? Or are most of these objects temporary manipulations of matter and energy? We must now ask if there could not be some validity to a hypothesis that the objects are *transmogrifications*, and that we rarely, if ever, see them in their real form.

In the "airship" flaps of 1896-97 and 1909, all kinds of objects were described, including winged cigars, dirigible types, and baffling "eccentrics." In 1909, there were innumerable "lights in the sky" reports that looked and sounded like *conventional airplanes*, even though the aircraft of 1909 could not equal the speed and performances of these objects.

While there were many "eccentric light" UFOs during the massive 1933-34 "flap" throughout Scandinavia, all of the "hard" sightings involved airplanes of a size and capability unknown for that period. These "ghostfliers" carefully flew over villages and military installations so that everyone could get a good look at them. They provided a "frame of reference" for the more distant and unusual "lights in the sky" that appeared simultaneously in the same areas.

The "dirigibles" of 1897 and the "airplanes" of 1909 and 1934 were used for the same purpose: to provide an acceptable *explanation* for the more mysterious UFO lights then operating. Nowadays, in the modern era, saucer-shaped "spaceships" are being deployed in the same way, to give us an acceptable frame of reference and an "explanation" for the real phenomenon. After reviewing all of the available data, it seems clear that the "hard" objects represent an organized, intelligent effort to *mislead and divert us* from the main phenomena. The "airships" and "saucers" exist temporarily, appearing to be solid, manufactured objects, when actually they are mere transmogrifications devoted to obfuscating the real "truth."

If you study the "lights in the sky" cases, you will find a lot of orbs and "mystery meteors," some of which seem to shapeshift. These orbs and meteors first appear as cyan-colored (bluish-green) objects, which then shift through the entire color spectrum. Their most stable state is a blinding white. When they descend or take off, they usually turn brilliant red. All of this suggests definite changes of frequency. They "enter" our environment by descending from the higher frequencies, beyond ultra-violet. (The many cases in which witnesses have suffered burned flesh and eyes suggest that ultraviolet radiation is coming from the objects.) They depart by passing into the red frequencies, going into infrared (producing those cases in which witnesses suddenly feel great waves of heat). We have been hearing about these "frequency changes" for years from the "kooks and contactees." The data actually supports it!

The objects may be composed of energy from the upper frequencies of the electromagnetic spectrum. Somehow, they can descend to the narrow (very narrow) range of visible light, and can be manipulated into any desirable form, including dirigibles, airplanes, and "flying saucers." Such transmogrifications would not actually be mechanical, although they could *appear* to be. They would simply adopt a form that would make sense to us. Once they have competed their mission and, say, led another police officer on a wild goose chase, they would revert to an energy state and disappear from our field of vision.

Perhaps Air Force intelligence officers worked all this out back in the 1940s, and recognized that most "flying saucers" don't really exist in the same way that Volkswagens exist. But having reached this conclusion, they realized there was no possible way for them to publicly prove it. The only course open was to deny the phenomenon altogether. So President Eisenhower suggested that UFOs were "hallucinations" in 1954. Secretary of Defense Robert McNamara called them "illusions" in 1966. In case after case, Air Force investigators bewildered witnesses and enraged UFO buffs by gently implying that maybe the witnesses had "a psychic experience."

In short, flying saucers might not be any more real than the "dirigibles" of 1897 and the "mystery airplanes" of 1934. Their existence as solid, manufactured physical objects cannot be proven. They may be nothing more than transmuted energy patterns coexisting with us in the unseen, undetectable high-frequency radiations that surround us. By day, when the ultraviolet and infrared radiations of the sun pour down on us, the objects are "washed out" and invisible to us. By night, when those natural radiations are absent, they become at least partially visible to us as green, red, and white lights bobbing around the skies. They are always there. The history books tell us that they have always been there. But they play outrageous games with our senses.

The intelligence behind them remains to be defined, just as their real purpose may be incomprehensible to us. We have watched them with interest for eons, and speculated on their origins, and they have cheerfully tried to oblige us by taking forms we would like them to take. In other epochs, they were "fairies" and "vampires." Now we have turned them into "spacemen."

While we seem to be co-authors in this cosmic script, one has to wonder if we aren't just part of the audience, watching a galactic "dinner theater" hoax in which we are led to believe we are equal participants.

THE SUPERIOR TECHNOLOGY

A "superior intelligence with an advanced technology" is busy keeping a benevolent watch over us, or so we have been told by assorted "author-ities" for years. Actually, the marvelous "spaceships" built by that "superior technology" seem to be made from spit and bailing wire. Let's take a look at the record.

Since 1897, there have been scores of reports in which the witnesses claimed to have observed the UFO pilots busily making repairs on their craft. *The damned things are always breaking down.* In case after case, we have been told how the ufonauts climbed out of their machines to examine the undercarriage or to hammer away, twist bolts, and perform various "handyman" repairs. (It is only a matter of time before one of the "spacemen" pulls out a roll of duct tape!)

The modern stories range from Signor Monguzzi's controversial 1952 account to Eddie Laxton's encounter on an early morning in March 1966. In both of these reports, a human-sized ufonaut dismounted to inspect the underside of his "superior technology" vehicle with some kind of flashlight.

There have been so many of these "repair" incidents that they constitute a pattern in themselves. It seems that the same action is carried out, over and over again, in different places, and in front of different witnesses. In addition, we have endless accounts of wobbling UFOs going out of control and even exploding. Charles Fort cited several examples. There were crashes and "repairs" in the Scandinavian flap of 1934. The things blew up repeatedly, all over Europe, during 1946. The first major UFO sighting of 1947, the weird Maury Island case, involved a donut-shaped object "in trouble."

Not only are the objects unstable and jerry-built, but they are constantly falling apart. Again and again, they have left debris behind after landing. Usually this debris was in the form of an oil-like composition, made up of silicon and alumina. All of these wretched things have leaky hydraulic systems! They also manage to dump small pieces of aluminum and magnesium all over the landscape. Pieces always seem to be falling off them while in flight.

A year ago, during a visit to New York's Kennedy Airport, I purposefully visited the runway maintenance crew. I wanted to find out just how much oil and metal junk was collected from the runways of one of the busiest airports in the world. I was told that it was rare for a piece of metal to turn up on the runways. Occasionally, a small part such as a bolt would drop off of a small private plane. But if even a fuel-tank cover fell off a big airliner, we would have a major disaster on our hands (if not from the spill, then when that piece of metal was sucked into another jet's intake). Infrequently, a hydraulic line will rupture and spew oil out. The plane is quickly grounded for repairs, and the oil slick is cleaned up.

Conclusion: our clumsy, crude, inferior flying machines are far more efficient and reliable than the wonderful "spaceships" of the flying saucer "people."

If you want to speculate, you can find a number of explanations for these "repair reports." This is a good way to make their descent and landing seem logical to the observer. In other words, the repairs are staged for the benefit of the witnesses. Or, the objects only land on our planet when they are in trouble. Or, a "space war" is going on, as some ufologists have suggested, and these accidents and UFO disasters are a result of the secret battle taking place in our sky.

One of the most intriguing "repair" stories I have seen comes from Seattle, Washington, in the summer of 1965. The witness awoke around 3 a.m. to see a small, football-shaped object fly into her window. She suffered akinesia (paralysis), and was unable to move or scream as tripod legs extended from the object, and it landed neatly on her bedroom floor. Half-a-dozen tiny people climbed out and went to work making repairs on their craft. When they finished the job, they hopped back in and flew off into the night.

This story is interesting for several reasons. I have been told of many "mini-people" encounters in the course of my investigations, but they are so seemingly absurd that none have been published. It is important that the witnesses nearly always suffer paralysis during these sightings. This same phenomenon is found in the many psychic accounts of "bedroom visitants." Parapsychologists have long speculated that the entities somehow manage to materialize by utilizing some form of energy radiating from the percipient. The more intelligent contactees speak of this as an "energy exchange." It is so common that I have labeled it "kinetic vampirism" – feasting upon the motivating energy of the percipient, thus inducing temporary paralysis.

The young lady in Washington thought she was awake and was actually seeing the "mini-people." Perhaps she was experiencing some form of hallucination. If you examine the vast "fairy," "elf," and "leprechaun" lore, you will find many incidents comparable to those in the UFO frame of reference. Kinetic vampirism has not really been discussed in the readily available UFO literature, but I have come across many reports.

For instance, on a warm June evening in 1962, Gregory Sciotti, then 18, woke up around 11:30 p.m. with the feeling that there was a prowler in the house. He was alone in his home near Turtle Creek, Pennsylvania; his mother worked on the nightshift in a nearby factory.

"There was a light in the room," Mr. Sciotti wrote to me in 1967. "I quickly tried to get up and found it impossible to move. I tried to turn my head to see where the light was coming from. This I also found impossible. It seems as though the only control I had was over my eyelids. The feeling I had was something like when you're very tired – just too tired to move. Then I heard something on the steps just outside the door – something like a heavy breathing sound. I heard it moving around. I tried to scream to find out if I was dreaming, but I couldn't do anything but move my eyelids. Then the 'light' went out. It was like I had been pushing on something heavy, and it suddenly moved."

He ran down the stairs, badly frightened, grabbed a rifle, and loaded it, and called for his dog, Teddy, who he knew was somewhere in the house. But Teddy was gone. He searched the grounds around the house with a flashlight. He had another dog that was kept in the yard. That animal was also gone.

The next night, he continued, he was sitting in his car in the driveway, talking with a girlfriend, when a strange object rose up from the woods behind the house. Four windows were visible on a dark, oval shape as it passed between the moon and the young couple. It was not an airplane, he declared, and no trace was ever found of the missing dogs.

In psychic literature, tales of nocturnal akinesia are almost unlimited. For example, in his book, *The Edge of the Unknown* (1930), Sir Arthur Conan Doyle (author of the *Sherlock Holmes* series) tells how it happened to him. He was, he said, "acutely awake, but utterly unable to move" as he heard someone walk over to him and whisper: "Doyle, I come to tell you that I am sorry." After a moment, his paralysis left him, and he turned to stare into the empty darkness.

Young Sciotti's alleged experience falls into this uneasy category. He was immobilized while his two dogs were removed forever. The next night, he saw a UFO.

When we were able to examine the experiences of UFO percipients in greater depth, we may find that akinesis is not an effect of a UFO apparition but is, instead, a *contributing cause*. The "mini-people" in that Seattle bedroom may have materialized by utilizing energy from the witness herself. The "little men" of M. Masse's lavender patch may have "used" him in somewhat the same way.

The "fairies" of Ireland paralyzed the folk, and they distorted reality in all kinds of "magical" ways. Whole villages have been involved in celebrated, well-documented "fairy" incidents. The "trolls" of Scandinavia and the "elves" of Germany's Black Forest may have been part of the same package, along with the "Stick Indians" and the legendary "Trickster" of the Southwest Pueblo culture. From time to time, our planet is overrun with these characters. They are not from outer space, but from some fantastic world beyond the range of our limited senses.

This means that many of our coveted UFO sightings are, in fact, merely induced hallucinations and distortions of reality. That "superior technology" may be a fantasy, and those endless "repairs" are merely part of the game that is being played on us.

Another part of the game involves artifacts. The "fairy" lore is filled with anecdotes about people who tried to capture "fairies" or proof of their existence, only to suffer in the end. In UFO lore, we have many game-like repetitions of the artifact factor. Antonio Villas Boas tried unsuccessfully to steal an instrument from the "spaceship." Betty Hill was given a book, briefly, but the "Captain" took it away from her again. Carroll Wayne Watts in Texas tried to swipe an instrument in the same manner as Villas Boas, but it was taken away from him, too. There are many lesser-known cases. A Long Island contactee whose story lurks in my files, far too sensational to be published, tried to steal an object while aboard a saucer, only to have it taken away from him at the last minute. This was in early 1967, before either the Hill story or Villas Boas case were well known to American ufologists.

So we have defined two of their games: the "repair" tactic and the "stolen artifact" gambit. Perhaps many of the "water" incidents we hear about also belong in this category. After all, fairies were often found by streams, pailing water. In April 1897, several contacts took place near wells and streams where the ufonauts were "replenishing" their water supplies. Why would they land on inhabited farms and draw water when they could have done it completely unnoticed along isolated streams and lakes? Need we spell out the answer? They *wanted* to be observed.

Why do they land on highways to inspect their landing gear? Why not land, instead, on remote hilltops and deserts? It is possible that they *chose* to land on that Italian mountain in 1952 *because* they saw Signor Monguzzi flourishing his Kodak.

Their broken-down "spaceships" will undoubtedly continue to land in front of isolated witnesses while "repairs" are effected. They will pose for more photographs and we, of course, will decide that the photographers are hoaxers and money-grabbing publicity seekers. We have been crying for "evidence" for over two decades, yet we have rejected nearly all the evidence they have handed to us on a silver platter. George Adamski and Carroll Watts took photos that were just "too good to be true." Therefore, they were obviously trying to "trick" us. Aluminum, magnesium, and silicon have turned up at UFO sites by the pound, but no self-respecting "superior technology" would use such ordinary materials, according to the "scientific" ET buffs.

It is my contention that a good part of all this has been planned and skillfully executed, not by random practical jokers, but by the UFO source itself. The problem has been our methods for evaluating these events.

If we wish hard enough and long enough, one of these things is really apt to land on the White House lawn. While the president and his staff watch, a little man, three feet high, will climb out with a flashlight and a monkey wrench, and go to work on the landing gear. A fleet of Jeeps and tanks will surround the area. Newsmen's cameras will be confiscated and the object will melt away. Then an army general will hold a press conference and announce that the whole thing was just a publicity stunt for a new science-fiction movie.

There is no other way to play the "game." It is a helluva lot easier to denounce the phenomenon than to try to explain it.

THE GLENDALE, CALIFORNIA, CONTACT CLAIM

Among the strange UFO stories circulated by the small American ufological publications in 1967 (but ignored by the national press) was the unearthly account of a woman in Glendale, California, who claimed a series of contact experiences beginning on Wednesday, July 26, 1967. Although she could not possibly have known it – even if she *had* read all of the UFO literature available – her narrative includes many of the significant details that are proving to be so important in this phenomenon. Pfc. Richard Hack, a serious researcher now in the U.S. Army, corresponded with the Glendale woman and asked her certain specific questions that I had relayed to him. Her response was intriguing:

> *The Tujunga Ledger* is very accurate in their story about me. I am a divorcee with a 12-year-old son, and Mike Kisner is a friend who does research with me. I have experienced the "unusual" for some years – since I was six years old, in fact. However, 1967 was the most active in all my life, and the most unusual. Mr. Kisner entered my life during 1967, and I feel he might be an instrument of unusual qualities.

> The experiences last summer happened all at once, while several of us were out driving to and from a beautiful park in the mountains some distance from Big Tujunga Canyon. One evening, Wednesday, July 26, to be exact, we encountered the unusual. A voice spoke to us, telling us to watch something unusual within 300 feet. Soon, a huge saucer appeared, sort of hanging on the cliff to our left. It was 20 feet in diameter, glowing with three beams of colored light emerging from the top of it. It followed us several miles, again looming up from the canyon on the opposite side. That night, it disappeared over the Tujunga mountains.

The second night we went back, we watched in the same spot for a reappearance. It came with the spacemen Kronin, Karaff, and one or more others speaking to us. The spacemen picked up our car and propelled it two or three miles down the road, and then set it down again. This was so frightening, because they controlled it. The car was lit up. We saw the blue beam to the mothership.

On the third and fourth nights, we met or heard from Kronin, but did not see the ship. Kronin then started making appearances at my home. I bought a tape recorder and recorded some of the conversations, which I use in my lectures. I have recorded several calls from spaceships, too.

Kronin stands very tall, but has no bones or eyes. His face and forehead light up on most visits, and there is extreme warmth emanating from his body. His legs are short. He is of a vegetarian substance – a "space robot encased in a time capsule," he says. He told me that their planet was being destroyed by radiation, and that there are 3,000 of them on our planet. He refused to say where they were, but I feel that it is Tujunga Canyon, because of so many similar sightings in the same area. I feel they are stationed underground near the big dam lake. There is a strange protrusion of rock jutting out in the spot where they always appear.

A week after my story was printed, there were three ships over my house, at around 9 p.m. Five UFO watchers in the neighborhood alerted me. Later, on Labor Day weekend, Kronin took over the controls of my car. He drove it some five miles and parked it. We sat in the car listening to Kronin. He talked about 15 minutes to us, and tried to bring the scout ship down to take us for a ride, but the airbase trainers were on maneuvers. We did get to watch two scout ships enter the mothership, and it was outstanding.

Throughout the fall months, we had several contacts. The last ships I saw were during the week of January 6, near Lancaster, CA. Mr. Kisner and I saw five huge saucers, with windows, remain stationary for about two hours. We stopped at a café and called all of the patrons out. Needless to say, there was commotion all around.

The events Kronin told us to watch out for occurred, down to the X-15 crash. I asked Kronin why he had picked me and my little son for all of this, and his reply was: "You are an earth angel!"

I have moved since the newspaper story broke. My name is Maris. You may use my name among your associates, but not the general press. Kronin's ruler has asked me not to give the press news of my future contacts with them.

Mr. Kisner is an Apache Indian, and subject to moods at times. Right now, he doesn't seem interested in writing to anyone. In fact, he can only write in the Apache language. You'll probably hear from him later. This story is true, and you can believe everything I say.

My 1966 study, which revealed that the majority of all *initial* contacts seemed to occur on Wednesdays, was not publicly revealed until June 1967, one month *before* this alleged event. Maris had not heard of this study. It was not published and widely circulated until copies of it had been distributed to a few of the ufologists attending the Congress of Scientific Ufologists, in New York, later that year.

There have now been several cases in which witnesses claimed to have heard "voices" before or during a sighting. Several times in the past few years, witnesses have testified that the objects and/or occupants seemed to take control of their automobiles in some inexplicable way.

Although they have been given no publicity, even among the UFO buffs (who usually regard them as hoaxes of some kind), there have been hundreds, perhaps thousands of phone calls, placed around the country, from the ufonauts to the witnesses. The voices usually speak in a dull monotone, carefully pronouncing each word. In many cases, background electronic sounds are audible. Since these calls have now occurred in every state and have all followed the same patterns, a common hoax or prank can be ruled out – unless the hoaxer has the equipment and funds necessary to conduct a rather pointless nationwide campaign, and is able to select his victims before they receive any publicity. (See *The Warminster Mystery* by Arthur Shuttlewood for a complete description of this type of "hoax.")

The boneless and eyeless description of "Kronin" is common in several of the "silent contactee" cases I have uncovered. Mr. Brad Steiger has independently come across this same "boneless" feature in cases he is currently investigating. Usually the witnesses claim that upon shaking hands or otherwise coming into contact with the entity, they were unable to discern any bone structure. In a series of "contacts" on Long Island in 1967, the witnesses told me that the entities were boneless and freely discussed the fact.

Witnesses have remarked to me that the entities seemed to have legs that were either too short or too thin to support their tall bodies. In one of my early interviews with the West Virginia contactee claimant, Woodrow Derenberger, he noted this odd feature.

In a number of confrontations, witnesses have noted that the eyes of the entities, when visible, appeared to be non-functioning. Luminous faces are common in religious as well as UFO lore. See *The Books of the Secrets of Enoch* for early descriptions of tall, radiant entities. The "angel" that purportedly appeared in the bedroom of young Joseph K. Smith, in 1823, was described as having a glowing face. Smith's encounter led to his establishment of the Mormon Church.

There are few if any correlations in what the contactees are *told* about life on other planets. These descriptions appear to be deliberate lies and probably have no bearing whatsoever on the problem. Since many of the contactees are remarkably honest people, albeit somewhat gullible, I believe that *they are lied to*. If the entities are deliberately lying about their origins, it seems probable that a very unexpected answer can be found somewhere in the "trivial" details of these stories.

"You are an earth angel" is apparently just a variation on what is told to every contactee – that they are somebody very special, and have been deliberately selected. Some are told they are reincarnations of great personalities from the past. Others are told that they have been chosen because they have exceptional psychic abilities. Still others are informed that they are actually "space people" themselves, and were planted here as very small children. Indeed, several contactees have proven to be adopted children of unknown parentage. Since most contactees are of humble backgrounds and low stations, they are flattered and pleased by such revelations.

The entities have the ability to ferret out flaws of character and to exploit them. Often they appeal to the ego. One very prominent American researcher underwent the contactee experience in August 1967, and he was promised that he would be given a cure for cancer, which would lead to his receiving the Nobel Prize in 1972. His ego thus led him into a labyrinth of disastrous manipulations that nearly caused him an emotional breakdown. He didn't get wise to this ploy until it was almost too late. He has since abandoned his interest in the subject.

The entities manipulate many witnesses into keeping silent by threatening to break "contact" if they reveal anything about their experiences. Since some witnesses believe they are undergoing a religious experience, they obey. Others, as cited above, are led to believe that if they keep quiet, they will eventually become rich and famous.

Certain contactees are *urged* to make public statements, however. George Adamski and Woody Derenberger were such contactees. The information revealed to them could have been nothing more than propaganda meant to foster belief in the extraterrestrial thesis, which has been foisted upon us since the 1950s. In most of the cases I have investigated, the witnesses have confessed that they were sorry they ever got involved, and if given another chance, they would not have obeyed the entities.

In Maris' case, which has been investigated by many researchers on the West Coast, we have a long line of sightings, many of which were witnessed by whole groups of people, and we have all of the minor elements that underlie the contactee phenomenon *but have never before been mentioned in print.* Determining the validity of this type of unprovable experience is less important than correlating the details of many such claims. If we are dealing with liars and psychopaths, the subject still deserves careful study. If we are dealing with actual entities of unknown origin, then every single detail of these stories demands full examination.

In nearly every case that I have investigated, the flying objects seem to have been used to *provide a frame of reference.* Once the contactee has accepted that the entity is a "spaceman" from the "saucer," the objects play a diminishing role in the contacts. Later contacts often involve the use of automobiles or unexpected materializations in the witnesses' homes. All of the talk about outer space, life on other planets, etc. may be employed merely to provide that frame of reference. The entities may be unwilling or unable to tell the witnesses where they are actually from. Perhaps the witnesses would be unable to comprehend it even if told.

Maris mentions that certain prophecies given to her proved to be accurate. It is common for contactees to be given precise predictions on future events. When those events occur as prophesied, the witness feels he or she has received proof of the validity of the entities' claims. If the witness begins to publicly repeat such predictions, false predictions are quickly passed along. When the witness repeats these with total conviction and they fail to occur, he or she is automatically discredited by their friends and the public.

The events in many UFO cases are obviously false or deliberately misleading. The truth lies not in the messages received, but in the manner in which those messages have been conveyed to us. It is now safe to guess that thousands upon thousands of people have been carefully selected, contacted, and "used" throughout history. We are only now becoming aware of the real phenomenon.

Our hopes that a "flying saucer" from another planet may someday land on the White House lawn probably have no foundation whatsoever. The phenomenon is historically consistent. The objects were as numerous in 1847 as they were in 1947, and they will probably still be aloof from us in 2047. But now that we are beginning to notice, we can also begin to make a serious study and forget all the childish controversies and nonsense of the past. We may be dealing with something very basic and very important to our own environment. Now we have a chance to find out what it really is.

CHAPTER 19

THE COSMIC BLOG – LETTERS TO AND FROM JOHN A. KEEL (JAK)

There is a danger that this letter may find its way into your "crank" file, but I am hoping you or one of your assistants will read it carefully and give it some consideration. I would hate to think of myself as being a "crank" or "crackpot." This letter concerns the perplexing stance taken by the U.S. Air Force on the subject of "flying saucers."

I am a professional writer, and author of a number of books and countless magazine pieces on a wide variety of subjects. Although I have extensive background as a globetrotting reporter and once served as Science Editor for *Funk & Wagnall's Encyclopedia*, I have been toiling in more recent years in the wasteland of television. Like most writers, I have a wide range of interests, a skeptical turn of mind, and an insatiable curiosity.

I have been collecting information on UFOs since the appearance of the mysterious "Foo Fighters" in World War II. But I did not fully believe in their existence until 1954, when I actually saw a "flying saucer" maneuvering over the Aswan Dam in Egypt. It was hovering at a low altitude, and was obviously a solid metal object, circular with a dome on top. After a few minutes, the outer rim started to revolve rapidly, and it moved off at very high speed. Similar objects – or the same one – were later reported over other areas of the Middle East. (For the record, I was employed as Chief of Continuity and Production for the American Forces Network in Europe, 1953-54.)

This sighting, however, has no bearing on the purpose of this letter. It was an isolated incident, and I have never written about it. In fact, I have never written anything about UFOs, but have left them up to the cultists and pseudo-scientists.

As you undoubtedly know, there was a considerable amount of UFO activity in 1965. They appeared in great numbers all over the world, and reportedly landed briefly in France, South America, and even in Minnesota. The U.S. Air Force, as usual, came up with a series of absurd explanations for them. By now, hundreds of thousands of people throughout the world have observed these things. A number of governments have issued statements to the effect: "They exist. We don't know what they are but, apparently, they are harmless." Our own government has been silent – even strangely secretive – on the entire subject.

Recently, I visited my hometown, Perry Township, NY, for the holidays.

It is about 50 miles from Buffalo and Niagara Falls. I learned that the area had been inundated with UFOs during October and November of 1965. Everyone had a choice story to tell me, and a number of people had managed to take photographs. I even saw a strip of 8mm movie film that clearly showed a solid, metallic disk hovering in the sky. Since Perry is a small town (pop. 5,000), the arrival of the saucers was a major event. Whenever one was sighted, everyone would jump into their cars and drive out to gawk at it. One hovered over the Perry-Warsaw Airport for about two hours one night, apparently causing the airport beacon to go out. These objects were "hedgehopping," and many people got a close look at them. I was told that groups of these things gathered nightly above Attica, NY for about a week. The descriptions were too graphic to be the product of some kind of mass hysteria.

It was during this period that we suffered the Great (Power) Blackout in NY. I found that everyone I talked to was convinced that the blackout was somehow caused by UFOs, particularly since there were a number of incidents in which automobiles stalled when the objects passed over, radios ceased to function, etc. – standard procedure with sightings all over the world.

Naturally, I didn't spend my whole visit discussing flying saucers. I hadn't been home for the holidays in 19 years. And since all of the reports were basically the same, there wasn't too much sense in pursuing the matter. Oddly enough, of all the witnesses I talked to, only *one* person had bothered to call the Air Force in Buffalo to report a sighting. Most people were afraid to report what they had seen for fear of ridicule. Many people expressed outright contempt for the Air Force's attitude towards UFOs.

A week ago, a UFO was sighted over New Jersey. It appeared at night and projected a powerful beam of light toward the ground. A number of people saw it, and they were all astonished and chagrined when the Air Force told them that they had seen a "helicopter." (There have been quite a few "searchlight" sightings over the past few years.)

So, at last, we arrive at the point of this letter. Hundreds of communities all over the United States have been sites of intensive UFO activity. Many thousands of people have seen these objects in one form or another (formations of moving lights, low-flying "fireballs," seemingly solid objects of various shapes, etc.) and they are all sneering at the U.S. Air Force for trying to tell them they have seen a distant planet, a weather balloon, or an ordinary aircraft.

The Air Force started out by trying to ridicule the notion that strange objects were maneuvering over our country, and now this approach has backfired. It is the Air Force that is looking ridiculous. In fact, our Air Force is beginning to look downright incompetent. The time has come for the Air Force to reassess their public attitude towards UFOs. Their present approach of "explanation and denial" is no longer acceptable to the American public. And this approach has caused them to lose the support of the public.

After wading through tons of literature on UFOs, and all available Air Force proclamations on the subject, I am forced to conclude that we have failed to investigate this mystery properly. It seems as if the Air Force knows no more about UFOs now than it did 19 years ago. Alien objects are traversing our skies, maneuvering at will above our cities, towns, and military installations, and we are totally helpless to do anything about it. Judging from the stepped-up UFO activity last year, we can expect more incidents in the future, and perhaps even greater numbers of these objects will appear. Public concern will certainly increase, and more demands for an adequate explanation will be heard.

A poll taken a couple of years ago revealed that 75% of the population believes in the existence of flying saucers, yet the Air Force continues to try to maintain its unbelievably naïve attitude. Or is it just trying to cover up its own inadequacy?

We know that UFOs have been around a long time. Historical records of sightings go back many centuries. And yet there is no concrete evidence that they have ever made a serious attempt to contact us. We can therefore assume that they will be around for a long time to come, and that they will remain aloof. Where they come from and what their mysterious missions are about is open to all kinds of conjecture.

I do not expect the U.S. Air Force to come up with any spectacular conclusions or out-of-this-world explanations. But I do expect it to stop playing the fool, and to stop calling baffled witnesses to this phenomenon liars and idiots. The average American knows the difference between a round metal disc that flies in total silence and a noisy helicopter. The average American knows that comets do not fly horizontally in "V" formations.

It is time for the Air Force to give the public whatever concrete information it has been able to gather. It is time for officials to tell the thousands of UFO witnesses that they *did* see something, and put to rest all of the rumors that are sweeping our country. This is not a serious situation yet, but a few more seasons like the one we had last year will really put the Air Force out on a limb.

Already, average sightings of UFOs no longer make the press. Newspapers are bored with reporting that Joe Schmoe saw something in the sky. Perhaps if the UFOs returned to Perry Township, NY tomorrow, they would cause less stir. But in the years to come, our skies could become filled with "Trojan Horses."

So I urge you to press Air Force officials for an improvement and expansion in their methods of investigating this situation. And I ask that a full and sensible appraisal be offered to the public.

-John A. Keel, letter to Senator Robert F. Kennedy 1/19/66

Thank you for your thoughtful letter on so-called "unidentified flying objects."

Many reputable scientists agree that there must be other beings in the universe. Dr. Harlow Shapely, for one, has stated that there is a high probability that there is other life in the universe.

To believe that there is other life in the universe is not, however, to believe that "UFOs" are manned vehicles. One explanation of this phenomenon connects the lights that are seen with gaseous tails of comets. A careful analysis of sightings to date has not given us any indication that "UFOs" are manned.

I appreciate hearing from you on this matter, and hope you will write again on matters of mutual interest.

-Senator Robert F. Kennedy, letter to JAK 2/7/66

On Jan. 19, 1966 I wrote to you outlining my misgivings about the manner in which the U.S. Air Force has been handling their investigation of "flying saucers." I received a reply from your office dated Feb. 7th. Since then, of course, the incidents in Michigan and elsewhere have stirred up great interest in the subject and, as I predicted, caused the national press to heap ridicule upon the Air Force.

I have been assigned to do an in-depth probe into this subject for *Playboy* magazine (whose present circulation is over four million). I will be arriving in Washington later this month to speak directly to the Air Force officials involved in this investigation. *Playboy* is writing directly to Project Blue Book to inform them of my plans, and to ask for their cooperation. I would be most grateful for any help you could grant me during my visit. If you are willing, I would like to meet with you briefly and get your point of view on this situation.

My files are bulging with well-documented "ammunition" that proves the USAF has handled their investigation in a horrifyingly incompetent manner over the past twenty years, and that they have been ruthlessly unfair to thousands of honest citizens. But I am anxious to hear their side of the story before I reach any final conclusion in print.

Judging from the cyclic pattern of the UFOs' activities, there will be a "flap" of fantastic proportions in the spring and summer of 1967. We must be prepared for it. The Air Force should certainly be ready to conduct a sensible and meaningful investigation when it occurs. I am about to expend a considerable amount of time, effort, and money in my research and, as I have already said, would appreciate any cooperation you might be able to extend.

-JAK, letter to Sen. Robert F. Kennedy 4/2/66

Out on the West Coast is a man you should talk with. Trace his information. His name is Fred Lee Crisman, of Tacoma, Washington. He flies to New Orleans steadily: in 1964, eleven times; 1965, seventeen times; 1966, thirty-two times; 1967, twenty-four times. He is the first man [JFK suspect] Thomas Edward Beckham called. Crisman was questioned by both the CIA and FBI in 1966. But he is able to call Washington, D.C. [for help]. They laid off of him in a hurry. He is very good friends with the Cubans and with Arnesto Rodriguez in Dallas, and Jorge Rodriguez Alvarado in New Orleans.

Mr. Crisman is a very odd man. He supplied the money for certain political campaigns and, in return, is very much protected by both Louisiana politicos and Washington State people. He has a diplomatic passport issued on the word of a chairman of a Senate committee. He seems to have no income, yet certainly spends a large sum of money on air travel. His private office has an unlisted number, and it is the meeting place for many odd characters, from Cubans to political figures.

Ask him to take a lie detector test, and then ask him where he put the $200,000 delivered to him by Beckham in Aug. of 1967 – money used to recruit killers…

Crisman is also a pilot. He is the man that paid off certain people. Is it not odd that he is a friend of Clay Shaw's? Is it not strange that he knew Officer Tippit? Crisman is the one who told Beckham to hide out in Iowa and to not go to New Orleans and make any statements about money or anything else. Have an investigator check out the amount of long-distance calls Beckham has made to Crisman in the past year, and the wild places Crisman calls. He is leaving for Europe in January. Keep digging, Jim, you have some odd fish on the run.

-Anonymous letter to Jim Garrison (reprinted by JAK) 1966

Here is an outline of the "Gray Barker" phone calls I have received. Since writing this up, there have been additional calls from a man identifying himself as "Samuel Guttenpoole, Attorney at the Lions Building, Clarksburg, West Virginia." These calls come from long distance. "Guttenpoole" claims he is a lawyer representing Gray Barker, and is threatening to sue a number of people for "defamation" of Gray's character.

In addition to these mysterious calls, someone has been calling various people in the New York area and on Long Island, claiming to be *me*, and leaving hysterical messages. These messages are left with people I do not even know. *Restaurants* have received these calls. As I told you the other day on the phone, it looks as if someone is trying to set up an elaborate "frame" of some sort – with me smack in the center of it.

I am, as you know, deep in some very important research, and I have a considerable amount of extremely important information and documentation in my possession. I intend to release this material very soon, perhaps within two weeks. A complicated and carefully planned hoax is being contrived by "someone" to shatter the validity of my findings, and throw a cloud of smoke over the whole issue. Gray Barker and others may be sucked into this situation unknowingly. I am convinced that the government, Air Force, CIA, etc. are *not* involved in any way. I have already been to the FBI with this. This thing is a lot bigger, and a lot more sinister, than any of the hobbyists suspect. We are dealing here with problems that go beyond mere military considerations.

Please file the attached material in a safe place. If anything should happen to me, print it. When you see Gray, give him the whole story and try to determine if he is involved in any way. I don't think he is.

To give you some idea of how horrifying this business is, the Pope is very likely to be assassinated in Turkey within the next few weeks. If that happens, all hell is going to break loose, and there will be UFO activity of a most unexpected nature. Believe me when I tell you that I have gotten to the bottom of things. The *real* UFO story is so weird, and so numbing, that even the hardcore believers and cultists will not be able to face the truth.

If, by any chance, any of your cronies are planting occasional hoax calls, get them to stop it. They will be needlessly involving themselves in a situation that could cost them their sanity or even their lives.

-JAK, letter to Jim Moseley 7/17/67

The piece in your July/August issue, called "Fantasy or Truth," got me thinking about a story I was told in West Virginia by a ufologist. Maybe it means a great deal. Here is his story:

> While interviewing UFO witnesses in West Virginia recently, a prominent community leader in a small town along the Ohio River asked me if the symbols of "triangles and squares" ever played a part in UFO reports. I asked him what he meant, and he told me his story.

> During the Korean War, he had served in the Air Police with the U.S. Air Force, and was assigned to a post in Germany. Sometime in 1951 or 1952, a Russian MIG fighter pilot decided to defect, and flew his plane across the East German border, continuing until he ran out of fuel and was forced to set down in West Germany. The Americans were, of course, delighted with this prize – a late-model MIG, intact. The witness and a buddy were assigned to guard the plane until the necessary vehicles could be mustered to collect it and haul it to the nearest Air Force base.

> The plane was guarded 24 hours a day until it could be moved, and the two men were given night duty. They were driven to the field, an isolated spot near Weisbaden, where they relieved the guards then on duty. They found themselves alone in the darkness, facing a long night. After a few minutes, they observed a bright light in the distance, moving slowly towards them. They assumed that it was a jeep. They watched as it appeared to move across the rough field to the plane, growing brighter as it came.

> Suddenly, the witness was astonished to find himself standing at a guard post *back at the airbase*. It was broad daylight, and he was on duty. Twelve hours had passed, somehow, and he had absolutely no recollection of how he had gotten back to the base, or what had happened. His buddy was also back on the base, and was equally baffled. They tried to make a few inquiries, but since no one seemed to think that anything

was out of order, they decided to say nothing further.

From that day on, the witness was plagued with recurrent nightmares in which triangular symbols appeared. He felt that the triangles were some kind of "doorways," and they frightened him. As the years passed, these dreams troubled him more and more. He claims he finally sought psychiatric help for a time, and the treatment seemed to pinpoint *that* single, unexplained evening. I suggested that he seek hypnotherapy from a qualified psychiatrist, and he is seriously considering it.

What happened to the two young soldiers in that distant field? Could he have spent those missing hours in the same twilight zone that engulfed Betty and Barney Hill? Perhaps hypnotic regression will produce some unexpected answers. We should take note of this story of induced amnesia, and watch for more stories like it from Europe during that period.

-JAK, letter to *Flying Saucer Review* 11/12/67

[Editor's note: the December 14th date for the mysterious "Happy Landing Incident," mentioned in the next letter, was the day before the collapse of the Silver Bridge on December 15th, 1967. Strangely, on December 14th, men in checkered jackets were reportedly seen climbing around and "tinkering" on the bridge.]

Here's the brief memo I promised you to boil down everything, which is, I suppose, better (and more private) than trying to do everything over the phone. Sorry I was so sleepy when you called. Woe to anybody who has to put up with a cover like I have, for the job worked my ass off Friday and Saturday. Though I got in early, by the time I gave everything a quick monitor, I practically fell into bed.

On the stuff that came in from AOK in Wisconsin, I would say it's mainly static, and A.W. is merely a nut of some sort. Let's not write it off, but put it in "inactive."

The Abernathy film doesn't check out. Write it off. The guy was clever, though. He was using high-speed film and solarizing the image into the film. The "solid object" was really an intense light source. You may not understand all this (and I don't entirely) but, anyway, this investigation is dropped, period.

In the case of B.D., the thing checks out. He did actually expose the tape with a cheap vidicon camera, and this one did originate as a tape – not as a film run on a film chain. The object moves with the camera movement and looks pretty good. There will be another investigation on this, though, before there's any okay on it.

When you send the report on Jim C., play up the part where there was "haze" and "fading in and out" of the landing gear. The old man loves this sort of thing, and this may get the heat off losing the files on Chandler.

"Happy Landing" is definitely set now for the *14th of December*. There will definitely be good play on this from all the "controlled" media. The others will have to pick it up. This will be a good one, though no Michigan. I know you have no part in this, but just be ready for it with the typical nutzine approach. (For godssake, I'm not giving you orders; just passing them along, so don't give me a Menzel on this.)

Regarding communications, G/144/1603 silent; G/144/1619 intermittent sampling; change G/144 1700 to an F/100 status; close analyses of the other suspected "foreign" G's on G/144 1622; change from IBM to Burroughs on G/144 1622-B. They now have the new 2" tape equipment, which should give more speed in monitoring. I learned this will all be done at Station C, and a feed made only when there is a "good program."

I think that is everything. I hope you're using the "suggestion box" and that the "suggestions" are being adopted regularly. Yours for transfer…

-Letter signed "Grunt," from Gray Barker to Jim Moseley (but mistakenly mailed to John Keel) 10/21/67

Though it is quite ridiculous to waste time on all this nonsense, here are the latest facts on *The Barker-Moseley Swindle*. These are confidential and not for publication.

With an opaque projector, I blew up the letter in question (the "Grunt Letter") and compared the type with previous letters from Gray Barker. Barker's typewriter was definitely used. You can check this yourself if you have any letters from Barker. (Take into account the minor distortions of the photocopying process.)

Both Moseley and Barker have referred to Barker in the past by the nickname "Grunt." The signature on the letter is *not* in Barker's handwriting. It is written in heavy, blue ink, probably with a flow-pen. It is possible that Barker had someone else sign the letter. If a hoaxer had somehow gained access to Barker's typewriter, they would most certainly have taken pains to *forge Gray's handwriting.*

The letter arrived in a Gray Barker envelope bearing a stamp from Gray's postal machine (#838511), postmarked Clarksburg, West Virginia, Oct. 21st. The envelope shows no signs of having been tampered with. Therefore, whoever sent the letter must have had access not only to Gray's typewriter, stationary, etc., but also used his postal meter.

I would have regarded this whole thing as a complete prank of some sort if the letter had not contained a reference to the December 14th "Happy Landing" incident. I have known about this date for some time, and have not mentioned it to a soul. This is not likely to be a Barker "fiction." He must have received this information from a *very* unusual source.

I copied the numbers in the next-to-last paragraph and sent them to Moseley. He called me on the afternoon of Oct. 27, 1967 and acted as though he did not know what they meant. I said I didn't know either, and that's why I had passed them on to him. Later that evening, Moseley called me back. He now appeared most perturbed by the numbers. I refused to tell him where they came from. He then suggested that perhaps the mail had gotten mixed up, and that maybe *I had received a letter meant for him.* I neither confirmed nor denied this.

If all of this was some kind of joke or maneuver on the part of Barker-Moseley, I do not intend to fall for it.

Regarding the Joseph Henslik ("missing UFO photographs") affair, I have now taped interviews with both Henslik and his mother, in which they admit to the MIB hoax and fully implicate Barker-Moseley in its conception and execution.

-JAK 11/22/67

Thanks for sending *UFO Warning* and your letter of Jan. 21st. *UFO Warning* reads like an amateurish effort to blow a single incident up to book size. If the stuff about the girl is at all accurate, then she apparently was hot for the book's author, John Stuart, and had some sexual hang-ups before her encounter with the "invisibles." There is so much derivative speculation in the alleged conversations that I tend to dismiss the whole case.

"Scott" certainly is a prolific letter-writer. There have been days when three notes from him have turned up in a single mail. For some reason, Jim (Moseley) seems to be ridden with guilt anxieties and a genuine fear of legal action. He does not seem to take my advice seriously, but applies his own hysterical logic to the trivia taking place.

A Long Island reporter pinpointed the identity of Princess Moon Owl months ago. He was going to write a piece about her, but her blatant bid for publicity disgusted him, and he tossed the whole thing in the wastebasket. Jim has nothing at all to fear from her. My comments in the last *Saucer News* were sufficient, and further exposure was unnecessary. If she wants to sue somebody, let her sue me. In a court of law, she would be obliged to prove that she is who she says she is. I just don't understand why Jim permits himself to take this kind of thing seriously at all, particularly after his having spent 15 years in this cockeyed field.

As for Jaye Paro, Jim and Mike made a very serious mistake in giving out the *unlisted* number of her family. The day after she gave Jim the number, their phone went crazy with hoax calls, and it has continued ever since, at all hours of the day and night. The phone company, at their request, attached both a tape recorder and a tracing device to the phone, and have been monitoring everything for three months. The FBI is also in on it. Some of the hoax calls were traced to Florida (while Jim was down there) and even to El Paso, Texas.

Jim cannot seem to realize the gravity of all this. He is not dealing with Miss Paro, but with her family, and they have considerable wealth and influence. Miss Paro is engaged to a prominent young man in Washington, D.C., and a few weeks ago she dumped all the telephone records, etc., in his lap. He turned them over to the proper authorities. I know this because they approached me a few days later to confirm the calls I had made out there. The whole thing is a hornet's nest.

To worsen matters, a few days ago, Mike Cleveland passed the Paro number onto Gene Barry, a Long Island character who caused Miss Paro some grief early last year. He called there, and then Jim and others called. It all seemed like part of the hoax pattern to the Paros. An FBI agent sat by their phone one afternoon last week, and took all incoming calls. In addition, they have been getting anonymous threats in the mail, and have been suffering other persecutions. They are fed up, and determined to take whatever action is necessary. I have tried to warn Jim, but he stupidly regards it all as some sort of "cover up," and goes blundering ahead. He may really end up with his ass in a sling if he doesn't learn to properly evaluate this kind of nonsense and steer clear of it.

The Paros are *not* fooling around. They are out for blood. Miss Paro isn't even involved in this current situation. She has quit WBAB and is now engaged in preparations for a new and more important job. Perhaps you can somehow hammer some sense into Moseley. I'm about ready to give up on him altogether.

As I have stated in print, I fear that some of these hoaxes are being engineered to frame or implicate innocent researchers. For that reason, we must take quiet, rational, responsible action. Jim has a tendency to fly off in all directions when these things happen. He unconsciously contributes to the circumstantial evidence that is mounting against him. I have been doing a lot of undercover investigation into these matters since last June, and now I'm preparing a very fat dossier of evidence and documentation on these telephone hoaxes. Irresponsible meddling by Moseley, Barry, etc. could blow my case (which is just what the hoaxers want).

I have learned the hard way that Jim cannot be trusted with any important information. He has chosen his friends and associates badly, and if he doesn't start playing it cool, he will end up in more hot water than he can imagine.

Back in June, I went to the FBI, accompanied by others who were suffering this kind of harassment. They have been working on this situation ever since. Special agents of the NY Telephone Co. have also been engaged full-time in this since last summer. It has all been a costly and time-consuming diversion, particularly when there are so many more important things requiring my attention.

I'm afraid Jim will never learn. His inane behavior is only contributing to his own destruction. I warned him months ago to beware of Gladys Fusaro, and I had good reason for doing so. But he ignored that advice, as he has ignored everything else I have tried to tell him. He just doesn't seem to be able to sit down and think these things through.

Try to convince him to stay out of these traps by avoiding the temptation to make phone calls, spread rumors, and harass people who do not want to talk to him. Get him to keep careful records of whatever hoax calls he receives, and to keep careful tabs on his own phone bills. We must always be suspicious of the obvious, and we must wait in silence until the authorities spring their own trap, which will be very soon.

-JAK, letter to Gray Barker 1/24/68

I received your letter this week, and was very happy that you are okay. With so many strange things happening, I worry about you when I don't hear from you (although I realize that you have more to do than write letters).

I had another strange visitor this week, who said he had first come to my office, but couldn't find me. Then he came to the house! Even Scotty thought he acted funny and looked very strange. He said he was an "electronics engineer" and worked in Newark, Ohio, but his home was in Michigan (he was "transferred" to Newark).

I cannot tell you the color of his hair. I guess it was white, but an odd shade, and never have I seen any hair that looked like it. I had this book you sent me about the UFO convention on a table. He nearly went wild when he saw it, and wanted to buy it, but I wouldn't let him have it.

He wore glasses, and when he took them off he had the funniest eyes I ever saw. They were back in his head, and the smallest I have ever seen. The color I could not tell you. I am sure he noted the strange look on my face.

The first question he asked me was just how well I knew John Keel. I said, "Well, I know him." I told him I didn't think it was anyone's business who my close friends are, or how close they are.

He said, "Do you know him well enough to speak to him?" I told him I spoke to everyone, but that doesn't mean that I was the best of friends to them. He said, "Did you ever get in his car and go anywhere?" I told him again that that was not a matter of discussion with anyone, and that I did not have to answer to anyone about where I went.

He then said, "Is this John Keel an investigator, or a writer?" I told him he would have to ask you. He tried to trick me by saying he was just wanted to go with me to see where John Keel saw these objects. I told him I couldn't, because I didn't know where they might have been.

He tried several times to get me to go with him, and to give him names of people who had been with you, but I told him I didn't follow you around to see who you talked with.

He also claimed he knew a girl that I knew in Columbus. His license number is JV0911 – Michigan plates. He said that he has been interested in UFOs for 20 years. With his glasses on, he looked 55 or 60, but with them off, he looked about 35 years old. His appearance changed completely with them off. Why, I cannot say.

-Mary Hyre, letter to JAK 3/25/68

After I did my column Sunday, it suddenly dawned on me that the "headless man" story I wrote about *could* have been the beginning of this whole (Mothman) puzzle here in this area.

In a very old newspaper clipping, I read a story with a headline "Legend of the Headless Soldier of Donohue's Lane Told With Early History Viewed." The story says that a distinctive type of farm-folk still dwell in Jackson County, West Virginia. Their land has been handed down from generation to generation since the early 1800s, until "the good earth" has become a traditional heritage. Around the fireside on a winter evening, you can hear a wealth of superstitions, like the story of the "Headless Soldier of Donohue Lane."

Sometime during the Civil War, Stuart Donohue, a federal soldier, returned from the Army of the Potomac to his home on Little Mill Creek. A few days later, he was warned that a detachment of "home guards," led by a native of the community, was on their way to arrest him as a "deserter" and return him to Virginia. Donohue met the home guard unarmed, having stuck his carbine in a decayed stump, and agreed to accompany them to Cottageville, where a hearing would take place.

After the party had crossed Little Creek at Click's Ford, a member of the guard shot Donohue in the back, inflicting a mortal wound. The murder became a local item of interest. Although the man who committed the crime went unpunished by civil law, there were mutterings after the war that the victim's family might avenge the killing. Perhaps it was their threat that kept the incident foremost in the minds of the people, and acted as a psychological effect on the happenings that followed.

Natives of the section began to report they had seen a strange and unaccountable phantom near a large beech tree – the spot where Donohue was killed. To some, the murdered man appeared as a black colt; to others, a ball of tawny dust. To an early United Brethren minister, he appeared as a headless soldier climbing through the rustic rail fence. As to what facts these stories are based on was not learned, but they had a paralyzing effect on the countryside. Grown men refused to travel the lane, children shunned the spot as if it held the devil for them, and the late traveler glanced frequently at the sinking sun and lengthened his stride.

One resident of the community, a brother of the deceased man, vowed that he met the strange figure one rainy night. The shock of the encounter sent him home as fast as his legs could carry him. When he came to Little Mill Creek, swollen by the spring rains, he plunged into the swirling waters and swam to the other side. Never again did he pass the spot where his brother died.

This didn't just happen in Jackson County, but also partly in Mason County (the county in which Point Pleasant resides). A few people are still reporting seeing unusual lights there (as usual). They will appear more often now that the weather is beginning to get a little better...

I think I am cracking up. I cannot seem to get that thick-glasses man out of my mind. I guess he will be coming for me. If they all look like him, I do not want to go.

When they come for me, I will let you know. As ever…

-Mary Hyre, letter to JAK 5/2/68

[Editor's note: The "scientist from Cleveland," who scared so many witnesses, was probably Fred Crisman, who attempted to pass himself off as a "scientific ufologist" from the Cleveland UFO Group. Woody Derenberger's daughter, Taunia, has identified Crisman as the man who came to their door after her father began his contacts with "Indrid Cold."]

I spoke to Jim Moseley a day or so ago. He tells me that you were in Hurley's from 9 to 9:30 the night we were supposed to meet. I arrived early, at about 8:45, and went into the RCA building to make a couple of phone calls. I returned to Hurley's shortly after 9:15, and sat at the end of the bar, by the door, until almost 11 p.m. I can't understand how we could have missed each other. I had a package of photos, clips, and other material that I wanted to pass on to you.

Now, about Point Pleasant… The key witnesses are now all dispersed. Roger and Linda Scarberry have now moved to Cleveland, Ohio. Roger was recently discharged from the Army. Steve and Mary Mallette have also moved, and will no longer discuss any of this with anybody (including me). Mrs. Hyre has been hounded so much, by so many people, that she may prove to be uncooperative. Connie Carpenter and her husband have moved northwards. Henderson in Ohio has been hitting the bottle pretty hard, as you undoubtedly know.

Others in the area have clammed up altogether, some after receiving a visit from "a scientist from Cleveland!" (???)

Mothman has not been seen for several months, but giant, hairy monsters have appeared in the area this spring.

The McDaniels are annoyed with you, because you never returned their clippings. Mrs. Bennett will probably refuse to see you. All in all, it is the old story. So many weird things have happened that most of these people just don't want to talk about it, or even think about it anymore. You must treat them very gently, and work to win their confidence.

One woman is now in a mental hospital with amnesia. Others have quit their jobs and disappeared. Officer Harmon has quit the police force and moved out of Pt. Pleasant. Unknown to the "natives," the FBI has been keeping the area under tight surveillance since the bridge collapse. At least one FBI man is likely to turn up at your convention at the hotel. The Air Force is not interested.

There are several contactees in the area, but they are not apt to reveal themselves to you. One man in the area is directly related to all of this. His identity is known only to me. He may approach you quietly, when you are alone. If he tries to get you to go with him somewhere in his car, beg off.

The strip mines in the hills, on the Ohio side of the river, are quite important to all this. Get over to them if you can. If you all want to go UFO-hunting some night, travel south along Route 2, to the sector between Gallipolis Ferry and Apple Grove. The Chief Cornstalk Hunting Area spreads eastward from there. It is thinly populated, and the site of much activity. Visit the Point Pleasant Chamber of Commerce on Main Street, and have a chat with Mrs. Belva Farley.

Try to keep a tight rein on aggressive, scoffing types like Timothy Beckley. A careless, tactless, snide approach will cause these people to clam up. The editor of the local paper is anti-UFO, as you probably know; so don't expect much help from him. Let me know how you make out.

-JAK, letter to Gray Barker 8/25/68

Regarding the question of why the U.S. has so many Men in Black cases, it is probably because the U.S. public was – due to the boom in sightings, far and above anything experienced elsewhere – made to be extremely conscious of UFOs. But I am happy to report that I am in excellent physical condition. The MIB have not gotten me. However, I am a little worried about my head. I can supply notarized affidavits from qualified physicians if necessary, but all the rumors and nonsense circulating in this country may yet drive me around the bend.

Am I really a "CIA agent" (as one widespread rumor has it), or am I just an inventive liar willing to sacrifice professional ethics – and thus jeopardize my reputation and livelihood – by "making up" UFO stories, which I then somehow con hard-bitten, skeptical New York editors into publishing? I do wish all of the rumor-mongers would get together and decide who and what I really am. The contradictions make me unhappy, and could turn me into some kind of schizoid.

In the past two years, I have published over 40 detailed articles on the

UFO phenomenon in major newspapers and national magazines. In those articles, I have clearly explained my position and conclusions repeatedly and, I thought, succinctly. There should be no mystery at all about my methods, my activities, or my interpretations of the data. Mr. Rankow, who should know better, somehow twisted my advice that he "research demonology" into the ridiculous and malicious claim that I "believe in Deros and devils." Now really!

As I have said so often in print, I have been unable to substantiate the extraterrestrial thesis in any manner, and I do not think it is even remotely valid. But if you read the Bible, it is chockfull of stories about "three men," and filled with obvious "contactee" events. It is a veritable ufological handbook (and I'm an atheist). I advise ufologists to also read textbooks on psychological warfare and police investigative methods. Such books are far more useful than speculative tomes on astronomy.

The phrase "find out what they eat for breakfast" is slang, in American journalism, for "find out *everything* about them." I thought this was made clear in my article that so confused Mr. Rankow.

The majority of my lengthy, heavily detailed reports go unpublished, but are privately circulated to trusted, serious ufologists around the world. Many of my findings are being confirmed and substantiated in numerous other areas. The editor of *Flying Saucer Review* has seen a number of these reports (at least the ones that haven't been intercepted in the mails), and fully understands why it is necessary to keep them "secret" at this time.

-JAK, letter to *Flying Saucer Review* 11/11/68

Charles Samwick's recent essay on the "saucer convention" in Point Pleasant (published in *Saucer News*) is incredibly naïve. I'm surprised you didn't set him straight. First of all, there were several "Mothman" sightings *prior* to the Scarberry-Mallette sighting, as you well know. It is absolutely inexcusable that none of you bothered to interview a *single* witness during your "convention" in Pt. Pleasant.

There are *hundreds* of UFO and Mothman witnesses in the immediate area. Residents on farms on Route 62, both north and south of the TNT Area, have had good sightings of Mothman. There are a number of families living deep within the TNT Area itself who have not only seen Mothman, but who have also seen UFO landings and other interesting phenomena. The old power plant, which lies on the *outskirts* of the 2500-acre area, was the site of only a few random incidents. There is an Indian graveyard deep in the hills to the rear, where some very strange activity seems to have been concentrated.

Before your convention, I mailed you a letter in which I named certain people who could have provided you with some very interesting information. Apparently, you never bothered to contact them. When PBL was planning two one-hour shows on UFOs in 1967, their teams visited the Ohio Valley three times, interviewed scores of people, obtained photographs and movies of UFOs, and dug up cases that I had missed. The programs were dropped because of "budgetary" problems. Most of their tapes, notes, and transcripts were eventually turned over to me. Among other things, they extracted interesting sightings and statements from sheriffs and policemen in other towns in the valley.

It is clear you made no effort to locate old or new witnesses (and there have been many incidents since my last visit). If you had spoken to Sheriff Johnson, you might have learned something. Both he and his wife have seen many UFOs. Mrs. Johnson is a rather avid UFO buff. Very few Mothman witnesses reported directly to the Sheriff or to the police.

I have taped interviews attesting to the reliability of the Scarberrys and Mallettes *at the time of their original sighting*. In 1967, Roger Scarberry did begin to display the symptoms of "mind control," and revealed certain "contactee" characteristics, but I am not all surprised by this behavior. In fact, I expected it.

I have never seen "fireflies" in the TNT Area. You should have interviewed the people on Camp Conley Road. The Lillys finally sold their house and moved last fall, because the poltergeist activity and telephone harassment had become unbearable. And, they were scared to death.

Two weeks after your convention, there was a huge wave of sightings throughout the Ohio Valley. Mrs. Hyre received hundreds of reports in a single week, but wrote only one short newspaper story about them. That same week, there was a North American flap, particularly in New England and in Montreal.

The Samwick essay falls into the same category as Allen Greenfield's recent report on his visit to an island in Georgia. Quite literally, it is like a school paper on "what I did last summer." Your convention delegates visited the place, poked around the abandoned power plant, didn't interview anyone, didn't see anything, and developed no facts, pro or con.

You listened to a lot of hearsay, but didn't bother to check any of it at its source. Unusual droppings *were* found in the old power plant in November 1966, and *were* collected by a county health official from Gallipolis, Ohio. I tried later to track him down and get his report, but I never succeeded in catching him in his office.

If you had bothered to visit the McDaniels, they would have shown you hundreds of clippings and letters from all over the area, recounting all kinds of UFO sightings and "monster" cases. But Mabel tells me you just called once, asked for Roger, and then hung up. I told you in my (prior) letter that Roger and Linda had moved to Cleveland in 1968.

You should have at least gone up to New Haven and talked with Lou Summers, the pharmacist who has been keeping track of things for NICAP. Instead, you, Jim Moseley, Tim Beckley, and Samwick engaged in a typical buffery "investigation." You went down there and looked at the sky *two years* after the main incidents had occurred. This was tourism, not investigation, Gray.

In 1967, you talked with some of the early witnesses immediately after their sightings. You have many clippings of those events (some belonging to Mabel). You should have been able to brief your gang properly. Instead, you permitted Samwick to compose a childish and irresponsible essay based upon speculation and nonsense. For instance, nobody ever told me that they thought "Mothman's wings" had caused the bridge to collapse. On the contrary, *two men were seen climbing around the bridge the day before the collapse.* The FBI suspected sabotage, which is why they went through the trouble and expense of reconstructing the whole damned thing.

Pfc. Richard Hack did visit Pt. Pleasant in January, and did conduct a thorough independent investigation, re-interviewing many of the witnesses named in my article, and checking out some of the more recent events. He is now preparing a detailed report for limited circulation.

I've just read the proofs of Woody Derenberger's book. It is thin and somewhat poorly done. In many ways, his account is identical to the Adamski and Schmidt stories. Unfortunately, he has left out a good deal. Some of the most important factors and events have been deleted.

The UFO situation has taken a very serious turn this year. I suspect there will be a new wave of "silencings" and Loftin-type deaths among the self-styled "ufologists" this year. It is highly possible that people like Hynek and McDonald will drop the subject altogether in the coming months. Vallee has already gone "underground," as have many others.

I have long been stressing the need for total in-depth investigations in flap areas, not superficial skywatching excursions. Since my *SAGA* "Mothman" article appeared, all kinds of wild-eyed teenagers and self-styled "ufologists" have visited Pt. Pleasant and bothered everyone. Most of them settled for spending a week sitting in the TNT Area staring at the sky! Some of the people named in my articles are now furious with me, because they have received so many idiotic, insulting letters and phone calls from tactless, irresponsible buffs.

I am really fed up with the buffery scene. I made every effort to cooperate with you characters, and devoted a lot of valuable time to writing for the various fan magazines. I have been repaid by groundless gossip, rumors, and maniacal nonsense. You and Moseley are directly responsible for much of it. It is little wonder that the subject has acquired such a disreputable aura. I don't pretend to understand your motivations, but I do wish you would adopt a more mature approach to the situation.

The monster and entity cases are actually nothing more than a variation of the age-old "elemental" phenomenon. Therefore, they prove little or nothing. The government has probably been well aware of this since 1946. By the same token, the infinite variety of shapes and reported objects is part of the same phenomenon, and a majority of all sightings result from hallucinatory effects. This is why the witnesses must be studied so carefully. We have to learn to weed the real from the unreal. Adamski's longhaired Venusians were really classic "elementals." He was tricked, as so many others have been.

You are certainly experienced enough by now to realize that the phenomenon is primarily concerned with the human mind, particularly the human subconscious. The UFO buffs have been caught up in a mischievous game for twenty years. They have been exploited, suckered, and conned. It is time for us to replace fantasy and speculation with logic, reason, and responsible, in-depth studies.

-JAK, letter to Gray Barker 3/15/69

During the past three years, we have received many "crank" letters and pieces of "anomalous mail." Some of these made direct threats against our person, while others were cleverly and carefully composed. We turned a few of the more serious-sounding items over to the FBI. We attempted to investigate other items through Postal inspectors. A total of four proved to be the work of mischievous "UFO buffs." The remainder are still unidentified or unsolved. Individuals involved in our investigations also received unusual letters, which added to our collection.

Here is a representative anomalous letter. On Nov. 30, 1967, this appeared in our mailbox in an Air Mail envelope (without a stamp). The word "Free" was typed in the upper right-hand corner of the envelope, with the words "International Bankers" typed in the upper left-hand corner. The letterhead on the note itself, bearing the words "The International Bankers," was well printed on high-quality bond paper. The paper was very slightly yellowed around the edges, indicating that it would have been on hand for some time. The envelope was of a type widely sold in post exchanges in Vietnam. Soldiers in Vietnam may send unstamped letters by writing "Free" in the upper right-hand corner. There was no postmark. The letter appears to have been typed on an electric typewriter:

> The year 1967 A.D. is rapidly coming to a close. Phase One and Phase Three are almost complete, so we take it upon ourselves to give you ample warning, Mr. Keel.

> Let us warn you that the year 1968 A.D. will have the color black as its symbol. So, Mr. Keel, be extremely cautious, and do not take much interest in things that do not concern you. We are a very powerful organization, Mr. Keel, and we can make things very uncomfortable for you and your friends who try to find out too much about Phase One, Phase Three, or anything concerning other parts of the Universe.

> If you do not heed our warning, Mr. Keel, we will be forced to visit you, as we did Mr. Henslik. We are always watching, Mr. Keel. We have eyes and ears that never sleep.

> Others have tried, without success, to find out things that did not concern them, such as Dr. Morris K. Jessup, Al Bender, and others who you do not even know about.

> Do not overstep your bounds, Mr. Keel. Even your own government cannot protect you from our powers.

> Remember, Mr. Keel: 1968 A.D. will have the color black as its symbol.

Keep in mind, certain words were misspelled (but have been corrected here). Misspellings of simple words are a common factor in mail of this sort. These often seem quite deliberate (i.e., a witness in West Virginia received a note containing the word "want" instead of the intended "won't").

The vague prediction that 1968 would be a "black year" proved disturbingly accurate. 1968 proved to be the year of widespread civil disturbances and the assassinations of Dr. Martin Luther King and Sen. Robert Kennedy.

-John Keel, letter in Anomaly magazine 12/7/69

The June/July *Merseyside UFO Bulletin* arrived yesterday (August 5) and has led me to order new suits (black) for my corps of Oriental-looking aides. I am sending them to England to carry out a kidnapping operation. You and Rimmer will be the first to disappear, for we need you desperately on this side of the Big Pond. This will be a new kind of "Brain Drain." My MIBs are looking for ufologists with open minds and a sense of humor. They scoured the United States systematically, for four years, and have failed to find anyone answering to these qualifications. But despite the petty conflicts and nonsense in British circles, I still suspect the general quality of ufology there is considerably higher than it is here. So pack your suitcase and wait for the 3 a.m. knock on the door. The password is "Stendek."

Now, whether you like it or not, here is my considered opinion.

Ufology should rightfully be a branch of psychical research. The psychical researchers have developed reasonably scientific methods for dealing with paranormal material. And they have quietly come up with some reasonable answers for much of it. I am not speaking of the innumerable crackpot cults and lunatic fringe believers. The "New Ufology" (Jerome Clark's term) must necessarily be concerned with *all* paranormal manifestations. It is folly to ignore and exclude cases that contain unsavory psychical elements, just as it would be folly for medical researchers to ignore leukemia because they don't like the sight of blood.

Ufology is not dying. It is in a transitional period – a most painful one for many. If our none-too-learned interpretations of the cave paintings are correct, UFOs have been buzzing this planet since man first appeared. They will very likely still be flying around long after we have blown ourselves up. Maybe they belong here even more than we do. We do make wonderful pets, and our antics are no doubt very amusing. Instead of debating the mathematical probabilities for life existing on other planets, the "New Ufologists" will be more and more concerned with the unseen (but frequently observed manifestations of) forces that exist here, right by our side. We seem to be currently suffering from psychical pollution. Perhaps the human mind itself is partially responsible, and is causing some peculiar interaction between "Us" and "Them." The "balance of the universe" is, indeed, upset. And the ufologists are the most unbalanced of all.

I have just been informed, from the most esteemed of authorities, that John Keel doesn't exist at all. An expert graphologist has examined samples of his handwriting and discovered that his many letters and articles were really written by Sir Francis Bacon. This finding should resolve some of the controversy.

-JAK, letter to *Merseyside UFO Bulletin* 9/11/70

I have just received the November and December issues of *Merseyside UFO Bulletin*. I was beginning to fear that sinister government agents might have confiscated your typewriter, and carried you off in the middle of the night to the Royal Air Force's super-secret prison-madhouse for "dangerous" UFO researchers. Glad you are still in operation and that postal service has resumed. The British Edition of *Operation Trojan Horse* is scheduled to be released on April 29th by Souvenir Press of London. I would greatly appreciate receiving any clippings of any reviews or comments that might appear in the British press. Frankly, I doubt if it will be widely reviewed, but one never knows.

Alan Sharp's comments in your November issue delighted me. His letter outlines all that has been wrong with ufology to date – the totally pragmatic approach (on the part of the scientifically trained element), and the tendency to denigrate opposite opinions and those who form them. Obviously, anyone who does not believe what "I" believe (he says in effect) must be a crackpot. Since my views are so different from his, this makes me "King of the UFO crackpots" (a phrase coined by Hynek's partner, William T. Powers, incidentally). Mr. Sharp is profoundly sane, of course, although I have yet to meet a truly sane astronomer.

Indeed, the two most insane areas of science are astronomy and archaeology. The classic characterization of the "crazy, absent-minded professor" is based solidly in fact. However, it is equally well-known that *writers* are the strangest, most eccentric breed of all. We are, undoubtedly, even weirder than the crackpot professors, A number of the latter group have been loudly advocating alien "visitations" for several years. Their evidence thus far has been on the same level as the evidence being used by the stalwarts of the Flat Earth Society.

I must take umbrage with Sharp's remarks about the value of "studying the movement of galaxies by watching a glamorous woman downing a scotch-on-the-rocks." I have, in fact, learned a great deal over the years by doing just that. The more scotch consumed, the more I learned. It is one scientific method I heartily endorse.

Perhaps Mr. Sharp misunderstands my entire thesis. I have stressed that the initial investigation must be a study of the witnesses, and must be conducted by psychiatrists and psychologists. As he put it, "the universe of mystery, incomprehensible in its complexity" is almost entirely the product of "the inhabitants of mental institutions." Many of our American UFO witnesses, contactees and researchers have ended up in mental institutions. The very basic promise of ufology is totally insane! The ideas and theories propounded by the ET believers are insane by almost *any* standard.

The strange urge to promote these insane ideas publicly, often at great personal expense and ridicule, has been detrimental to any public acceptance of the phenomenon. Such efforts are *evangelistic*, not scientific. And the people who advocate irrational, unsubstantiated ideas should be medically examined. Since 1965, Dr Hynek himself has stressed the examination of witnesses, and has often complained that no UFO case has ever been given the "FBI treatment" (i.e., a thorough study of all aspects). In my investigations, I have attempted to apply this treatment within my (admitted) limitations.

In my two books, I carefully outlined my methods, my findings, and my conclusions. I suggested numerous ways in which my "discoveries" could be tested in the field by intelligent investigators. The results of my efforts have been interesting and – psychologically speaking – curious. A polarization has taken place on the American UFO scene. Those who have been directly involved in UFO investigations and bizarre events, and who have yet managed to retain an open mind, are quietly swinging over to my side (if I have a side). They *know* what I'm talking about.

Unfortunately, many of them have chosen to discontinue their publications, terminate their membership in UFO organizations, and more or less withdraw from the UFO *mainstream*. Apparently, acceptance of "Keelism" (another choice Hynek phrase) destroys interest in mainstream evangelism. The result is that the remaining "hardcore" ET buffs are virulently anti-Keel. I dismiss their beliefs, so I am an "enemy." Most of the UFO publications that have survived are therefore antagonistic to the new "Keelist ufology." They go on censoring and distorting the items that come their way, and continue to advocate the old causes and beliefs, most of which are based on the peculiar logic denounced by Sharp: the philosophy of the mischievous "elementals," who have been playing silly games with the human race since Og crawled out of a cave.

Some time ago, a West Coast UFO publication carried an absurd, even slanderous, quasi-review of *Operation Trojan Horse*. Jerome Clark wrote to the journal in "protest." He was duly informed that I was "banned" from its august pages and, even if I wanted to bother, would not be permitted to reply to the perverse charges leveled against me.

Other American publications have employed tired tactics, such as quoting me out of context. One took a direct quote from Howard Menger – found in my book – and credited it to *me* as "proof" of something or other. Another sad fact is that the extreme right-wing groups (political ultra-conservatives) have *infiltrated* ufology here, and are lending their own sick, paranoid notions to the already disoriented American UFO scene. Right-wing smear tactics (quoting out of context, attacking through innuendo, etc.) are becoming the "norm" in American UFO publications. Recently, NICAP's illustrious bulletin made some inane crack about my waiting for "girlie magazines." Of course, I avoid such magazines. My main field has always been the men's *adventure* magazines, which are quite separate and distinct from the "girlie" field. NICAP doesn't know the difference, I suppose. Should they stumble upon one of my pieces in *The New York Times Sunday Magazine*, they would undoubtedly condemn me because that same publication is usually filled with advertisements of winsome ladies posing in their underwear.

The trend, unfortunately, is for newly enlightened "Keelist" ufologists to stop beating the ET drum, and to drop out of sight, leaving the field to the steadily shrinking but loud-mouthed fanatics and fringe types. I would hate to see this sad pattern repeated in Great Britain. History demonstrates that believers and fanatics shoot people, start wars, and generate all kinds of useless controversies and conflicts. Ufology has been following the patterns of the religious groups. You don't need a background in sociology to discern this.

Alan Sharp and many others have responded emotionally to my findings and conjectures. They have failed to recognize the main thrust of my work – a return to objectivity and the consideration of *all* theories and intelligent investigation, and the testing of each and every one.

Here in the U.S., there some large, well-organized groups that are loudly battling our government's mental health programs. I have interviewed and written about some of the leaders of these groups. It is clear that what they *really* fear is that such programs may be directed at *them* because, deep down, they *know* they are crazy. When the Condon Committee first swung into action, they called Ray Palmer and other hardcore ufologists and generated considerable outcry because, logically enough, a large part of the committee consisted of psychologists, and they were asking psychological questions.

The ufologists instinctively feared that Condon was out to prove they were crazy. Most of ufology adopted this same stance, and most ufologists frothed at the mouth when psychiatry was even mentioned. Why? For the same reason that anti-mental health groups are battling efforts to enlarge and improve our mental institutions and psychiatric techniques. If careful studies were to prove that contactees, witnesses to landings, etc., were hallucinating or suffering from mental aberrations akin to religious ecstasies, then the believers would only scream "whitewash," "fraud," or "conspiracy," because all of their beliefs are based entirely on blind acceptance of the physical reality of such experiences.

If ufology can ever be set upon the right track, we stand to learn amazing things about the human condition generally, and about psychology, religion, the myth-making mechanism of the human mind, and reality itself. Along the way, we will certainly abandon, one by one, all of the concepts and beliefs that have been popular this past quarter-century. By 1980, ufology may be dead; that is, ufology as we now know it. But it will hopefully be replaced by a new, more rational science that studies everything, considers everything, and does not attempt to support any particular belief. Recently, Dr. Frank Drake, our famous radio astronomer, stated that discoveries in the last five years have forced astronomy to discard many of its most beloved theories and truths. All astronomical textbooks will have to be completely rewritten in the next thirty years. We are making a grand discovery – the grandest of all. We are learning just how ignorant we really are. Ufology is but another road leading us to the same discovery. Once we recognize our sublime ignorance, we can stop searching for answers, and try instead to frame the proper questions.

The U.S. and Soviet moon shots taught us one horrible fact. After peering at the moon for hundreds of years, we really didn't know a darned thing about it. And most of what we *thought* we knew has been proven erroneous, overnight. Man's ego really can't take this kind of punishment. And the ufological ego is the largest of all. It is easier to deny new facts than to re-fashion old acceptances. The American ufologists don't like what I have to say, so they have banned me from some of their periodicals. One American group even tried to get Bowen to ban me from *Flying Saucer Review*. These are the same people who have been wailing for two decades about alleged government *censorship* of UFOs, official conspiracies, and so on.

Now I must get back to work and write a crackpot article for a "girlie" magazine. All the best...

-JAK, letter to *Merseyside UFO Bulletin* 6/1/71

I must admit I felt very embarrassed for Alan Sharp when I read his emotional critiques in *Merseyside UFO Bulletin*. I'm a bit puzzled you would choose to devote so much space to this Menzelian/Keyhoe type of attack. It seems like something right out of the 1950s. Poor Alan has denuded himself, exposing his astonishing ignorance of ufology and his apparent inability to read the English language. Since my clearly stated position is really "anti-UFO," one wonders what his position is. Is he a super-believer or a super-skeptic?

Several years ago, I was assigned to write a technical article on meteors, comets, bolides, etc. I naturally contacted the leading authorities and I was taken aback to discover how little hard data actually exists. Mathematical formulae and spectrographic analyses do not impress me at all. The astronomers have been proven totally wrong in almost every important area in the past decade. But I am very aware of all that is being done. For example, a group of Canadian astronomers went to great lengths in 1967 to check the course of a meteorite, interview all those people who saw it, etc. When I read their thorough report, I could only wonder why no one had over really conducted the same kind of investigation into a UFO transit.

Operation Trojan Horse (*OTH*) was written in 1967-68, and was completed long before *The Condon Report* appeared. In fact, I was reading the proofs when *Condon* reached me. I penciled in a number of minor references and corrections, added items about Vallee's book (which appeared after *OTH* was written), etc. For example, the item about the closing of Blue Book (p.293) was added to the galleys. Much of the chapter "Charting the Enigma," which Sharp takes exception to, was published in my *Flying Saucer Review* article, "Beyond Condon," in 1969. A detailed paper on the results of the investigation into the Allende meteor was published long after *OTH* appeared; as near as I can recall, it was in the Feb. 1971 issue of *Science*. My material came largely from *The Christian Science Monitor*, a newspaper that regularly contains the best science coverage. (It was a delightful "coincidence" that the name "Allende" should be associated with this incident.)

Many of the things commented on by Sharp had been repeated over and over again in the ufological lore, and my own tack was to ridicule items such as Prof. Agrest's crackpot theories on the ancient city of Baalbek. My original section on tektites was deleted from *OTH* and later worked into *Our Haunted Planet*. If Sharp re-reads that chapter of *OTH* (Chapter 4), he will see that I give full credit to the creators of the various theories outlined. If he reads it carefully, he will see that I do *not* take these theories seriously.

Sharp's critique seems like a rather pointless exercise in egomania. He has clearly not bothered to research any of the subjects he is attacking. Rather, he is trying to draw conclusions and create explanations from sketchy summaries of cases drawn from more detailed articles in *Flying Saucer Review* and elsewhere. He thinks he is attacking Vallee and myself, but all he is really doing is demonstrating his own ignorance of the UFO literature. He has produced a classic example of the nonsense I ridicule in my introduction to *Our Haunted Planet*. The UFO field should have outgrown this kind of childish, churlish, irresponsible, and highly personalized form of attack.

When I prepared "Beyond Condon," I included a rather extensive glossary of terms. An extended version of this glossary was included with the manuscript of *OTH*, but remains unpublished. I am a professional lexicographer, having served as Science Editor for Funk and Wagnall's encyclopedias, and as Geography Editor for their *New College Dictionary*. (You will find my name listed in their publications). The etymology of ufology has been one of my interests from the start. In *Anomaly*, I have frequently published glossaries of important terms. It is both presumptuous and pretentious of Sharp to complain about my use or abuse of the language. Although my books have been deliberately "written down" to my audience, Sharp obviously suffers from semantic difficulties.

Many of the things I discussed with deliberate vagueness were actually based upon research now being conducted by many disciplines. For example, at the IEEE Symposium in New York this March, Dr. Robert O. Becker revealed experiments that found that very low frequency EM waves could promote healing of bone fractures and rapid healing of skin ulcers and burns, thus verifying my speculations about "miraculous" UFO healings.

The U.S. Bureau of Radiological Health, a bureau of the Dept. of Health, Education, and Welfare, has been studying these things for years. DHEW's National Institute of Mental Health is very concerned with schizophrenia, a subject closely allied to the UFO phenomenon. It is no secret that I have been working as a consultant to DHEW here in Washington.

Sharp's credentials are certainly far more limited. In fact, mineralogy is almost as useless to ufology as astronomy.

As for Peter Rogerson's review of *Our Haunted Planet*, my astonishment is multiplied. The book, largely derived from deleted sections of *Operation Trojan Horse*, was clearly and pointedly an examination of the theories and beliefs of all the crackpot cults – a deliberate appraisal of the "pseudo-scientific garbage" believed by mankind. It summarized many of the major and minor beliefs of these cults, but certainly did not support any of them. Yet Rogerson was apparently blinded by emotionalism when he read it, and inverted the meaning of everything. I simply pointed out that the basic beliefs of the assassination buffs were identical with the beliefs of cultists using other frames of reference. And in the last chapter, I summarized the beliefs of the present youth culture. Many youth are particularly interested in Indians and Indian lore, most of which is founded on visions – mediumistic and drug-induced hallucinations.

Quite a few scientists – all operating outside the UFO field – are working to find the cause(s) of the UFO "effect." In England, a group of scientists now have a funded program to investigate the "religious experience." In the Soviet Union, work along these lines is now very advanced. It is really most difficult to define UFOs, per se, until we can properly separate the *possibly* real from the totally subjective. And the world's greatest philosophers and thinkers have been attempting this for 2,500 years.

Sharp and his ilk want us to lapse back to what Husserl termed "phenomenological reduction." Back in 1967, I published a little essay in *Saucer News*, in which I said that the ufologists, like cuckolds, would be "the last to know," because they are blinded by belief, and because they have an urge to simplify complicated situations and accept those simplifications as "truth."

In my three books, I have tried to at least touch upon all the popular theories and the "evidence" used to support them. I have never accepted any of that "evidence." Rather, I have tried to explain why I have *rejected* all those theories. The "ultraterrestrial theory" is merely a new, more workable frame of reference (new to the UFO field, but hardly original or new in the strictest sense). The first step to understanding this mess is rejection of the extraterrestrial hypothesis. But there is a long and difficult road ahead for anyone who tries to go beyond it.

My work has been aimed at uncovering and interpreting the cause of these events and experiences. A great deal of headway has been made in recent years, and it constantly appalls me that so few ufologists seem capable of actual research; of visiting a technical library and examining the literature for themselves.

Many of the things Sharp complains about were, in fact, more fully documented in my many articles published here in the U.S. I wouldn't expect him to be familiar with those articles, but I would expect him to exercise suspension of judgment until he was more familiar with the massive material used by Vallee and myself as the basis of our conclusions. He is rejecting the history of mankind out of hand. In *Our Haunted Planet*, I clearly state, "All of this may be absolute nonsense, but we cannot overlook the unhappy fact that these 'truths' were completely believed for thousands of years by the leaders of the world, and therefore had an appalling influence over human events and destiny."

Vallee and I realized that the core of the problem was belief, and that the rational, philosophical study of belief was necessary to understand the whole. From 1967 onwards, I pointedly classified UFOs as manifestations and anomalies, divorcing myself from the concept that they were machines piloted by Venusians. While others have been trying to "prove" their beliefs or, in some cases, their sanity, I have been searching for the underlying causes.

That search has led me to reconsider all of man's beliefs, particularly his religious concepts. While many readers do not fully understand this consciously, they can and do react emotionally on other levels. They suspect I an attacking them in some manner, because I am attacking their beliefs. Eric Hoffer explains all this in his book *The True Believer*. In that book, he really defines the average UFO or ET buff – the Menzel/Sharp types, who exploit ufology to gratify their own emotional needs.

Millions of people welcome and accept subjective experiences as the basis for their beliefs in ghosts, the afterlife, Christ, and spacemen. Arthur Shuttlewood is one of those. It is both pointless and vicious to attack Shuttlewood for what he believes, and for his earnest, honest attempts to communicate those beliefs. We can reject the beliefs of such people *without* rejecting the people themselves. From the little I know about the man, Shuttlewood's sincerity is beyond question. On the other hand, the intellectual integrity of people like Menzel and Sharp can be seriously questioned.

Before closing, I might add that I contacted some of the religious cults that are concerned with miracles, particularly Fatima, and they showed me documentation of their search to locate the photos and newsreels taken in Fatima on that day. Apparently, someone *did* go to great expense to collect all of the photos. Whether it was the Catholic Church (very likely) or our Men in Back is anyone's guess. The Vatican waited 13 years before classifying Fatima as a "miracle," and did so reluctantly, bending to enormous public pressure.

-JAK, letter to John Harney 5/19/72

While packing my effects before moving from D.C. back to New York City this week, I came across the enclosed diatribe, which was written in response to Alan Sharp's rather incredible critique in *Merseyside UFO Bulletin*. For some reason, it never got into the mails.

I have been amused by the ufological reaction to *Our Haunted Planet*. Many reviewers, including your Peter Rogerson, seem to have missed the main point of the book altogether, although I tried to spell it out in the introduction. *Our Haunted Planet* was a compilation of the beliefs of mankind, including ufological beliefs, demonstrating how those beliefs are largely based upon the rather fiendish manipulations and manifestations of the unknown power or phenomenon that surrounds us. None of the manifestations has any genuine meaning, so we have always labored to interpret them and give them our own meanings. Like Charles Fort, I question the sanity of the phenomenon *itself.*

Perhaps our real problem is that so few ufologists are schooled in history, philosophy, and such sciences as archaeology. They are all peering through telescopes and wondering about "ET" life. Alan Sharp complains about the things that were left out of *Operation Trojan Horse.* In an earlier essay, he attacked cases that were summarized in *Operation Trojan Horse* because they were so well known. I am baffled that he took so many reportorial remarks as implications of some personal belief. I took pains to label silly theories as such in both *Operation Trojan Horse* and *Our Haunted Planet.* Alas, very few of the theories accepted in mainstream ufological circles really hold up under close scrutiny.

-JAK, letter to John Harney 9/25/72

I have for years been haunted by a very intense group of UFO followers called "ufologists." I have seldom responded to any of their questions or requests. I had several reasons for not doing so:

1. I soon learned that no matter how logical or straightforward I wrote, it was always turned into something that I did not mean or did not say.

2. Aside from one short period in my experience, I have not had the slightest interest in the world "out there."

3. My life is my own. My travels – what I do and where I go – are of no interest to, or business of, the general public.

The years that have passed have not dimmed the horror of those days. The spot on Maury Island has never re-grown the brush and trees that were destroyed. I am still in full contact with Hal Dahl. I spoke with him yesterday.

I appreciate the kindness with which you handled me in your book.

-Fred Crisman, letter to JAK, printed in *Anomaly #10*, 1973

I haven't heard from you in a long time. I imagine the current superflap is keeping you hopping. All hell has broken loose this year, from the widespread appearances of chimeras to awesome MIB activity.

The stuff that has been coming in the last few weeks seems to support the validity of the "great circle route" theory. UFOs seem to be sweeping in over the Great Lakes region from Canada, while another wave has been moving up the Mississippi and Ohio Valleys from the Gulf of Mexico. These patterns are followed in *every* flap. Ohio should produce several new landings and contact cases in the next few weeks.

One significant new trend that is not receiving much publicity, for obvious reasons, is the deliberate contacting of *sheriffs and police chiefs*. We've had plenty of police contacts in the past, but now they seem to be selecting the top law officers in various areas. Keep your ears open for contacts of this sort in Ohio. Also, be alert for new amnesia cases.

Finally, all year, we've been having a rash of large, unmarked helicopters from California to New York. Usually, the law decides they are sophisticated cattle rustlers. But, as you know, I have been following this "phantom helicopter" phenomenon for years, and these new incidents are following the patterns. Animal mutilations have also been on the increase this year, again blamed on human cattle rustlers. But would rustlers also butcher dogs, geese, and chickens?

The current great wave will probably subside shortly. But I expect a December flap, probably in the Massachusetts area, and a Florida flap in January of 1974. March of '74 could bring the biggest flap of all. Then things will quiet down until about 1978. The 1979-81 flap I am predicting could be a kind of grand climax to the whole business. I hope you can keep me posted on what's happening in your part of the country.

-JAK, letter to "Bonnie" 10/22/73

For many years now, I have been quietly interviewing warlocks, trying to develop a book based on the actual experiences of natural witches and warlocks – people who are born with the ability to perceive and control the elementals. They seem to be several steps beyond mediums. Mediums are used *by* the phenomenon. Warlocks, on the other hand, are able to use these forces. Unfortunately, most of them seem to come to a tragic end – suicides, murders, and bizarre deaths.

But it is apparent that thousands of people in each generation suffer from this uneasy talent. I think I had it when I was an adolescent, but I diverted my attention by studying physics, chemistry, etc., and lost it by the time I was 18. At 18, I woke up one night in a furnished room near Times Square, and had what can only be described as an illuminating experience. For a few brief moments, I suddenly understood *everything*. I was really one with the cosmos. The next morning, I could remember very little of it, but I'm sure it was all entered into my subconscious.

-JAK, letter to author Colin Wilson, 1974

The Fred Crisman summoned to testify in the Clay Shaw "JFK" trial was the same Fred Crisman who was involved in Tacoma's "Maury Island (UFO) Affair." He is *also* the same Fred Crisman who claimed to have shot his way out of a cave in Burma, receiving a hole the "size of a dime" in his arm from a "raygun" wielded (he said) by the Dero ("detrimental robots"). His exact words to me were: "For God's sake, drop the Shaver cave stories! You don't know what you are dealing with here!" He is the same Fred Crisman who offered to go into a cave in Texas and bring out some of the "ancient" machinery used by the Dero, if only I would send him $500 expense money.

It was not Clay Shaw who was ruined financially, personally, and physically by the JFK trial, it was Jim Garrison who was ruined. He was subjected to an IRS audit, and finally won the case in court, but at tremendous financial cost (which was the goal of the IRS in the first place). Garrison was also libeled, framed in a drug ring, and hounded from office, finally losing out in a re-election run.

I have Garrison's letter stating that they (all these Fred Crismans) are one and the same man. I also have my reply letter to Garrison, predicting that Crisman could not be subpoenaed – that he was CIA, and tremendously powerful.

There is a definite link between flying saucers, the Shaver Mystery, the Kennedy assassinations, Watergate, and Fred Crisman.

There is one common denominator for everything that is happening in the world today. That common denominator is right where Shaver said it was, no matter whether you prefer "caverns," or the "lower astral," or "another dimension."

-Ray Palmer, letter to JAK 1976

My usual fee for allowing my handsome countenance to be used on the cover of scurrilous publications is $5,000. However, in this case, you will be an exception. I have instructed my lawyer to sue you for everything you've got.

One of my mysterious informants sent me a copy of the review you sent to *FATE*. I understand the ET ding-a-lings have lined up to write (negative) reviews of *The Eighth Tower*, so your noble efforts probably won't be used, thus sparing you from a second lawsuit. Instead, some whacked-out "true believer" in ETs will undoubtedly vilify me further (if that's possible) as a pawn of the CIA and/or Dr. Condon's illegitimate son.

Despite my valiant efforts to reduce everything to the simplest possible language, my "message" seems to float majestically over the heads of all my readers, except Jacques Vallee. He borrows freely from me. And now, even Dr. Hynek has taken up the habit (see *Edge of Reality*). Both may actually be *unaware* of how deeply my gilded words have infiltrated their consciousnesses.

Line after line in Vallee's *Invisible College* are only slightly paraphrased from *Operation Trojan Horse* and *Our Haunted Planet*. The latter books dealt extensively with Fatima, Lourdes, the Mormons, etc. at a time when Vallee (in *Passport to Magonia*) showed a strange reluctance to examine the religious implications of the phenomenon. I assumed this was because he was Catholic, or at least had undergone training in Catholicism in his childhood.

The ideas he now extols (though in a vague, diaphanous way) were fully explored by me in the 1960s, and were graphically discussed in the book I published five or six years ago. During that period, you may recall, Vallee, Hynek, and others in their crowd were attacking me openly, and pooh-poohing the "occult connection." Now that they are executing a classic right-angle turn, they are adopting my once-hated concepts and claiming them as their own. Vallee has even lifted some of my favorite citations (*Oahspe*, *The Book of Mormon*, etc.), although he obviously has not read the books I cite.

Dr. Hynek first revealed the existence of the "Invisible College" in 1966. Vallee has had ten years to get his act together. I expected Vallee's book to reveal the results of ten years of effort. Instead, *The Invisible College* could have been written by any New York City hack with my books at his elbow. No vast international network of scientists was necessary, nor are they even dimly apparent in *The Invisible College*. Only one episode suggests their presence: the scientists in Europe and France who were *taken in* by the obviously *terrestrial* UMMO affair. The book is part Vallee, part Keel, and part bullshit.

The "Invisible College" is *still* just as invisible as ever. It apparently exists in the same way that *Project Blue Book* existed – more a myth than fact. A handful of scientists are named, but their contributions are uncertain. Vallee seems to rely more on Aime Michel, who is a brilliant fellow but no scientist (Michel is the "Brad Steiger of France"). One of Vallee's favorite cronies, Jacques Bergier, recently did a rewrite of *Our Haunted Planet* and called it *Secret Doors of the Earth*.

Incidentally, a nervous editor made me delete a passage about *The Book of Mormon* in *Operation Trojan Horse*, which pointed out that Mormonism was probably a partly human hoax. He didn't want all those Mormons to come down on our necks. I compared the Mormon bible with other "inspired" works, and noticed a curious, yet serious, flaw. It is written in a clumsy, semi-literate imitation of the style in *The King James Bible*, and totally lacks the literary quality of other inspired books. This is really strange, and a rather glaring deficiency when you've read as much of this kind of garbage as I have. Joseph Smith sat behind a screen and dictated the book to his wife, who sat on the other side. Ostensibly he was translating the gold plates but, actually, I suspect he was in a trance, and no real translating was taking place.

From *The Invisible College* and *Edge of Reality*, I gather that Hynek and Vallee are now at roughly the point I reached in 1968-69, but they are proceeding slowly, possibly because they instinctively realize – and fear – that if they pursue the evidence to its logical conclusion, they will have killed off their beloved boondoggle. The simple truth is that there is nothing whatsoever to the UFO phenomenon. There is nothing to be gained by a "scientific" study of the matter. The extraterrestrial thesis is nothing but a trick – a propaganda device that has been foisted upon us. Historically, the overall phenomenon has done considerable damage to the human race, and is responsible for the deaths of many millions of people. It is human to indulge in wishful thinking and hope that it is leading us somewhere, but it has always led us down dead-ends to destruction, and I don't think the situation is suddenly going to change.

Vallee has absolutely no sense of history. (As to whether or not this is due to his Catholic upbringing, you'd have to ask a psychiatrist.) And Hynek, of course, is completely out of his element in this kind of study. Hynek has spent ten years trying to raise millions of dollars for a scientific study of UFOs. In articles published in 1967-68, I pointed out that the U.S. had already spent millions on the subject, and that no amount of money, and no number of scientists, could ever solve the "mystery." Now, at least, Vallee has swung to that point of view. He has finally recognized the fundamental fact that a *subjective* phenomenon cannot be explored with technology.

On the other hand, if the ET believers are right – if UFOs are real machines from some other planet – then the historical record suggests only one proper avenue of approach. The subject is a matter exclusively for a highly trained, highly secret group of intelligence agencies, and *not* a matter for amateur investigators. If UFOs are real (regardless of where they come from), then the situation is so grave that all amateur groups should ruthlessly be crushed, all UFO news censored, and the general public kept in total ignorance for as long as possible.

Apparently, the government *did* try to implement such a program, on a modest scale, in the early 1950s, but it was fragmented, poorly financed, and inefficient. The phenomenon itself has so many built-in contradictions that it doesn't need any outside help. If the government had found real cause for alarm, you can be sure that people like Donald Keyhoe, Coral Lorenzen, and Jim Moseley would have been jailed on trumped-up charges, and no civilian UFO movement would ever have had a chance to organize.

My famous beard is gone again. The CIA put some powder in my shoes, which caused all of my hair to fall out. Gene Duplantier's drawing of me is really unnecessarily flattering. What did he use for a model, that old post office "Wanted" poster of me? This letter will self-destruct in 30 seconds.

-JAK, letter to Gray Barker 2/3/76

The legendary "Skyhook" balloons were the "swamp gas" of their day, and were blamed for many UFO incidents, not just the Mantell case. Actually, the Skyhook balloons didn't have much purpose, and were used in only a few tests. I well remember how, two weeks after the burst of continuous UFO sightings over Farmington, New Mexico (March 17-19, 1950, when literally hundreds of witnesses reported sightings of massed flights of *hundreds* of flying discs), all was blamed on an exploded Skyhook balloon. The U.S. Air Force tried to convince us that the good people of New Mexico were seeing tiny pieces of the balloon floating around the area for two weeks!

Regarding the famous "giant UFO" flight detected by radar over the Pacific during World War II (*Flying Saucer Review*, vol. 29, issue 4), this was reported in an article called "Our Skies Are Haunted," in *The Saturday Evening Post* in 1947. I came across it when researching *Operation Trojan Horse*. Unfortunately, I can't recall the date or author, and my notes are long gone. Keyhoe just lifted it. (Considering his great fame in the field, Keyhoe did very little original investigation and research.)

We have had a massive UFO wave here in the Northeast this year, beginning in March and continuing through May. Unfortunately, few investigations have been made, and the news media are, in general, disinterested. In fact, our newspapers and television stations offer very poor coverage of *everything* these days. They have fewer reporters than they used to have, and the whole news-gathering network is slowly collapsing. Major news events are now slighted. Hundreds of newspapers, large and small, have quietly gone out of business throughout the country. This is, of course, just part of the larger cultural breakdown that is occurring worldwide.

-JAK, letter to *Flying Saucer Review* 7/13/84

As I wrote in "The Contactee Key" (published in the now-defunct magazine, *UFO Reports*, in February of 1979), it is apparent that the Men in Black often employ the same techniques as elusive government agents. In many cases, it appears that two different MIB groups are involved, and that these groups are actually working *against* each other. A kind of underground war of nerves is taking place around the world.

A large part of the UFO mystery is nothing more than myths based upon the speculations of bewildered outsiders. The government successfully diverted civilian research for two decades, and if Howard Menger and others like him are correct, official brainwashers may have actually worked to *create* the extraterrestrial theory to misdirect the civilian ufological establishment, while some other covert government agency quietly tried to get at the real truth.

The rub is that the very nature of these investigations makes it necessary to keep the identities of the witnesses secret. The deeply personal aspects of the UFO experience, and the privacy protections within psychiatry, have an automatic silencing factor. In essence, when a responsible investigator does stumble onto something important – some hint of official brainwashing, for instance – he finds that he cannot reveal it publicly without getting sued or seriously affecting the lives of the witnesses. This is undoubtedly why some of the early government investigators advised certain witnesses to keep quiet.

However, today, when someone tries to report a UFO sighting to the U.S. Air Force, a Public Information Officer (PIO) usually refers them to a *civilian* UFO investigator! Several UFO contactees have been sent to me by USAF personnel in recent years. Indeed, government officials have often referred to me as "the world's leading authority on UFO contactees"

– a title I don't deserve and constantly have to disown.

We now know that most genuine contactees have a fragment of special information planted in their subconscious minds. It is apparent that the government tried to extract such fragments in the early days. Contactees continue to receive this programming, but the government is apparently no longer interested. It is probable that this programming process has been going on since the beginning of the human race. All kinds of cover-ups have been employed to keep the truth from us, with particular emphasis on religious, occult, and political beliefs. The extraterrestrial concept is simply a 20th-century propaganda device that has now effectively reached every country, every society, and every belief system.

Motion pictures of the past 35 years have spread the Extraterrestrial Thesis everywhere, and today there is not a single world leader, scientist, or journalist who is not conversant with it – and in many cases, a whole-hearted believer. UFO buffs can no longer cry: "Why don't they contact us?" They *have* contacted us. The whole population of the planet has been exposed to the extraterrestrial idea, and *has accepted it without a single shred of actual evidence!*

No government has been able to cope with this propaganda movement. No government has been able to censor the UFO movement. It is as unstoppable as the Christian movement of 2,000 years ago (no scholar or archaeologist has been able to produce any evidence whatsoever that Christ ever actually existed).

The bottom line is that we are dealing with forces that can distort reality and manipulate the human mind. Governments and agencies like the CIA and KGB are incapable of dealing with, or even recognizing, such forces. If we were actually able to interfere with this mysterious programming process, the human race would probably cease to exist.

-JAK, letter to *Flying Saucer Review* 6/29/85

It was exactly ten years ago that I was in London, and met with you and your secret society. I was in rather poor health at that time, unfortunately. I am now struggling to write a book on quantum physics – on how all phenomena actually *represent* the real reality, thus making our perception of reality completely askew.

Still, I really think some of us are going to figure everything out by the end of this century, and that the effect will be the total dissolution of our civilization (a process or "deprocessing" that is already well under way).

Time is going backwards now!

The UFO scene here is very static. The only big event this fall was a Bigfoot attack in West Virginia. Two of the creatures scared two hunters badly.

-JAK, letter to Flying Saucer Review 12/14/86

The UFO scene here has suddenly come alive again! The conventions have drawn huge crowds this year, and interest is really high.

Budd Hopkins and Whitley Strieber have "reinvented the wheel." They have turned the clock back to the 1950s, and are rediscovering the whole contactee thing with its doppelgangers, its insidious little games, and its mimetic hallucinations. But they are totally unaware of all that has gone before. They think they have found something new in age-old "Devil's Marks," forms of astral projection, and tired demonological manifestations.

We hear the claim being made: "I alone know the cosmic truth…" We have heard it all before, over and over again.

-JAK, letter to Flying Saucer Review 7/1/87

CHAPTER 20

Andy Colvin (AC): Did *The Mothman Prophecies* come out the way you wanted?

John A. Keel (JAK): Well, they took a lot of stuff out. They especially took out my profound, mind-bending philosophy...

AC: What was that?

JAK: I don't know, just my *usual* mind-bending philosophy. I went through all that so many years ago. Now I'm just concerned with keeping the planet Earth going. I don't think we have much of a future here. I think it's time for us to build a rocket and go to Mars or something.

AC: Do you think that there's something to these stories about the Mayan calendar and 2012 being the end of the world? Are we coming to a turning point?

JAK: Well, they've predicted the end of the earth every few years for all my life, and of course a lot of religions are based on Armageddon. It always seems like we're right on the edge of extinction, yet we keep going. All the things that are happening in the Middle East now are reasonably outlined in the Bible. People who read the Bible carefully get scared to death that these things are coming to pass.

AC: I have a little theory that this *recent* blackout in New York may have been the one that was predicted in 1967, and mentioned by you in *The Mothman Prophecies*. Mothman witnesses were having premonitions of a blackout in New York. And I think a *partial* one did occur at that time, when the president flipped the switch on the Christmas tree.

JAK: Oh, yes, President Johnson… He was having a high-level meeting with the Russians in Glasborough, New Jersey. When he flipped the switch, the lights failed in Glasborough, and they had a lot of trouble with telephones and things. There were a lot of predictions in that book that came to pass, like Martin Luther King's assassination. There were a lot of predictions of the assassination of the Pope. And there *were* assassination attempts. As you know, he got shot, which is not very healthy. Also, a renegade priest tried to stab him.

It's tough being the Pope.

AC: The reason I bring it up is because, as I told you, we built a shrine to the Mothman as children. The Mothman showed up, and we had a premonition of 9/11 in New York in 2001. Having had that experience, it seems to me that some of these prophecies were way ahead of their time – maybe 35 years or more. This led me to think that maybe the 1967 prediction, of a big blackout in New York, was actually a premonition of this most recent one in 2003. It just took that long (35 years) to occur.

JAK: Right… Now the attack on the World Trade Center… None of our psychics saw that coming. Normally if we have a major event, like the assassination of President Kennedy, hundreds of people foresee it. But this thing at the World Trade Center took everybody by surprise – even the psychics. The pundits on television are telling us that London is now next. There have been a lot of predictions about something happening in London. Of course, that's a major city full of people, and it's pretty hard to protect. But very often, these predictions just lead us astray. While we're watching London, they're doing something in Cairo… The prediction business is very hazardous.

AC: Whitley Strieber talks about this topic in his *Secret School* book. He says that he thinks that these premonitions are warning tools that arise in humanity as we reach cataclysmic times. Premonitions allow for changing the future or a bad outcome, before it gets here. Do you think there's anything to that?

JAK: I don't think we can change the future. If we knew exactly what was going to happen six months from now, we couldn't do anything about it. We're not that well organized – that civilized. If we were, we could have a perfect world. But the world becomes more *imper-fect* all the time. I've given a lot of thought to the future. It seems to me that for people to see the future, the future would have to exist in some form. Otherwise, they *wouldn't be able to see it*. I have written about finding a way to tap into this universal mind. *Then* we could see the future. Once we can see the future – the future of the human race – then we are at "childhood's end." And it's all over… We can let the dolphins and the Mothmen have the planet. We don't seem to be doing very much for this planet, anyway. We're systematically destroying it, and everything on it – killing off all the lifeforms. I'm not sure that's a real plan for this planet.

AC: I should clarify that our 9/11 vision showed *greater* damage than what actually occurred, which makes me wonder if there isn't some wriggle room in changing the future. Perhaps events can be changed by the prior awareness of many people? Now earlier, you said that you're trying to keep ecological ideas going – trying to find a way to live more in harmony. Is that what keeps you coming back to Point Pleasant?

JAK: I don't know what keeps me coming back to Point Pleasant. It's pretty much the way they said it in the movies, where Dr. Leek warns Richard Gere *not* to go back to Point Pleasant. I had a lot of warnings like that. I can't see that Point Pleasant is the center of any universal harmony or whatever. There are other places in the United States where people who are more "attuned" gather with that kind of thing in mind. But the people in West Virginia are just people. I've run into very few psychics here.

AC: In my case, I approached the Mothman from a desire to see him. Most people just stumbled across him. It frightened them. Do you think there's a difference? If you're a person who wants to find the Mothman, like you or me, does that change the way the encounter might play out?

JAK: Well, I know this happens to many people. They want to see a flying saucer. They want to see Mothman – something to confirm their beliefs, whatever their beliefs are. There are people who sit cross-legged in a cave for 30 years to attain Godhead and become part of God. We had this group a few years ago that committed suicide, thinking *that* was the way to join the flying saucers – the Heaven's Gate cult.

AC: My theory on that? I don't know if you remember this, but that was the same day that the Martin Luther King family came out and said that they thought James Earl Ray was *innocent*. They felt that it was *the government* that had killed MLK.

JAK: And they went to court and won! It was too late for James Earl Ray, but they had a big court event claiming that another man was the mastermind behind the whole thing – a businessman who lived in the South. They had the evidence on him, and the jury agreed with them. And it didn't make the newspapers at all! The only press it got in New York was in one of the Harlem newspapers. The other papers just avoided the subject.

AC: Yes, that businessman was Jowers, the owner of the bar across from the Lorraine Motel. He had taken the gun and shuffled it out. Speaking of conspiracies, I was listening to a talk recently by Walter Bowart. He wrote an influential book in the 1970s called *Operation Mind Control.* He is now saying that the cutting edge of mind control research has to do with UFOs. But he didn't really go into the details of it. I was wondering if that rings a bell with you at all. Do you think that there is manipulation going on within this "phenomenon?"

JAK: I had a friend, Ivan Sanderson, who was a real scientist. He had looked into the UFO stuff and written a lot about it. He kept referring to the "mind patrol." He felt that people's minds *were* being somehow tampered with, and there was nothing we could do about it. As you know, we've seen a lot of people who are obsessed – who go way out on a limb with this stuff. Whitley Strieber is a good example. He started out just wanting to be a writer, and he's ended up with his mind opened up to all kinds of things. He's now back in Texas with a radio program. Did you read his book about the coming storms and strange changes in the weather? It came out two or three years ago. It did *not* become a bestseller. Of course, timing is very important in any book. If you come out with the biggest, best-written book of all time at the same time Hillary Clinton's book comes out, people are going to buy Hillary's book, not yours. That kind of thing happens over and over…

AC: In terms of trying to maneuver through this minefield of paranormal phenomena, I've speculated that it's important for people to look at their own experience, and try to figure out if it was a "natural," bio-energetic event, or if there was some sort of a "synthetic," governmental, or human influence on it. It seems to me that it's important to figure that out – to try and look at your own situation and separate the two.

JAK: Well, the thing that works against all these conspiracy theories is that the government is very stupid. They try conspiracies against each other, but they're very stupid, almost all the time. Mostly, governments consist of either madmen like Adolf Hitler and company, or small-town lawyers who have suddenly talked their way into a big position handling billions of dollars. But they can't even handle their own bank account! And there are other things at work here that we don't understand, like the fact that *somebody runs everything*, yet we don't know who it is. That's what it amounts to… If you look at the economic situation very closely – the oil situation and all – you see that there's somebody running this thing, and that they had it planned for a long time. *But we don't know who they are.* They're sitting on a mountaintop somewhere, or in a penthouse somewhere, keeping a very low profile. And when they die, they don't even get an obituary. *These* are the people we really have to think about and go after. George Bush spends a lot of his time on his ranch. We have the Arabian countries run by very wealthy men who have no real interest in running countries. They just want to run their oil business, or whatever they are running. There's got to be some guy out there – like a Howard Hughes type – who is really visionary and has knowledge of what he's doing and how he's doing it. For a while I *did* think it was Howard Hughes, because he fit into all of the patterns. He was a recluse; he was a nut; he was filthy rich; and he was capable of almost anything. When he moved to Las Vegas, he got them to *stop the testing of atomic bombs* in Nevada. Not many men have the power to do that. Nobody ever really found out where all of his money went. He did contribute heavily to the CIA. And there must be people in the CIA who are operating on their own or with overseas bankers.

AC: *The Gemstone File* claims Hughes was kidnapped by Onassis and held on an island for 20 years, while being force-fed heroin. Onassis, the CIA, and the Mormons supposedly appropriated Hughes' money. But I wanted to ask whether or not you run into problems with people (like cryptozoologists) who think that if you're both a paranormal witness *and* researcher, your credibility somehow goes down. I was talking to you the other day, and you said that you *started off* as a "ridiculous," low-credibility figure. As a result, did that issue – of their trying to lower your credibility through ridicule – become moot? How does one defang the spooks, dupes, and paid skeptics?

JAK: I spent years of my life writing jokes for television. I wrote Merv Griffin's ad-libs at one point. There are a lot of people writing ad-libs. You see these comedians on television, and you think they're very funny people; they aren't. They've got ten guys behind the scenes writing jokes for them. Take Regis Philbin and his show *Do You Want to Be a Millionaire*... Regis sits in front of a television set, and they have three or four guys sitting backstage. For every situation that comes up, these guys (who are crack-humorous) immediately type in a joke, and Regis reads it off the TV screen. Everybody says, "That Regis is really fast-witted and funny." Well, the guys who are fast-witted and funny are sitting backstage earning $10,000 a minute. Jay Leno has twenty writers writing all of his monologues and jokes. Johnny Carson used to have a script with him onstage.

You'd see him shuffling papers. If you were an outsider, you'd say, "What the hell are those papers?" They were the scripts. He had jokes for all the visitors that came on. The writers had prepared jokes ahead of time. And there would be subjects that people didn't want to discuss. Those would be listed there. Carson would follow the instructions.

AC: If people knew this sort of thing, they'd have more appreciation for what we are doing here today. We are having a real conversation. There are no cue cards here.

JAK: Oh, I wrote cue cards, too. *[laughter]*

AC: Have you talked much about your childhood? I remember reading that you had some paranormal experiences as a child, with some lights in your room.

JAK: Yes. Around the age of 12, I was living in an old farmhouse, upstairs. Everybody else was sleeping downstairs. There came a knocking on the wall. At first I thought it was squirrels in the attic or something. I did my "scientific" investigation of the whole house. I couldn't find anything. This went on for several weeks. I couldn't find any explanation for these knockings. Then I learned that you could communicate with them, just like the Fox sisters had – you know, "knock three times for this, and two times for that." As a 12-year-old, I didn't have many interesting questions to ask, but I was communicating with this thing that was knocking in the wall. This drove me to the public library to find any books I could on psychic phenomenon. They only had about three books. Up until the 1960s, all of this stuff was really taboo. You don't realize today how taboo it was. It was almost illegal. They'd almost put you in jail for getting into psychic phenomena or parapsychology. There have been like five "New Ages," and each New Age has brought us to another level. Every few years, somebody like Shirley Maclaine starts up again. It's a phenomenon in itself. It's like there's a timetable, and every generation is elevated a little bit. Did you ever read *Childhood's End*? I'm always quoting that. It's an Arthur C. Clark science-fiction book. Basically, his story was that we eventually evolve into something else. We evolve into a spiritual thing; then we don't need all of the trappings that go with being human beings. We abandon our bodies and just become spirit.

AC: Speaking of spiritual beings, there are stories now that the Sasquatch are psychic. When you were in Nepal, you saw a couple of them, didn't you?

JAK: Well, I saw animals from a distance, and the Natives told me it was the Yeti. At that time, interest in the Yeti was very high, and the publisher asked me about it. I told him, "Probably a bear." And he said, "We'll make it into a Yeti. It'll sell."

AC: Apparently there is an alternate form of bear up there, too, which Reinhold Messner, the great climber, has seen.

JAK: I read his book. He believes in it enough that he *moved* to Tibet. I think he's still chasing it. I don't think he's caught it. But the Chinese and the Russians are very big on this. They have financed big expeditions to go to these areas where they are seeing them. So far, they've turned up very little. Meanwhile in the United States, in the state of Washington, somebody gave five million dollars to one of the Bigfoot chasers. He got helicopters out, and all kinds of expensive equipment. Every time the phone rang, they'd all jump into the helicopter and try to go to the scene. They spent the five million dollars. They lived *very* well while they were chasing Bigfoot, but they never caught Bigfoot.

AC: A fellow named Lapseritis has written a book called *The Psychic Sasquatch*. He claims that you need to go into the forest and quietly meditate for several days. If you follow certain rituals and meditations, the Sasquatch will telepathically contact you. Do you think there's anything to that?

JAK: No, but it just wouldn't apply just to the Sasquatch. It would apply to almost anything. You know, so much energy has been spent on these subjects – writing about them and exploring them. And yet, we've always ended up with nothing. That's not made me sour on these subjects, but I know that we have to take another approach that's entirely different. In the 1960s, we had people sitting in the TNT Area all night long, simply because someone else had seen something there once. They still came, for years afterwards, to the TNT Area. Some of those who are into witchcraft and the black arts were obviously in the TNT Area, because they had put graffiti up in all the buildings. But Mothman may have been a very temporary or sporadic thing, just like most of the Bigfoot sightings there.

AC: In really old Buddhist paintings, they often have the Garuda floating above the Buddha. He's a deity to the Buddhists.

JAK: It may be that when they "saw" the Garuda, they thought it to be a spiritual entity. It was *so* different that they included it in their spiritual drawings and paintings. As you know, in Indonesia they have belief in the Garuda going way back. The American Indians believed in the Thunderbird for generations. In some cases, they thought the Thunderbird was very dangerous and would attack you. This may be true, because if a giant creature attacks you like that, there's not going to be any evidence left of the attack. It's going to carry you away and eat you.

AC: Sort of like that situation in Braxton County, West Virginia that you wrote about, where some teenagers went missing.

JAK: There were a lot of disappearances of teenagers in those days. They were hitchhiking, which used to be legal. That was the way kids got around. They were hitchhiking to the football games and would never show up. The police tried to keep it as quiet as they could, which they always do. We had things happen here in Point Pleasant that they tried to keep quiet. It especially annoys them when someone like me shows up.

AC: The Men in Black probably weren't happy, either.

JAK: The MIB would show up alongside UFOs and tell the witnesses to shut up. They drove black Cadillacs – expensive antique ones – and they were showing up all over the country. But most people are not going to report this to anybody. If someone gets out of a black Cadillac and takes a picture of your house, you're going to think it's a real estate agent. I thought I would have a better chance of catching an MIB than Mothman, because I can't fly. But the MIB were always one step ahead of me. If I were driving to a small town in West Virginia, they would show up two or three hours before I would get there. And they would take pictures of people's children – especially children *who had seen Mothman along with their parents*. I was concerned for these children. One parent, a dentist, had to deal with the black Cadillacs trying to nab his kids as they walked home from school. This was long before we had all of the perverts and serial killers, so it was really horrible. It stood out. I was also concerned for Mary Hyre, because her office was right next to the Silver Bridge, and the MIB were always coming in there. She hadn't slept for three days when I finally contacted her after the bridge collapse... And there were *female* MIB, too. I have had mysterious encounters, particularly on trains, with very beautiful ladies. They looked like movie stars. They were obviously assigned to talk to me, so I wouldn't tell them anything. When the train got to the station, they would always disappear, even if I had been talking to them for three hours.

AC: We found that the rivers in West Virginia seem to be where most of the Mothman sightings occur – along the Ohio, Poca, Coal, Elk, and Kanawha rivers. Do you think there's something about water that aids the paranormal process?

JAK: Oh yes – water, and also blood. In the Mothman days, the ufonauts seemed to have a real interest in blood. This also is sort of a taboo subject, especially if you're being interviewed for television. They don't want to talk about that. They usually are waiting for me to say something in particular; you never know what. In a two-hour interview, they may only take 30 seconds and put *that* on the air.

AC: Well, *we're* going to use the whole interview.

JAK: We've got so many mysteries on our hands. It's better to be normal and not pay any attention to mysteries.

AC: Are you still actively investigating?

JAK: Not actively... We had a bunch of sightings of Bigfoot up in the Catskill Mountains two or three years ago. The only reason I went up there was that my informant was one of the game wardens. We had very good witnesses. Whatever these things are, they vanished as fast as they came. I've had reports where witnesses have seen a Bigfoot reach down to the ground and catch the hand of another Bigfoot, and then pull it up out of the ground – the solid ground. Then the two of them would walk away. That's a pretty good indication that it's something *other* than a physical animal we're watching. We are watching the behavior of a *paraphysical object*.

AC: A friend and I saw a Bigfoot in the Catskills once, in the early 1980s, while camping after the Anti-Nuke Rally in New York City. Actually we never saw the creature, as it seemed to be *invisible*. The spot was fairly remote, and it came up to us soon after we got out of the car. How did it know where we were going to pull over? We heard the crunching of heavy steps, and I got this frightening chill up my spine. When we saw the tall vegetation parting – with *nothing* there – it was terrifying. Later, I decided it must have been Bigfoot. This was on Bear Mountain.

JAK: I know Bear Mountain. The recent paraphysical activity I mentioned was near there. So you got "the chill," huh? Some people just see two red eyes in the woods, and it scares the hell out of them. These are experienced people who camp out all the time. These two huge, red eyes, each the size of a dinner dish, will appear in the woods. They don't see any forms besides that. They're terrifying, whatever they are. And with Mothman, they always reported that it had those red eyes.

AC: I have a friend who saw the red eyes in his *bedroom*. He said the bed started shaking violently. He saw the red eyes and then blanked out. He doesn't remember anything that happened after that.

JAK: I went into the old power plant in the TNT Area with one of the early Mothman witnesses. The power plant, you know, was a pretty big place. It had all kinds of steel stairways in it. It was a good place for a Mothman to hide. She volunteered to go with me into this plant, and she became hysterical. I didn't see anything, but she claimed she saw the eyes – just the red eyes. She saw something red in there, that's for sure. We had a policeman standing outside the plant while we were in there. He wouldn't go in. I was such an idiot then – the "fearless John Keel." I was convinced that I was right, and the world was wrong, and therefore nothing was going to happen to me when I faced off with these entities.

AC: Well, that power plant story reminds me of something in Gray Barker's book, *The Silver Bridge*. He has a couple of chapters in there where he describes things from *Mothman's* point of view.

JAK: Well, you have to be very careful with Gray Barker. He was an intelligent, complex person with a very good sense of humor. In his *Silver Bridge,* he has people flying around in flying saucers with Indrid Cold and all that. He was having some fun. If you read his famous book *They Knew Too Much About Flying Saucers* carefully, you can see that there's a point where he sort of gives up and starts fictionalizing. He just says, "To hell with it," and throws in everything. That book was so popular, a copy of it was found in the home of the Heaven's Gate people.

AC: Do you feel the Indrid Cold story is bogus?

JAK: Yes, *but* I think his original story had *some* substance to it, because he was scared enough to go to the police. Nobody's going to go to the police with a bogus story. They might come to you or me with a bogus story, but they're not going to go to the cops. Like Barker, Derenberger was a complex character. His daughter called me a couple of years ago, very upset that some television show had done something about him. He had "given the whole thing up" in the 1970s or '80s, and moved to Ohio. People were always writing to me. They wanted to contact Derenberger, because they wanted to contact Indrid Cold. Indrid Cold became a real entity to them.

AC: What about the other witnesses, who said they saw the "spacecraft" parked in front of Woody's truck? Do you think there may be a *part* of the story that's real?

JAK: Yes, two men who lived outside of Point Pleasant had pretty much the same experience. They were going to report it, but one of their sons came by and talked them out of it. I knew all the details, and was going to use some of it in a book or article I was doing. In short, the witnesses got talked out of it.

AC: Switching gears, it sounds like you have a sense that we need to change direction as a civilization. Do you have a soundbite or a mantra for how to start that process?

JAK: No, and it would take somebody with great leadership ability to have any affect. As you know, the Bible and Nostradamus and everybody are predicting that a man is going to come out of the Middle East and start this process going. So we're over there, now, bumping off all the Arab leaders we can find.

AC: A lot of the old Sumerian tablets over there are being destroyed, too.

JAK: That's another habit we have, of destroying so many of these ancient artifacts. When we finally arrived at Easter Island, they had a lot of writings carved into wood, because all they had were trees there. The early explorers destroyed all of the writings. Of course it would have been a job to interpret them (similar to cracking the Egyptian hieroglyphs), but those slabs of wood should have been safely stored somewhere.

AC: If you were interviewing a witness like me – who comes up 30 years later and says they had this bizarre Mothman experience as a kid – what would you say?

JAK: I would ask: "Why are you still obsessed with this?" You've got to explore your inner self. This happens to many of the people who get involved, who would never think – in a million years – to get involved in something like this. It suddenly changes their whole lives, and they may not really understand what's happening to them. But it has opened up the minds of many people. I always recommend reading *The Elegant Universe*. Before we can understand the "paranormal," we've got to understand the "normal" universe a little bit. The people who have been chasing the "Bird" (Mothman) are *not* bird experts. The people chasing the Loch Ness Monster don't know a damn thing about fish. I'd study the forms in the ocean before I'd really get serious about Loch Ness. Of course, now the

British government has come out with a very firm statement saying that they have spent a lot of money at Loch Ness, and that there is *nothing* there. Well, that only convinces many people that there *is* something there.

AC: Would you say that you got into this originally as part of a self-journey?

JAK: Yes, it started when I was very young. I had a very bad childhood. My mother and father parted when I was about 3 years old. In a sense, I'm an orphan who raised *myself*. I was reading my own books, and reading books on many subjects. When I was a kid, there were many poltergeists in our farmhouse. It was a terrible farm, with an unheated outhouse (fun in the winter) and no electricity. It was so damn primitive. It had no insulation, and we heated it with kerosene lamps. You had to pump the water from a well, and it tasted sulfuric. It was still the Great Depression, and we didn't really realize how bad it was… But I would get these knocks on my bedroom wall. I would tap to it, and it would tap back. Maybe it was Mothman. I worked out a primitive code and asked it questions like, "Who will win the war?" I developed an interest in the paranormal, but was mostly interested in writing jokes. I read the works of Will Rogers and so on. Around the same time, I wrote a letter to the editor of the local newspaper, and he thought it was so funny that he asked me into his office. He had inherited the newspaper, and he offered me two dollars a week to write a column. This was a big deal in those days. Some of those columns were really awful – really "scraping the keel" – but I did it for several years. It takes discipline to do that, so it was good practice. I was able to take off from there. I never finished high school, but people assumed I had a doctorate, because of the subjects I was able to write about at such an early age. By the time I was 17, I was really on my own, all by myself. I came to New York with 75 cents. It never occurred to me that this was a very dangerous thing to do. I just knew that I had to be in New York; that was where I was supposed to be. New York has been my home ever since. Even though I've traveled all the time, I keep going back to New York. I've met a lot of fascinating people there…

AC: Well, your *Mothman Prophecies* book certainly is fascinating. When I ran across it in 1993, it put it all together for me. At least, it got me thinking that I wasn't crazy…

JAK: Right, and that was my intention. That was a carefully done book. I really aimed that book at people who had had experiences, whether it was experiences with Big Bird, or small bird, or Loch Ness, or whatever. I've heard from thousands of them since. They know that they're not crazy, and they know that they are learning. It's a shame that the whole world doesn't go through this learning process, but they don't. It's only a small percentage... I did a lot research into parapsychology and psychic phenomenon. The Bird was here in the Ohio Valley for at least three weeks. I was convinced at the beginning that the Bird was a real bird – that it physically existed. But the sightings stopped after a month or so, so I figured it had moved on to another nesting area, or was looking for food somewhere else. However, it has turned up in other areas of the world ever since, so there *is* something to it. But no birdwatchers have ever seen it, and they are always looking. Whatever the hell Mothman is, it put a big scare into a lot of people here in Pt. Pleasant. Nowadays, they argue about it. Some say there is no such thing; others say there is. I am convinced that this thing we call "Mothman" *is* out there, but we haven't learned much about it. We need more specialists on giant birds, or perhaps *interdimensional* birds, since we can never seem to find any Moth-scat or other proof that it is physical.

AC: Even though interdimensionality is proven by quantum physics, many naturalists still tend to doubt it.

JAK: *The Elegant Universe* is heavy reading, but it is the best book on this subject. It defines what we know, in general terms, about our place in the universe. Our home is a bubble of water filled with billions of peculiar lifeforms. They keep telling us they are finding new planets, but usually there is no life on them. If the earth were in just a slightly different position relative to the sun, we would either burn up, or be freezing. We will never be able to settle Mars like we did Virginia. We landed on the moon over 30 years ago – an impossible dream when I was a kid – but we haven't been back for a long time. If we decided to go back again, it would take us ten years to rebuild the equipment, because the blueprints do not exist; they were supposedly "destroyed." We should probably have a plan for getting off the planet, since the earth may eventually be hit by a comet and burn to a cinder.

AC: Is there *really* a way out?

JAK: I've run out of bad advice to give people, because I think so much of it is hopeless. We will never know what's going on. People have been chasing ghosts since the beginning of times – for 5000 years or more – and we still don't know anything about ghosts. There are many theories about "dead people returning" and so on, but we have no proof. What would be rapping on my wall when I was 12 years old? Maybe it was something inside of me that needed expression – that wanted to come out. We are doing more studies now of the human being than we ever did before. We need to learn a lot more about the human being. Why do young men go off to war? Why do we do these stupid things? This planet has so much on it that still has to be explored, and billions of lifeforms in every shape and form. If I were a young person going into science, I would just pick one of these forms and study it. There are plants thousands of feet below the ocean. The middle of the desert is filled with all kinds of living things. Life can adjust to anything on this planet; it has for a long time. Birds survive by eating all the insects and worms, or by eating each other. Hawks take other birds home for dinner. That's the way nature has worked it out. Today, we go out and hit a cow on the head with a sledgehammer. (We have improved methods now.)

AC: Technology increases efficiency. Where would cattle mutilators be without black helicopters?

JAK: That's why scientists specialize. If you want to study poison ivy, you have to study it for years. There are doctors who do nothing but study one organ. This is the age of specialization. And it is the same with writers, who specialize in all sorts of different things. Mark Twain – whose family was from Point Pleasant, incidentally – would write about everything. But writers today just write about one thing – usually politics. They waste their lives this way. The political writing from two years ago is useless today. Why did they bother? Most of it wasn't true to begin with! We have big problems with education, and thus with logic and reason. If you meet someone who has been investigating UFOs, Bigfoot, and the like for twenty years, they are basically pretty crazy. Like any religious fanatic, they have usually lost all credibility. Some of them go on the lecture tour, because there are people who like to go to these conventions. People go to these lectures like they go to lectures on how to grow flowers. It doesn't amount to much in the end. I have had many offers to do lectures on Mothman, but I rarely do. I have only given three or four lectures on Mothman in 35 years.

AC: That makes this interview all the more special. Thanks. I will take your advice and put a time-limit on my Mothman project, so that I don't go crazy. But I *have* to do it.

JAK: That's okay. The "coincidences" you have found between yourself and the other witnesses are really interesting. Just remember to pay attention to human psychology.

In September 2003, John Keel made his last public appearance in West Virginia, at the unveiling of the Mothman Statue in Point Pleasant. He was most gracious, and spent all of his free time with the local investigators, touring old and new sighting locations. His presence seemed to set off a long series of interrelated paranormal events in the lives of those investigators, which persisted until after his death on July 3, 2009. His "magic" and humor, as well as his valuable research, will be missed.

LIST OF ILLUSTRATIONS

Oruro Birdman, Bolivia... 46

Trunk Carrier Satellites and Defense Logistics Agency, West Virginia 54

"Mothman" at 9/11 Disaster, New York City... 91

John Keel and Mark Twain Historic Sign.. 125

Jim Creek and Kimball "Birdman" UFOs.. 136

Mothman Statue and Garuda "Karasu Tengu"... 165

Ring UFOs... 171

"Mothman" Crop Circle, Holland.. 183

Mothman by Frank Frazetta 205

Keel and His Grandmother 220

Keel at Mothman Statue Unveiling... 274

INDEX

3-M, 8

Adamski, George, 66, 123, 145, 157, 214, 219
Aenstria, 158
Aldrin, Buzz, 47
Algeria, 50
Allen, Ray, 130
Alligewi Indians, 70-71
Allingham, Cedric, 157
aluminum, 45, 74-79, 166-171, 211, 214
Alvarado, Jorge Rodriguez, 225
Amazing Stories, 118-122, 148-149
Anasazi Indians, 70
Anomaly magazine, 106, 108, 241, 248, 251
Aphloes, 58
APRO, 16, 28, 30, 124, 146, 158, 164, 169
Argentina, 40, 170, 199
Arkansas, 24-25, 133-135, 170, 175-178, 186, 189
Arnold, Kenneth, 59, 63, 66, 121, 144, 171, 189
Asia, 48, 71
Asimov, Isaac, 118
Aswan Dam, 196, 221
ATDA, 50
ATIC, 148-151
Australia, 48, 109, 139, 189, 194

Backstrom, Terry, 131
Bacon, Sir Francis, 242
Bandit, 90
Barker, Gray, 153, 158, 226, 229-230, 232, 236, 240, 256, 269
Barry, Gene, 231
Battelle Memorial Institute, 154
Bear Mountain, 268
Becker, Robert O., 248
Beckham, Thomas Edward, 225
Beckley, Timothy, 236
Bell, John, 98-99
Bell Witch, 98-99
Belyayev, Pavel I., 52
Bennett, Marcella, 85
Bergier, Jacques, 255
Bering Straits, 71
Berlitz, Charles, 117
Bermuda Triangle, 40, 117, 126, 128

Bernard, Raymond, 149
Berry, Homer, 134
Beyond Condon, 108, 208, 247-248
Bigfoot, 80, 117, 147, 259, 266, 268, 273
Binder, Otto, 44
Black Knights, 51
Bock, Ken, 134
Bormann, Frank, 48
Bowart, Walter, 263
Bowen, Charles, 161
Boyd, Lyle G., 158
Bradbury, Ray, 118
Braxton County WV, 90, 267
Brazil, 28, 103, 167, 169-170
Briggs, Ben, 141
British Columbia, 140
Brown, Jack, 82
Brown, Townsend, 123
Browne, Howard, 119, 122, 125
Bruton, Dempsey, 52
Buddha, 196, 266
Burma, 253
Bush, George, 264

Caidin, Martin, 49
California, 7, 20, 22-24, 29, 32, 80, 105, 135, 186, 199, 201, 215, 252
Camp Conley Road, 238
Campione, Michael, 168
Canada, 21, 28-29, 33, 35, 37, 39-40, 67, 69, 79, 109, 131, 138-139, 141, 143, 186, 189, 252
Cannon, Brian, 140
Cape Canaveral, 51
Cape Kennedy, 51-52, 66, 198
Carmody, Bob, 131
Carpenter, Connie, 83, 235
Carpenter, Faye, 85
Carpenter, Scott, 49
Carson, Johnny, 264
Case, Leo, 179
Catholic Church, 61, 250, 254-255
Central America, 70, 156
Central Park, 198, 201
Cernan, Eugene, 50
chaff, 75-79, 169
Chant, C.A., 35
Chaplin, Grant, 139
Chaput, Leo Paul, 137
Charleston WV, 72, 74-75, 95
Chartrand, Gerry, 138

Chasson, John, 139
Chicago, 19, 24, 26, 118, 180
Chile, 40
China, 48, 54, 195
Chop, Al, 152
Chosi City, 74, 169
CIA, 65, 120, 122-123, 152, 154, 162,
    225-226, 236, 253-254, 256, 258, 264
Clarion, 158
Clark, Jerome, 242, 244
Clarke, Arthur C., 151, 161
Cleveland, Mike, 231
Cold, Indrid, 114, 198, 235, 269
Colombo, Bartholomew, 68
Colombo, Cristoforo, 67-68
Colorado, 29, 35, 94
Columbia Pictures, 201-203
Columbus OH, 20, 154, 233
Colvin, Andy, 13-14, 136, 260-273
Condon Committee, 17, 20, 94, 245
Connecticut, 20, 58, 153
Cooper, Gordon, 48-50
Corrales, Luis, 51
Courson, Frank, 179
Cramp, Leonard G., 155
Creighton, Gordon, 15, 161
Crisman, Fred Lee, 121, 225-226, 235, 251, 253

Daigh, Ralph, 122
Daniken, Erich Von, 161
Dare, Virginia, 67, 70
Davidson, Leon, 154
Davis, Lonnie, 179
Day, Russell B., 28
De Polo, Anthony, 92-95, 194
Defense Logistics Agency, 46, 54, 125
Delaware Indians, 70
Denmark, 68, 109
Denton, William, 11, 156
Department of Defense, 50
Derenberger, Taunia, 235
Derenberger, Woody, 11, 116, 198, 219, 235,
    239
Dermody, Pat, 131
Deros, 119-121, 124, 149, 237, 253
DHEW, 248
Dickson, Homer, 180
Dione, R.L., 161
dolmen, 68
Dominguez, Ernesto, 34

Dominican Republic, 28
Donnelly, Ignatius, 117
Donohue, Stuart, 81
doppelganger, 105
Doyle, Sir Arthur Conan, 213
Drake, Frank, 246
Drasin, Dan, 99-100
Dunavin, Velma, 134
Duplantier, Gene, 140, 256

East India, 50, 55-57
Ecuador, 70
Egypt, 68-69, 94, 195-196, 221, 270
Eighth Tower, 254
Einstein, Albert, 114
Eisenhower, Dwight, 109, 150, 209
EM effect, 27, 53, 99-102
England, 30, 36, 40, 58, 68, 108, 129, 138,
    150, 157, 160, 171-172, 188-189, 194-195,
    238, 242, 249
Engstrom, Walter, 180
Enoch, 155, 218
Eskimos, 41, 195
Extraterrestrial Hypothesis (ETH), 145,
    150-152, 156, 158, 162-164

FAA, 166
Fairhall, Allen, 169
fairies, 137, 198, 210, 213-214
Farish, Lucius, 22
Farley, Belva, 236
Fatima, 250, 254
FBI, 91, 225-226, 231-232, 236, 239-240, 244
Ferguson, William, 157
Flatwoods Monster, 80, 90
Flick, David, 155
Fluornoy, Theodore, 156
Flying Saucer Review, 80, 92, 145, 160-161, 206,
    228, 237, 246-247, 256-259
Fodor, Nandor, 98, 167
Folkerts, J.H., 178
Ford Motor Company, 86, 99
Fort, Charles, 106, 117, 147-148, 167-168, 170,
    211, 251
Fort Meade, 178
France, 27, 29, 58, 68, 138, 145, 160-161, 168,
    194-195, 221, 254-255
Frazetta, Frank, 165, 205
Freeman, George P., 75
Frenzel, Lawrence, 130
Friedman, Stanton, 164

Fry, Daniel, 157
Frye, Charles, 38
Fuller, Curtis, 121, 149
Fuller, John, 43, 145, 159, 162, 190
Funk & Wagnalls, 106

Gaddis, Vincent, 117, 145, 159
Gallagher, Cornelius E., 173
Gallipolis OH, 89, 236, 238
Gardiner, Jack, 140
Garner, John, 133, 176
Garrison, Jim, 226, 253
Garuda, 165, 266-267
Geiger, Herb, 133
Gemini, 47-48, 52-53
Georgia, 19-20, 29, 207, 238
Gere, Richard, 262
Germany, 49, 75, 109, 151, 167, 213, 227
Gernsback, Hugo, 118
Giant Rock, 7
Gilbreth, J.W., 133
Glendale CA, 6, 215
Glenn, John, 49, 52
Goddard, Victor, 163
Gordon, Keith, 83
Goulart, Ron, 119
Gould, Rupert T., 117
Gran Chaco, 46, 54
Grant, W.V., 157
Great Britain, 68, 160, 245
Great Circle Route, 40, 252
Great Depression, 117, 271
Great Lakes, 69, 252
Greenfield, Allen, 15, 238
Greenland, 70, 172
Griffin, Merv, 264
Grumman Corporation, 51
Grunt Letter, 229
Gulf of Mexico, 29, 34, 252
Guttenpoole, Samuel, 226
Gypsies, 104

Haagland, Mrs. Richard, 178
Hack, Richard, 215, 239
Hall, Richard, 158
hallucinations, 17, 107-108, 210, 213, 249, 259
Halstead, Millard, 81
Hanson, Mrs. Harry, 178
Happy Landing Incident, 228
Harmon, Harold, 87

Harney, John, 250-251
Hawaii, 23, 48, 50
Heard, Gerald, 150
Hecht, Ben, 148
Hefferlin, W.C., 121
Henderson, Willard, 100
Henslik, Joseph, 230, 241
Herrick, Darlene, 130
Hickman, Warren, 109
Hill, Barney, 103, 162, 228
Hill, Betty, 45, 214
Hitchcock, Alfred, 202
Hitler, Adolph, 263
Holiday, F.W., 160
Holland, 183
Hollow Earth, 149, 151, 158
Holly, Lester, 79
Holmes, Sherlock, 213
Holy Bible, 11, 46, 104, 155-156, 237, 255, 260, 270
Hopi Indians, 156
Hopkins, Budd, 259
Hubbard, L. Ron, 118
Hudson, Charles, 73
Hughes, Howard, 264
Husserl, Edmund, 107
Hynek, J. Allen, 20, 147, 152, 164, 183, 202-204, 239, 243-244, 254-255
Hyre, Mary, 59, 73, 87, 90, 267

Ice Age, 71
Idaho, 5, 126, 128-129, 135, 186
Illinois, 29, 38-40, 126, 135, 179-180, 182, 186, 189, 203
Indiana, 29, 40, 73
Indus Valley, 69
Instant, F.D., 139
International Bankers, 240-241
International Fortean Organization, 148
Invisible College, 164, 254-255
Iowa, 32, 37, 135, 159, 180, 186, 201, 225
Iron Curtain, 52
Israel, 199

Jackson, Andrew, 98-99, 101-102
Jacobs, David Michael, 123
Jansonius, Jake, 180
Japan, 74, 169-170, 195
Jessup, Morris K., 18, 36, 42, 45, 145, 154-155, 241
Jesus Christ, 202, 250, 258

Jewel, Walter, 140
Jim Creek Radio Observatory, 136
Johnson, Lyndon B., 260
Jowers, Loyd, 262
Judson, Frank, 51

Kachina, 156
Kaiser Aluminum, 74, 78-79
Kansas, 24, 38-39, 180-182, 186
Karasu Tengu, 165
Karlsefni, Snorre, 67
Karlsefni, Torfinn, 67
Keel, Edgar, 7
Keel, Mary, 9
Kennedy, Robert F., 13, 114, 224-225, 241, 253
Kennedy, John F., 13, 64, 253, 261
Kentucky, 69, 126, 178, 184
Keyhoe, Donald, 52, 122-124, 145, 148,
    150-153, 158-159, 164, 246, 256
Khauga, 157
Kimball, Paul, 136
King, Martin Luther, 114, 241, 260, 262
Kisner, Al, 181
Kisner, Mike, 215
Klass, Philip J., 159
Kolberg, Ronald, 179
Korendor, 158
Kronin, 216-217

La Paz, Lincoln, 51
Lacey, Howard W., 141
Laika, 29
Lanulos, 114, 198
Lapseritis, Kewaunee, 266
Layne, Meade, 42, 156
Lear, William, 123
Lemuria, 120, 148
Leno, Jay, 264
Leonov, Alexei A., 52
Lewis, C.C., 90
Liveright, Horace, 148
Loch Ness, 117, 147, 160, 270-272
London, 40, 113, 140, 243, 258, 261
Long Island, 20, 32, 55, 57-59, 73, 94-95, 100,
    105, 187, 214, 217, 226, 231
Lore, Gordon, 22, 24
Lorenzen, Coral, 124, 146, 256
Louisiana, 30, 175, 225
Lourdes, 254
Lovell, James, 47

Lucas, Cecil, 89
Luhm, James, 132, 135

Mackay, Ivar, 161
Maclaine, Shirley, 265
Maffei, Risvaldo, 167
magnetism, 99-101, 141, 171
Magor, John, 140
Mallette, Mary, 81, 235, 237-238
Mallette, Steve, 81, 235, 237-238
Manitoba, 29, 40, 140, 208
Manly, Raymond, 84
Mars, 66, 115, 128, 157, 191, 199, 260, 272
Martin, John, 144
Maryland, 110-112, 114, 178
Mason County, 83, 87, 89, 234
Massachusetts, 11, 20, 29, 156, 186, 189, 252
Maury Island, 167, 170, 211, 251, 253
McClintic Wildlife Station, 81
McDaniel, Park, 82
McDivitt, James, 48
McDonald, James, 164
McKay, Henry, 138
McKenzie, Patrick, 131
McLaren, John, 137
McNamara, Robert S., 104, 173, 182, 210
Mela, Pomponius, 68
Melnichuk, Alexei, 33
Men in Black (MIB), 12, 31, 57, 59-60, 62, 82,
    84, 88-89, 102, 105, 127, 230, 236, 252,
    257, 267
Menger, Howard, 30, 157, 244, 257
Menzel, Donald, 152, 155, 158-159, 229, 246,
    250
Merritt, A.A., 148
Merseyside UFO Bulletin, 241-243, 246, 250
Mexico, 20, 28-29, 34-36, 41, 51, 157, 168,
    170, 252, 256
Michael, Cecil, 157
Michel, Aime, 41, 255
Michell, John F., 159
Michigan, 20, 23-25, 31-32, 35, 37-40, 73,
    80, 135, 140, 166, 169-170, 177, 186, 224,
    229, 233
Miller, Jack, 131
Miller, R. Dewitt, 155
Minnesota, 21, 70, 102, 130-135, 175-177,
    185-186, 221
Mississippi, 29-30, 69-70, 81, 175, 252
Montana, 40, 178, 186
Moore, Olden, 31

Mormons, 156, 218, 254-255

Moseley, Jim, 9, 227, 229, 235, 239, 256

Mothman, 9, 46, 58, 80-83, 85, 88-91, 136, 165, 183, 205, 233, 235, 237-239, 260-262, 266-274

Mothman Prophecies, 9, 165, 205, 260, 271

Mount Palomar, 123, 157

Muir, J. Sloan, 178

NASA, 48-50, 52-54, 64, 66, 174, 185, 197-198

National Enquirer, 44

National Security Agency, 65

Native Americans, 42-43, 55-57, 67-71, 94, 102, 117, 157, 195, 217, 237, 249, 267

Navajo Indians, 70

Nebel, Long John, 58, 157

Nebraska, 20, 28-29, 35-40, 135, 168, 170, 172, 184, 186-187, 189, 191, 208

Nelson, Linda, 133

Nevada, 35, 264

New England, 36, 40, 68, 189, 238

New Hampshire, 43, 73

New Haven, 83, 85, 89, 239

New Jersey, 19, 29-30, 32, 73, 76, 100, 126, 134-135, 157, 168, 172-173, 175, 184, 186, 188, 222, 260

New Mexico, 28-29, 35-36, 41, 51, 157, 168, 170, 256

New York, 29-30, 33, 35, 40, 55, 58-59, 74, 91, 99, 104-105, 114, 122, 126, 129, 135, 151, 157, 168, 170, 184, 186-188, 198, 201, 203-204, 211, 217, 226, 236, 248, 250, 252, 254, 260-262, 268, 271

NICAP, 11, 16, 28, 30, 43, 52, 106, 123-124, 153, 158-159, 161, 164, 169, 239, 245

NORAD, 35

Norman, Eric, 161

North American Newspaper Alliance, 84, 88, 176

North Carolina, 21, 135, 173, 189

Nostradamus, 270

Nyls, Raymond, 177

Oahspe, 104, 254

Oberth, Herman, 151

Office of Naval Research, 154

Ohio, 9, 20, 25, 29, 31-32, 40, 44, 58, 69-70, 72-73, 78, 81, 83, 87, 89-93, 95, 100, 108-110, 122, 135, 147, 154, 186, 191, 194, 227, 233, 235-236, 238, 252, 268-269, 272

Ohio Northern University, 25, 44, 108, 110, 191

Ohio River, 20, 70, 78, 87, 90, 100, 227

Oklahoma, 20, 25, 43, 135, 175, 177, 184, 186, 188-189

Olmecs, 70

Onassis, Aristotle, 264

Ontario, 29, 40, 137-143

OOFs, 106, 148

Operation Trojan Horse, 9, 108, 243-244, 247-248, 251, 254-256

Oregon, 20, 187

Oriental, 41, 55, 61, 82, 199

Oruro, 46

Osborn, Louis, 134

Osborne, Virgil, 181

Pacific islands, 71

Palmer, Ray, 117, 119-120, 123, 146, 148, 158, 245

Paquette, Edgar, 138

Parks, George, 166

Paro, Jaye, 231

Partridge, Newell, 90

Paulus, Charles, 184

Peck, Donald, 183

Pennsylvania, 19, 40, 69, 73, 120, 167-168, 183-184, 212

Pentagon, 47, 51, 75, 78, 89, 143, 151, 153

Perry Township, 221, 224

Peru, 40, 189

Philbin, Regis, 264

Phoenicians, 68

Pikal, 130

Playboy, 224

Pliny, 68, 72

Point Pleasant WV, 22, 46, 54, 72, 80-82, 85-91, 99, 114, 125, 165, 187, 189, 205, 234-237, 262, 267, 270, 273-274

poltergeists, 26, 87-88, 97, 271

Porterfield, R.W., 72

Portugal, 68

Potter, Bob, 131

Powers, William T., 243

Princess Owl Moon, 56

Project A, 108

Project Blue Book, 23, 26, 28, 30, 44, 63, 75, 78, 110, 138, 143, 151-155, 158-160, 163, 184, 186-187, 207, 224, 247, 255

Project Grudge, 122, 149-150

Project Ozma, 199

Project Saint, 47

Quebec, 137, 142-143
quebracho, 46, 54
Quintanilla, Hector, 78

RAF, 163
Ravenswood WV, 78-79
Ray, James Earl, 262
RCA, 184, 235
Reed, Graham, 127
Reid, Stanley, 141
Reid, Wesley, 143
Rennie, Michael, 151
Roanoke, 67, 70
Robertson Panel, 110
Rodriguez, Arnesto, 225
Rogers, Will, 271
Rogerson, Peter, 248, 250
Rolph, Herbert, 35
Roman, Bonita, 147
Rowles, Phyllis, 178
Ruppelt, Edward, 41, 44, 63, 110, 138,
    151-152, 154, 159
Russia, 45, 167
Rutledge, William, 183

Sagan, Carl, 163
Samwick, Charles, 237
San Francisco, 22-24, 121, 199
Sanderson, Ivan, 97, 106, 263
Sandhill Road, 72
Sasquatch, 265-266
Saucerian Press, 12
Saunders, David, 145
Savannah River Project, 19
Scandinavia, 67, 189, 208, 213
Scarberry, Linda, 235
Scarberry, Roger, 81, 238
Schirmer, Herbert, 168
Schirra, Wally, 50
Schmidt, Reinhold, 29-30
Sciotti, Gregory, 212
Scully, Frank, 145, 150
Secret Commonwealth, 148
Seymore, Paul, 134
Shalett, Sidney, 150
Shapely, Harlow, 224
Sharp, Alan, 243, 245-246, 250-251
Shaver, Richard, 120, 125, 148
Shaw, Clay, 225, 253

Shertzer, Beau, 190
Short, Norma, 147
Shuttlewood, Arthur, 217, 250
Silence Group, 9
Silver Bridge, 114, 228, 267, 269
skiamachia, 107
Sky People, 60, 156, 160
Smith, Helene, 156
Smith, Joseph K., 156, 255
Smith, Mrs. Homer, 177
South Africa, 28-29
South America, 30, 40, 46, 50, 54, 58, 70-71,
    139, 157, 188, 194-195, 200, 221
South Dakota, 37, 130, 133, 176, 186
Soviet Union, 33, 42, 45, 47, 51-53, 64, 149,
    162, 172, 246, 249
space grass, 73-75, 79, 169-170
Spielberg, Steven, 201
Stafford, Thomas, 50
Steiger, Brad, 145, 159, 162, 217, 255
Storgaid, Judy, 140
Strieber, Whitley, 259, 261, 263
Sugar Grove WV, 54
Sullivan, G.L., 181
Sullivan, Walter, 42
Summers, Lou, 239
Swedenborg, Emmanuel, 155

Tacoma, 22, 59, 225, 253
Tashkent, 33
Tass, 53
Tennessee, 29-30, 98-99, 103, 175
Texas, 20, 25, 28-29, 45, 144, 154, 164, 169,
    191, 214, 231, 253, 263
Thayer, Tiffany, 148, 153
Thomas, Ralph, 85, 90
Thompson, Robert, 140
Thule, 172
Tippit, J.D., 225
TNT Area, 46, 54, 81-83, 85-88, 90-91,
    237-239, 266, 269
Tombaugh, Clyde W., 51
Toronto, 35
Tougas, Charles, 39
Trench, Brinsley Le Poer, 160
Twain, Mark, 125, 273
Twin Towers, 91
Tyo, Dennis, 135-136

U.S. Air Force, 16-17, 23, 30, 52, 63, 65, 78,
    96, 106, 110, 122, 138, 148, 150, 152-155,

158, 160, 172, 174, 187, 200, 207, 221-225, 227, 256-257

U.S. Coast Guard, 29

U.S. Department of Interior, 7

UMMO, 254

University Of Colorado, 17, 21, 65, 99, 145, 160, 163-164

Ury, Tom, 83

Vadig, 110-111

Vallee, Jacques, 21-22, 27, 145, 156, 159, 161, 254

Varo Corporation, 154

Varo Edition, 45, 155, 159

Vatican, 250

Venezuela, 28, 40, 51, 189

Venus, 66, 128, 156, 183, 188, 193, 195

Vikings, 67

Villas-Boas, Antonio, 103

Virgin Mary, 46

Virginia, 36, 52-53, 67, 70, 124, 171, 189, 234, 272

Walker, Joe, 48

Wallops Island, 52

Wamsley, Marvin, 91

Wamsley, Raymond, 85, 91

Wanaque Reservoir, 19, 32

Warnock, Mrs. Ned, 177

Washington D.C., 31, 49, 65, 75, 110-111, 123-124, 151-152, 154, 188-189, 224-225, 231, 248

Washington State, 20, 22, 63, 136, 144, 212, 225, 266

Watergate, 253

Watts, Carroll Wayne, 45, 214

Weehunt, Ron, 181

Wells, H.G., 148

West Virginia, 7, 20, 42, 46, 54, 58-59, 69, 72-75, 77-81, 83-84, 89-91, 94-95, 99-100, 105, 113-114, 125-126, 140, 153, 165, 169-170, 187, 189-190, 192, 199, 218, 226-227, 230, 234, 241, 259, 262, 267-268, 274

Westbrook, Jack, 38

White, Edward, 48

White, Robert, 49, 143

White House, 12, 32, 205, 214, 220

White Sands, 28, 50, 157

Wilcox, Gary, 111

Wilkins, Harold T., 155

Williamson, George Hunt, 157

Wilson, Colin, 253

Winfield WV, 72, 74

Wisconsin, 118, 122, 132-133, 135, 149, 175, 186, 228

World Trade Center, 261

Wright, Robert, 187

Wright-Patterson Air Force Base, 75, 78, 89, 122

Wyndham, John, 104

Wyoming, 38-40

X-15 jet, 48-49, 216

Yeti, 266

Young, John W., 48

Zamora, Lonnie, 168

Zechariah, 11-12, 46

Ziff, William B., 118

Zomdic, 158

38691367R00161

Made in the USA
Lexington, KY
20 January 2015